D0240371

A LEGAL OVERVIEW
of the NEW STUDENT

A LEGAL OVERVIEW

of the

NEW STUDENT

as Educational Consumer, Citizen, and Bargainer

By

ROBERT A. LAUDICINA, Ph.D.

Dean of Students
Fairleigh Dickinson University
Madison, New Jersey

JOSEPH L. TRAMUTOLA, Jr., J.D.

Professor of Business
Fairleigh Dickinson University
Madison, New Jersey

CHARLES C THOMAS · PUBLISHER

Springfield · Illinois · U.S.A.

Published and Distributed Throughout the World by
CHARLES C THOMAS ● PUBLISHER
Bannerstone House
301-327 East Lawrence Avenue, Springfield, Illinois, U.S.A.

This book is protected by copyright. No part of it
may be reproduced in any manner without written
permission from the publisher.

© *1976, by* CHARLES C THOMAS ● PUBLISHER
ISBN 0-398-03575-X
Library of Congress Catalog Card Number: 76-14879

With THOMAS BOOKS *careful attention is given to all details of manufacturing and design. It is the Publisher's desire to present books that are satisfactory as to their physical qualities and artistic possibilities and appropriate for their particular use. THOMAS BOOKS will be true to those laws of quality that assure a good name and good will.*

Printed in the United States of America
R-2

Library of Congress Cataloging in Publication Data

Main entry under title:
   A Legal overview of the new student, as educational
   consumer, citizen, and bargainer.

   Includes index.
   1. College students--Legal status, laws, etc.
--United States--Addresses, essays, lectures.
I. Laudicina, Robert.   II. Tramutola, Joseph L.
KF4243.A75L45   344'.73'079   76-14879
ISBN 0-398-03575-X

for Our Parents

CONTRIBUTORS

Joseph Bevilacqua

Neil S. Bucklew

Irving Buchen

Jonathan Flagg Buchter

Alan C. Coe

John Coleman

James Giles

Tom Heaton

David Hill

Robert A. and Eleanor Laudicina

Richard D. Rowray

Charles Selden

Alexander G. Sidar, Jr.

Joan S. Stark

Richard L. Tombaugh

Sandra L. Willett

INTRODUCTION:
THE CHANGING STATUS of STUDENTS

A N intense search for students and the funds to support their interest in college has become for educational administrators a pervasive concern. A complex series of social, historical, and generational forces has precipitated dramatic changes in college curricula, student lifestyles, and student-administrator relationships. Students now come to the university with specific rights and privileges of their own grounded in judicial and legislative *desiderata*.

A new administrative mode presently exists in higher education — the educational administrator has become a broker who helps shape and arrange policies and programs by persuasive rather than authoritative technique. This book examines contemporary student-institutional relationships and recommends a viable legal framework to encourage commitment and reciprocity among all campus citizens.

College and university administrators no longer enjoy easily accepted commitments from students based on prerogatives of their administrative offices. Unquestioned authority has been effectively replaced during the last several decades by successive stages of modified relationships between students and institutions they may attend. Briefly, the college administrator's role has evolved from rule by administrative fiat, through benevolent counselor relationships, to rule by contract — where students come to the university with a specific means of exchange for goods and services requested.

The inducements offered by a college or university through its respective admissions offices, in many instances, no longer are predicated upon academic and personal review of student needs, but rather the need to satisfy projected student quotas. Such quotas usually represent minimum income figures necessary to satisfy overhead and operational costs a particular institution may experience.

Legal adult status for most students now requires that financial assistance officers reassess criteria traditionally utilized (parental income) when distributing economic support. Changes in the age of majority, moreover, have had substantial impact on the status of students who may now be considered consumer-contractors with concomitant rights in accessibility to and confidentiality of academic and personal records maintained by institutions they attend.

Student services, including residence, food, and health, which traditionally were furnished in house and thereby reinforced student-university relationships are increasingly being delegated to professional service organizations. Such delegation has in large part been caused by the inability of educational institutions to manage certain services effectively in today's precarious economy. Students, as consumer contractors, also have contributed to the use of outside contracted services by demanding an equitable return for their dollar.

The evaluation of a student's academic performance now requires supportive documentation by individual professors and administrators to justify grades and/or recommendations. In addition, academic, social, and psychological guidance now takes on an additional legal dimension because of the potential liability for professional malpractice.

Changes in the legal adult status of students, the advent of the collective bargaining on college and university campuses, and the desire on the part of students to be participants in the formulation of rules, regulations, and policies that may affect them have intensified student demands and involvement in decision-making arenas which formerly were restricted to faculty and administration.

The future administrator must wrestle with not only diminished fiscal and administrative prerogatives, but also must contend with a changed environment where students may now be considered consumer-contractors having concomitant legal privileges.

CONTENTS

A LEGAL OVERVIEW
of the NEW STUDENT

The authors hope this book will become an important reference for present educational administrators and those in training. Readers should recognize that this book serves best as a resource rather than as a replacement for legal counsel or as a substitute for individual administrative judgment.

The authors acknowledge and extend their appreciation to those administrators who have attended and supported the series of legal symposia held annually at Fairleigh Dickinson University which have helped make this book possible. They also are grateful to their wives, Eleanor and Mary Ann, for their patience, understanding, and encouragement during the preparation of this manuscript.

Robert A. Laudicina
Joseph L. Tramutola, Jr.
Fairleigh Dickinson University
Florham-Madison, N. J.

CHAPTER ONE

A LEGAL TIME FRAME FOR THE EDUCATIONAL ADMINISTRATOR

ALL public questions, sooner or later, seek judicial resolution. Courts, in general, and the Supreme Court, in particular, help formulate much public policy. Institutions of higher learning are cloaked with substantial public interest and, therefore, are highly vulnerable to involvement in judicial controversies. Campus unrest in the sixties brought students, faculty, and administrations all too often to the courtroom door, where administrative discretion yielded to judicial interpretation. Legal adulthood for most college students, moreover, now prefigures a rearticulation of student-institutional relationships. Upon what bases should those relationships be formed?

As a means of examining the kinds of relationships that exist between students and institutions today a review of previous relationships is in order. What common characteristics, for example, epitomized student-institutional relationships in 1936? What kind of disciplinary structure was common to colleges and universities? What kinds of rules might apply, and who interpreted these rules?

ENVIRONMENTAL CONDITIONS

The changes noted in the time frame on the following page have obviously been at work over a long period of time, and result from a complex series of social, historical, and generational forces impinging upon the university. Not all such changes can be clearly enclosed within a discrete time period. Nevertheless, administrative authority clearly has been diluted over the last several decades. Students, quite obviously, enjoy rights, privileges, and equal bargaining power unheard of and unthinkable in 1936.

The new forms of contractual association emerging on the

TIME FRAME

	Rule by Administrative Fiat 1936	Lord of the Realm 1956	Counselor 1966	Rule by Contract 1976	Rule by Strict Constructionism or DeCommunitatis 1986
	Authority-dominated administration (Vertical Rule).	Authority-centered administration (Vertical Rule).	Consensus-centered administration (Horizontal Rule).	Consensus-dominated administration (Horizontal Rule).	Authority or consensus rule.
	The dean as in loco parentis surrogate father.	The dean as benevolent father.	The dean as friendly articulator of options.	The dean as professional articulator of responsibilities.	Bureaucratic and impersonal rule or contractual commitment (Bilateral and multilateral).
	Administrative judgment re: educational development of students - unquestioned.	Administrative judgment re: educational development of students - sometimes questioned by students.	Administrative judgment re: educational development of students questioned by students and sometimes by courts.	Administrative judgment re: educational development of students questioned by courts.	Administrative judgment re: educational development of students questioned by courts and community.
	Education restricted to some of those who are rich and intelligent.	Education a privilege for all the rich and intelligent.	Education a right for all who wish the opportunity.	Education a contractual relationship between student and institution (Student to have a specific means of exchange).	Education a citizen-governmental body relationship (Colleges as a community resource).

college campus, including financial aid expressed in voucher terms, residence contracts, student union fees, and learning contracts, have vastly altered and complicated student-institutional relationships. If faculty and deans once were in the position of defining values and goals for students, it is now the student himself who defines personal perspective and academic objective. Indeed, the student comes to campus with rights grounded in judicial and legislative *desiderata*.

Judicial decisions of the sixties and early seventies have crystallized and brought into sharp focus the full extent of revolutionary changes affecting the roles of college administrators, their relationships with student constituencies, and their relationship to a wider network of social and political linkages. Emphasis on the individual and independence from parents filters through recent legislative history of financial aid legislation. The goal of antidiscrimination regulations issued under Title IX of the Education Amendments Act of 1972, while laudable in purpose, further restrict administrative discretion and promote horizontal rather than hierarchical relationships between students and institutions they may attend.

The two most salient legal phenomena of the 1960's with regard to the rights of students are (1) the recognition of First Amendment freedoms as essential and fundamental to the American theory of education, and (2) the recognition that the requirements of due process of law are fully applicable in student disciplinary proceedings.

In *Tinker v. Des Moines School District*, 393 U. S. 503 (1969), Justice Fortas noted that personal intercommunication among students is as much a part of the educational process as formal classroom teaching. In controversies involving free speech, assembly, association, and media publication, public institutions of learning may justify prohibition of a particular expression of opinion only when the free exercise of that right would "materially and substantially" interfere with the operation of the school.

The *Tinker* case brings the constitution to the classroom door and forces college administrators* to find new sources of legiti-

---

*College Administrators, indeed, may be liable to money damages under 42 U.S.C., Section 1983 if they act without regard to a student's clearly established constitutional rights. See *Wood v. Strickland* 420 U.S. 308 (1975).

mation for their authority and their capacity to define the rules by which their institutions will be governed. From a time when colleges and universities were similar to feudal baronies with regard to their relationship to the state, colleges and universities have now been brought into the framework of constitutionalism, the rule of law, and social contract.

The second significant judicial decision, involving the right of due process, grew out of the case of *Dixon v. Alabama*, 294 F. 2d 150 (1961). In this case, the Court of Appeals for the Fifth Circuit stated "Whenever a governmental body acts so as to injure an individual, the constitution requires that the act be consonant with due process of law." The *Dixon* case represented a landmark decision in that it signified recognition by the court that state-supported educational institutions, as well as judicial, legislative, and administrative bodies, are subject to the constitutional requirements of the Fourteenth Amendment.

It should be noted here that there are two separate and distinct forms of due process, procedural due process and substantive due process. Both have important implications for administrative actions against students. Procedural due process involves the basic question of what procedures for hearing and notice are legally required to ensure fairness in student discipline. In the area of procedural due process, the case of *Esteban v. Central Missouri State College*, 417 F. 2d 1077 (1969), set up the general requirements for state institutions. These entail the following guarantees: (1) There must be adequate notice in writing of specific charges and the nature of the evidence against the student; (2) the student must have the opportunity to present his own position, explanations, and evidence; and (3) no disciplinary action should be taken on grounds which are not supported by substantial evidence. It is important to note, however, that the court did not go so far as to require legal representation, public hearings, confrontation and cross-examination of witnesses, warnings of self-incrimination, applications of the principles of double jeopardy, or compulsory production of witnesses.*

---

*See R. Laudicina and J. Tramutola, Jr., *A Legal Perspective For Student Personnel Administrators* (Springfield, Thomas, 1974), pp. 95-98. See also the guidelines for campus-based tribunals at the end of this chapter.

The second form of due process, substantive due process, emphasizes not means, but the motivation behind regulations and administrative decisions, e.g. what activities constitute a proper cause for a student's suspension? Although there have not been many test cases in this area, it is entirely possible that the day may soon come when, for example, rules against "misconduct" as grounds for dismissal may be declared unconstitutionally vague. In the *Dixon* case mentioned earlier and in the case of *Soglin v. Kauffman,* 418 F. 2d 163 (1969), the court stated that, while obviously disruptive activity need not be specifically proscribed, rules for conduct must be drawn with enough specificity to make a reasonable person aware of just what conduct would be prohibited.

Although the full weight of the preceding decisions falls upon state institutions, their ultimate impact on private institutions remains open to conjecture. In the case of *Zerbo v. Drew University,* 1 FBA 27, U. S. District Court., District of N. J. (1973), and again in the case of *Grossner v. the Trustees of Columbia University,* 287 Fed. Supp. 535 (1968), the courts ruled that receipt of money from the state was not enough, without a good deal more, to make the recipient an agency of government. In order for the rules of due process to apply to private institutions, then, it will be necessary to demonstrate a substantial and relevant connection between the state and the private university. In this sense, private institutions continue to remain somewhat apart from "the long arm" of the law, but current economic realities, as well as other economic and social forces, may foster increasing interaction between public and private educational sectors, eventually encouraging further review of the due process clause as it applies to private schools.

The implications of *Dixon v. Alabama* go well beyond the due process clause. *Dixon* now compels viewing public colleges and universities as integrated instrumentalities of the state subject to those rules and regulations that might be applied to other state institutions. The judicial legacy of *Dixon*, indeed, vitiates the kind of special relationship to the state which once made it possible for college administrators to wield vast amounts of power over the lives and lifestyles of students within their institution.

NEW STUDENT-INSTITUTIONAL RELATIONSHIPS

Both *Tinker* and *Dixon* together with subsequent federal district and Supreme Court decisions hold profound meaning for college administrators. In a little more than one decade (1960-1969), the courts have systematically stripped away the privileged status of administrators and the aura of a special expertise with regard to student clientele. Due process of law is therefore applicable to students, and the wide shield of First Amendment freedoms will serve to immunize students where no substantial interference with institutional operation can be shown.

Legislation enacted in almost all states reducing the age of majority from twenty-one to eighteen years is a consequence in large part of judicial decisions made during the last twelve to fourteen years. The judiciary, then, has helped redefine values and determine a new legal footing for both students and administrators. Students as well as administrators are no longer separate from the law but legitimately and closely tied to its processes. A new administrative mode can be said to exist — it is parallel and horizontal, not vertical and hierarchical.

The ramifications of legislation changing the legal age necessitate serious review and reassessment by college administrators of certain conventional administrative practices. For example, there is no longer a legal justification for sending institutional transcripts and reports to parents in those states where the legal age is eighteen. The examination of family financial resources may no longer be as relevant as an audit of an individual student's financial means. Requirements that students maintain residence, eat in the student cafeteria, and pay mandatory fees for services they do not want, use, or require prefigure difficulties for college administrators.

Students are persons, administrators are persons, and both live and learn within the same legal environment. The judiciary has introduced two substantially different options in the relationship which will in the future prevail between student and dean. On the one hand, deans can adopt a purely bureaucratic, impersonal, and authoritative mode of interaction in which students and administrators eye each other warily across the demilitarized zone of the law, *or* administrators can accept the new challenges and opportunities implicit in these judicial decisions. In effect, the judiciary has provided a new opportunity for administrators to work with students as junior colleagues, fostering a spirit of mutuality and reciprocity and a campus spirit in which contractual commitment and *DeCommunitatis* replace *in loco parentis*.

APPENDIX: RECOMMENDED PROCEDURES
FOR DUE PROCESS COMPLIANCE

Campus judicial systems should permit aggrieved parties to register complaints against students with the dean of students. If the complaint warrants review, the dean will notify the accused of the complaint and ask that he meet with him. If the dean determines that the complaint has merit, the student should be advised of his options, i.e. an administrative hearing or a quasi-formal hearing before a campus tribunal. Appeal on grounds of passion, prejudice, or new information should be available through the institution's chief executive or his designate.

JUDICIAL PROCESS FLOW CHART

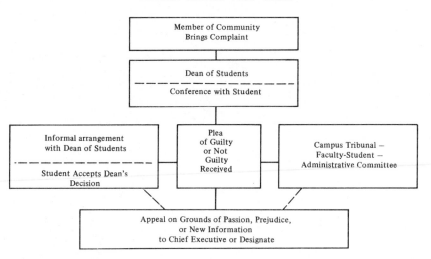

Family Rule Procedure
(Plea: Guilty)

(1) Meeting called to order.
   Introduction.
(2) University member states the charges.
(3) Chairman of the tribunal asks the defendant whether the dean should be present at the rest of the hearing.
(4) The defendant admits to the charges.
   (a) Defendant gives statement to the event in question.

      (b) Tribunal members question the accused about the event.
(5) Chairman thanks the accused, and defendant leaves.
(6) Tribunal makes a decision.

Formal Procedures*
(Plea: Not Guilty)

(1) Meeting called to order.
      Introduction.
(2) University member states the charges.
(3) Chairman of the tribunal asks the defendant whether the dean should be present for the rest of the hearing.
(4) The defendant pleads not guilty.
(5) Witnesses for the complainant examined.
(6) Defendant and witnesses examined.
(7) Final statement by complainant.
(8) Final statement by defendant.
(9) Tribunal excuses the defendant and advises him he will be given written notice as to judicial determination.

---

*Students should under most circumstances be given the option of a closed or open hearing.

CHAPTER TWO

ADMISSIONS:
A CHANGING MARKETPLACE

UNTIL at least 1970, admission officers were in the unique situation of being both counselors and salesmen. Traditionally, the role of counselor was emphasized, particularly in terms of helping a student select an appropriate institution and/or program given his aptitude, abilities, and goals. After World War II colleges and universities were in the enviable position of searching for ways to accommodate all of those students who wished to enroll in their institution. In this seller's market, the primary responsibility of admission officers was to ensure that new student profiles were similar to previous ones in terms of intellectual skills and prior educational experience. This responsibility was relatively easy to fulfill given increasing numbers of students during the 1950's and 1960's who wished a college education. Problems for admission officers then were essentially concerned with counseling and selection, rather than active recruitment of applicants to fill an ever increasing number of vacancies.

CHANGING PATTERNS IN COLLEGE AND
UNIVERSITY RECRUITMENT

The systematic growth of state and community colleges, especially since the early 1960's, combined with presently static enrollment levels, has resulted in serious downturns in student registration at some institutions, fatal declines for others, and enrollment concerns for all colleges and universities.

Certain private institutions whose tuition income represents the major portion of their entire revenue now face a highly uncertain future, especially because of a declining birth rate, a national leveling of numbers of students attending college, and a drop in the number of males seeking college entry.

One typical private college with a nine million dollar break-even budget was compelled to use previously restricted monies to satisfy an outstanding deficit of one million dollars caused by a 10 percent drop in enrollment.* Once this institution, like many others, engaged primarily in a selection process of those who had applied, carefully examining personal and intellectual credentials. Today, this institution actively seeks and recruits students by means of sophisticated merchandising techniques. With the eighteen-year-old population approximately 20 percent less than originally forecasted for the seventies, increasingly colleges and universities are desperately seeking new student clientele. Their search has led many institutions to use commercial marketing devices which include the following:

(1) direct mail-order advertising,
(2) media advertising,
(3) contracted outside services,
(4) academic packaging,
(5) sales-oriented admission training programs.

Commercial marketing devices coupled with a philosophy of salesmanship rather than counseling and selection provide the promise and potential of puffery, exaggerated claims, misrepresentations, and other related abuses. Consumers who usually would expect and be sensitive to such sales approaches when purchasing conventional goods and services may be taken unaware by the use of such techniques by the academic community. In fact, some naive parents whose children have received numerous letters and telephone calls from admissions and academic officers may be under the mistaken belief that this undue interest on the part of the university is precipitated by the exceptional qualifications of their children, rather than the enrollment requirements of an institution in difficulty.

Recruiting by mail-order advertising has been one of the most widely adopted business procedures in the present recruitment of

---

*Per unpublished study compiled by authors of enrollment and student tuition and fee costs at New York and New Jersey private institutions.

students. The College Board's Student Search Service, which uses academic and demographic selectors to reach college prospects, is seen by admissions officers as a viable alternative to commercial direct-mail services. The College Board's service lacks the unfortunate connotation of a crass business approach and is, therefore, welcome to most college administrators. It is not seen as injurious to institutional integrity.

Media advertising, including radio, television, newspaper, and/or magazine presentations, has become a permanent part of an admissions officer's tools of trade. Public relations officers and/or consultants have become as much an established entity on the campus as financial aid officers or business managers. With the same zeal used to sell toothpaste and mouthwash, advertising agencies address their talents to devising provocative, imaginative, and exciting appeals for prospective students. Inducements may emphasize a particular kind of night life, the alleged beauty and availability of females, or the distance to local beaches, ski areas, and other recreational centers. The scope and quality of academic offerings receive — at best — minimal attention.

Contracted outside admissions services may include organizations which consult on enrollment problems as well as, in some cases, physically assume the role of an admissions officer. Such contractors may help an institution to professionally package its academic programs in an attractive and commercial fashion similar to those utilized by business organizations.

Admissions training programs sponsored by national professional organizations as well as educational consulting groups often emphasize sales approaches rather than counseling and academic selection process. There can be little doubt that the growing enrollment crisis afflicting many institutions requires more imaginative approaches and a more active search for appropriate student recruits. As the survival needs of the institution begin to outweigh the personal and academic needs of the potential students to whom appeals are made, the traditional standards of honesty and fairness characteristic of academic institutions may appear increasingly less compelling.

The fundamental problem with the sales and marketing approach to college admissions is that colleges, perhaps unintentionally and perhaps unwittingly, may be luring students with emotional appeals and overstated claims into attending institutions whose course offerings are inappropriate for their actual future goals. Similarly, students may be pressured into programs, less because of their individual aptitudes than because of the college's need for high enrollments to sustain existing faculty and contractual commitments. Most serious, perhaps, is the tendency of sales pitches to create unrealistic expectations concerning the future income potential or other success criteria related to enrollment in a specific program.

TRUTH IN EDUCATION: A CONSUMER APPROACH

Commercial marketing devices are not necessarily inappropriate in an academic environment; nevertheless, potential for abuse exists. Consequently, truth-in-education laws have been proposed to protect student interest. Such laws may be compared to consumer legislation. Truth-in-education laws which already have been proposed recommend full disclosure of information required by college entrants to make intelligent decisions with regard to program of study and institutional choice.

Recommendations by the Education Commission of the States for truth-in-education legislation have included:

state licensing of all postsecondary educational institutions with adequate bonding and annual review;

state licensing and bonding of all persons involved in recruiting students;

full disclosure by each institution of costs, contract terms, and accreditation reports;

substantiation of all claims made in advertising and recruiting, including disclosure of its placement record if the institution cites job prospects for its graduates in its advertising or recruiting;

written contracts as the basis for relationships between students and the institution;

clear statements by each institution of what is expected of students by instructors, the institution, and employers;

student choice of arbitration or court action for redress of grievances;

greater student involvement in consumer issues in postsecondary education) persons to be appointed as student representatives on boards and commissions should be selected by "recognized student organizations");

counseling of prospective students before they enter a program to help determine whether it is appropriate for them;

drafting of model legislation and other initiatives under leadership of the Education Commission of the States.*

The use of marketing devices by colleges and universities will continue to be a permanent part of admissions' procedures and processes. Such devices have a justifiable validity. Nevertheless, serious damage to an institution's integrity may result if an overzealous and uncontrolled use of commercial sales techniques is employed. Indeed, colleges and universities which continue to include conventional merchandising tools in recruitment programs soon will be compelled to assume a position of mutuality, i.e. institutions will be legally as well as morally obligated to full disclosure of actual standards of selectivity, substantiation of ratios of students to teachers and counselors, student dropout rates, and student placement records.

The ethical implications surrounding the use of commercial techniques requires college administrators to ask at least the following questions:

(1) Do students have reliable and meaningful information about the colleges they attend?

(2) Are contractual terms which obligate students to loans, residence, and tuition fees properly explained?

(3) Are students aware of the ways in which they may hold the university responsible for the fulfillment of contractual terms?

(4) Are the terms of the educational contract sufficiently described so that students can monitor institutional performance?

By providing full disclosure of contractual terms and access to relevant financial, academic, or institutional data, students will be able to pursue intelligent, informed, and aware choices about their futures. If college administrators are unwilling to discipline

---

*The Chronicle of Higher Education (April 1, 1974). See also, *Consumer Protection in Postsecondary Education,* Report Number 64 of the Education Commission of the States, March 1975.

themselves, they surely at some point in time invite restrictive governmental regulation of their activities and increasing disaffection, discontent, and distrust among students.* Indeed, the likelihood of increased student legal claims concerning educational malpractice, including the worth of a degree, particular courses, and inadequate services is a serious concern for most college administrators. Rules now in effect issued by the Office of Education under its Guaranteed Loan Program require

(1) a limit of $100.00 to be retained by the institution for students who withdraw prior to the commencement of the academic semester;

(2) a fair and equitable policy for the refund of tuition and fees for withdrawal after the commencement of the academic semester (to determine whether such policy is truly equitable, the critical factor is the actual costs expended rather than those which are merely speculative);

(3) each institution to make a good faith effort to communicate to prospective students information regarding tuition, fees, programs, faculties, and facilities;

(4) each institution providing career education to include information in its literature regarding the relevancy of student employment to the curricula in which they are enrolled, and to include salary data for graduated students.

Rules concerning the administration and enforcement of various civil rights laws issued by the Office of Civil rights include institutional self-evaluation and maintenance of records in the following areas:

(1) application, admission, and assignment of students;

(2) recruitment of students, faculty, and staff;

(3) financial aid administration;

(4) recruitment, salary, training, demotion, and separation of employees;

(5) grievance procedures and effectiveness thereof;

(6) disciplinary rules and application thereof.†

---

*See in this regard, The Student Financial Aid Act of 1975, Hearings before the Subcommittee on Postsecondary Education, Committee on Education and Labor, House of Representatives.
†See "Title IX Consolidated Procedural Rules" at the end of this chapter.

College administrators have all, in one way or another, become increasingly — perhaps painfully — aware of a dramatic shift in the relationship between students and the institutions they attend. The benevolent authoritarianism which once provided the foundation for this relationship has given way to far more equitable, balanced arrangements as students now assume important responsibilities and articulate needs which they expect to be met. The growing stature of students as participants within the campus community has been reinforced as well by judicial and legislative changes giving students rights and responsibilities as members of the civic as well as the college community.

This is an age of consumerism. Buyers are no longer willing to placidly accept shoddy merchandise, misrepresentation in advertising, or inadequate services. Just as students have forced legal support for their new standing within academic institutions, they will soon seek — and no doubt find — legal support for their standing as consumers of its educational output.

Policies of disclosure will serve to restore equilibrium to the traditionally unbalanced relationship between student and institution. Emphasis on the individual's right to know and the opportunity for equal bargaining can only have a salutory effect on student-institutional relationships.

DISCRIMINATION AND ADMISSIONS

The Education Amendments Act of 1972, particularly Title IX, with certain exceptions prohibits sex discrimination in all federally assisted education programs and amends relevant portions of the Civil Rights Act of 1964. A large number of controversial areas are covered by this legislation such as admissions policies, scholarships, financial aid, curfews in dormitories, counseling and testing that may have a sex bias, and financial aid for one-sex organizations. With the notable exceptions of physical education in virtually all age groups and sex education in primary and secondary grades, Title IX bans sex-segregated classes.*

Denial of admission by an institution of higher education has been the subject of unresolved constitutional controversy. Typi-

---

*See Chapter VII for a discussion of Title IX and relevant excerpts from the Department of Health, Education, and Welfare's official interpretation of institutional obligations.

cally, such controversies have been based on the equal protection clause of The Fourteenth Amendment. Distinctions between private and public institutions which formerly were of some importance in determining prejudicial exclusion, no longer appear to have any significance. Given the proscriptions of Title IX which preclude sexual discrimination in both private and public institutions receiving federal financial assistance, it is not inconceivable that all forms of discrimination will be prohibited regardless of the private or public nature of the college or university.

The U. S. Supreme Court in *DeFunis v. Odegarrd,* 416 U.S. 312 (1974), declined to rule whether the University of Washington Law School had properly rejected Marco DeFunis, an applicant, while admitting thirty-eight members of minority groups with lesser academic credentials. The Corut held that because Mr. De Funis had been admitted as a result of lower court rulings he no longer had status to bring legal action.

It is unfortunate that the U. S. Supreme Court did not find a justiciable issue in this case, and the unique question of reverse racial discrimination was not resolved. Justice Douglas in a notable dissent indicated that segregated admissions processes which would seek to admit a particular number of minority candidates in preference to equally or better qualified nonminority applicants created a presumption of inferiority which placed an unfair burden on favored minority groups.

The U. S. Supreme Court hinted that, while racially based criteria would be unconstitutional, the judicial door would be left open in similar controversies which might arise in the future in cases where other forms of discrimination might be employed, such as economic class.*

Alevy v. Downstate Medical Center, 78 Misc. 2d 1091, 359 N. Y. S. 2d 426 (1974), a medical school's minority admissions procedure which considered "academic achievement in the light of attendant educational, financial, and cultural disadvantage," was upheld even though nonminority candidates had no such consideration. The court found that "only minority students who are qualified and whose entire record demonstrated to the committee that they possessed potential to successfully complete the program were accepted." The court noted that Downstate's admissions procedure would have been declared unconstitutional only if race alone were used as an admission criterion.

CASE: DENIAL OF ADMISSIONS

Admissions: Discrimination

Marco DeFunis, Petitioner, v. Charles Odegarrd, President of the University of Washington, 94 Supreme Court 1704 (1974) Decided April 23, 1974.

PER CURIAM.

In 1971 the Petitioner, Marco DeFunis, applied for admission as a first-year student at the University of Washington Law School, a state-operated institution. The size of the incoming first-year class was to be limited to 150 persons, and the Law School received some 1,600 applications for these 150 places. De Funis was eventually notified that he had been denied admission. He thereupon commenced this suit in a Washington trial court, contending that the procedures and criteria employed by the Law School Admissions Committee invidiously discriminated against him on account of his race in violation of the equal protection clause of the Fourteenth Amendment of the United States Constitution.

DeFunis brought the suit on behalf of himself alone and not as the representative of any class, against the various respondents, who are officers, faculty members, and members of the Board of Regents of the University of Washington. He asked the trial court to issue a mandatory injunction commanding the respondents to admit him as a member of the first-year class entering in September of 1971, on the ground that the law school admissions policy had resulted in the unconstitutional denial of his application for admission. The trial court agreed with his claim and granted the requested relief. DeFunis was, accordingly, admitted to the law school and began his legal studies there in the fall of 1971. On appeal, the Washington Supreme Court reversed the judgment of the trial court and held that the law school's admissions policy did not violate the Constitution. By this time De Funis was in his second year at the law school.

He then petitioned this Court for a writ of certiorari, and Mr. Justice Douglas, as Circuit Justice, stayed the judgment of the Washington Supreme Court pending the "final disposition of the case by this Court." By virtue of this stay, DeFunis remained in law school and was in the first term of his third and final year when this Court first considered his certiorari petition in the fall of 1973. Because of our concern that DeFunis's third-year standing in the law school might have rendered this case moot, we requested the parties to brief the question of mootness before we acted on the petition. In response, both sides contended that the case was not moot. The respondents were permitted to stand; the petitioner could complete the term for which he was then enrolled but would have to apply to the faculty for permission to continue in the school before he could register for another term.

In response to questions raised from the bench during the oral argument, the counsel for the petitioner informed the Court that DeFunis registered "for his final quarter in law school." The counsel for the respondents so made clear that the law school would not, in any way, seek to abrogate this registration. In light of DeFunis's registration for the last quarter of his final law school year, and the law school's assurance that his registration was fully effective, the insistent question again arose as to whether this case was not moot.

(1,2) The starting point for analysis is the familiar proposition *"that federal courts are without power to decide questions that cannot affect the rights of the litigants . . . before them."* Although as a matter of Washington State law it appears that this case would be saved from mootness by "the great public interest in the continuing issues raised by this appeal," the fact remains that under Article III "(e)ven in cases arising in the state courts, the question of mootness is a federal one which a federal court must resolve before it assumes jurisdiction."

(3) The respondents represented that, without regard to the ultimate resolution of the issues in this case, DeFunis would remain a student in the law school for the duration of any term in which he was already enrolled. *Since he had registered for his final term, it was evident that he will be given an opportunity to complete all academic and other requirements for graduation, and, if he does so, will receive his diploma regardless, of any decision this Court might reach on the merits of this case. In short, all parties agreed that DeFunis was entitled to complete his*

legal studies at the University of Washington and to receive his degree from that institution. A determination by this Court of the legal issues tendered by the parties is no longer necessary to compel that result, and could not serve to prevent it. DeFunis did not cast his suit as a class action, and the only remedy he requested was an injunction commanding his admission to the Law School. He was not only accorded that remedy, but he now has also been irrevocably admitted to the final term of the final year of the Law School course. The controversy between the parties thus clearly ceased to be "definite and concrete" and no longer "touch(es) the legal relations of parties having adverse legal interests."

It might also be suggested that this case presents a question that is "capable of repetition, yet evading review," and is thus amenable to federal adjudication even though it might otherwise be considered moot. But DeFunis will never again be required to run the gauntlet of the law school's admissions process and so the question is certainly not "capable of repetition" so far as he is concerned. Moreover, just because this particular case did not reach the Court until the eve of the petitioner's graduation from law school, it hardly follows that the issue he raises will in the future evade review. If the admissions procedures of the law school remain unchanged, there is no reason to suppose that a subsequent case attacking those procedures will not come with relative speed to this Court, now that the Supreme Court of Washington has spoken.

(4) *Because the petitioner will complete his law school studies at the end of the term for which he has now registered regardless of any decision this Court might reach on the merits of this litigation, we conclude that the Court cannot, consistently with the limitations of Article III of the Constitution, consider the substantive constitutional issues tendered by the parties. Accordingly the judgment of the Supreme Court of Washington is vacated, and the cause is remanded for such proceedings as by that Court may be deemed appropriate.*

Mr. Justice Douglas, dissenting.

I

The University of Washington Law School received 1601 applications for admission to its first-year class beginning in September, 1971. There were spaces available for only about 150 students, but in order to enroll this number the school eventually offered admission to 275 applicants. All applicants were put into two groups, one of which was considered under the minority admissions program. Thirty-seven of those offered admission had indicated on an optional question on their application that their "dominant" ethnic origin was either black, Chicano, American Indian, or Filipino, the four groups included in the minority admissions program. Answers to this option question were apparently the sole basis upon which eligibility for the program was determined. Eighteen of these thirty-seven actually enrolled in the Law School.

In general, the admissions process proceeded as follows: An index called the Predicted First Year Average was calculated for each applicant on the basis of a formula combining the applicant's score on the Law School Admission Test (LSAT) and his grades in his last two years in college. On the basis of its experience with the previous years' applications, the admissions committee, consisting of faculty, administration, and students, concluded that the most outstanding applicants were those with averages above 77; the highest average of any applicant was 81. Applicants with averages above 77 were considered as their applications arrived by random distribution of their files to the members of the committee who would read them and report their recommendations back to the committee. As a result of the first three committee meetings in February, March, and April 1971, seventy-eight applicants from this group were admitted, although virtually no other applicants were offered admission this early. By the final conclusion of the admissions process in August 1971, 147 applicants with averages above 77 had been admitted, including all applicants with averages above 78, and ninety-three of 105 applicants with averages between 77 and 78.

Also beginning early in the admissions' process was the culling out of applicants with averages below 74.5. These were reviewed by the chairman of the admissions committee, who had the authority to reject them summarily without further consideration by the rest of the committee. A small number of these applications were saved by the chairman for committee consideration on the basis of information in the file indicating greater promise than suggested by the average. Finally during the early months the committee accumulated the applications of those with averages between 74.5 and 77 to be considered at a later time when most of the applications had been received and thus could be compared with one another. Since DeFunis's average was 76.23, he was in this middle group.

Beginning in their May meeting the committee considered this middle group of applicants, whose folders had been randomly distributed to committee members for their recommendations to the committee. Also considered at this time were remaining applicants with averages below 74.5 who had not been summarily rejected, and some of those with averages above 77 who had not been summarily admitted, but instead held for further consideration. Each committee member would consider the applications competitively, following rough guidelines as to the proportion who could be offered admission. After the committee had extended offers of admission to somewhat over 200 applicants, a waiting list was constructed in the same fashion, and was divided into four groups ranked by the committee's assessment of their applications. DeFunis was on this waiting list, but was ranked in the lowest quarter. He was ultimately told in August 1971 that there would be no room for him.

II

Applicants who had indicated on their application forms that they were either black, Chicano, American Indian, or Filipino were treated differently in several respects. Whatever their averages, none were given to the committee chairman for consideration of summary rejection, nor were they distributed randomly among committee members for consideration along with other applications. Instead all applications of black students were assigned separately to two particular committee members: a first-year black law student on the committee, and a professor on the committee who had worked the previous summer in a special program for disadvantaged college students considering application to law school. Applications from among the other three minority groups were assigned to an assistant dean who was on the committee. *The minority applications, while considered competitively with one another, were never directly compared to the remaining applications, either by the subcommittee or by the full committee. As in the admissions process generally, the committee sought to find "within the minority category, those persons who we thought had the highest probability of succeeding in law school."* In reviewing the minority applications, the committee attached less weight to the Predicted First Year Average "in making a total judgmental evaluation as to the relative ability of the particular applicant to succeed in law school." (82 Wash. 2d 11, 21, 507 P. 2d 1169, 1175.) In its publicly distributed *Guide to Applicants,* the committee explained that "(a)n applicant's racial or ethnic background was considered as one factor in our general attempt to convert formal credentials into realistic predictions."

Thirty-seven minority applicants were admitted under this procedure. Of these, thirty-six had Predicted First Year Averages below 74.5 and thus would ordinarily have been summarily rejected by the Chairman. There were also forty-eight nonminority applicants admitted who had Predicted First Year Averages below DeFunis. Twenty-three of these were returning veterans (see n. 2, supra), and twenty-five others, presumably admitted because of other factors in their applications making them attractive candidates despite their relatively low averages.

It is reasonable to conclude from the above facts that while other factors were considered by the committee, and were on occasion crucial, the Predicted First Year Average was for most applicants a heavily weighted factor, and was at the extremes virtually dispositive. A different balance was apparently struck, however, with regard to the minority applicants. Indeed, at oral argument, the law school advised us that if the minority applicants were considered under the same procedure as was generally used, none of those who eventually enrolled at the law school would have been admitted.

The educational policy choices confronting a university admissions committee are not ordinarily a subject for judicial oversight; clearly it is not for us but for the law school to decide which tests to employ, how heavily to weigh recommendations from professors or undergraduate grades, and what level of achievement on the chosen criteria are sufficient to demonstrate that the candidate is qualified for admission. What places this case in a special category is the fact that the school did not choose one set of criteria but two, and then determined which to apply to a given applicant on the basis of his race. The committee adopted this policy in order to achieve "a reasonable representation" of minority groups in the law school. (82 Wash. 2d 11, 20, 507 P. 2d 1169, 1175.) Although it may be speculated that the committee sought to rectify what it perceived to be cultural or racial biases in the LSAT or in the candidates undergraduate records, the record in this case is devoid of any evidence of such bias, and the school has not sought to justify its procedures on this basis.

III

The equal protection clause did not enact a requirement that law schools employ as the sole criterion for admissions a formula based upon the LSAT and undergraduate grades, nor does it prescribe law schools from evaluating an applicant's prior achievements in light of the barriers that he had to overcome. A Black applicant who pulled himself out of the ghetto into a junior college may thereby demonstrate a level of motivation, perseverance, and ability that would lead a fairminded admissions committee to conclude that he shows more promise for law study than the son of a rich alumnus who achieved better grades at Harvard. That applicant would not be offered admission because he is black, but because as an individual he has shown he has the potential, while the Harvard man may have taken less advantage of the vastly superior opportunities offered him. Because of the weight of the prior handicaps, that black applicant may not realize his full potential in the first year of law school, or even in the full three years, but in the long pull of a legal career his achievements may far outstrip those of his classmates whose earlier records appeared superior by conventional criteria. There is currently no test available to the admissions committee that can predict such possibilities with assurance, but the committee may nevertheless seek to gauge it as best as it can, and weigh this factor in its decisions. Such a policy would not be limited to blacks, or Chicanos or Filipinos or American Indians, although undoubtedly groups such as these may in practice be the principle beneficiaries of it. But a poor Appalachian white, or a second generation Chinese in San Francisco, or some other American whose lineage is so diverse as to defy ethnic labels may demonstrate similar potential and thus be accorded favorable consideration by the committee.

There is no constitutional right for any race to be preferred. The years of slavery did more than retard the progress of blacks. Even a greater wrong was done the whites by creating arrogance instead of humility and by encouraging the growth of the fiction of a superior race. There is no superior person by constitutional standards. A DeFunis who is white is entitled to no advantage by reason of that fact; nor is he subject to any disability no matter his race or color. Whatever his race, he had a constitutional right to have his application considered on its individual merits in a racially neutral manner.

The reservation of a proportion of the law school class for members of selected minority groups is fraught with dangers, for one must immediately determine which groups are to receive such favored treatment and which are to be excluded, the proportions of the class that are to be allocated to each, and even the criteria by which to determine whether an individual is a member of a favored group. There is no assurance that a common agreement can be reached, and first the schools, and then the courts, will be buffeted with the competing claims.

The key to the problem is consideration of such applications in a racially neutral way. Abolition of the LSAT test would be a start.

The argument is that a "compelling" state interest can easily justify the racial discrimination that is practiced here. To many, "compelling" would give members of one race even more than pro rata representation. The public payrolls might then be deluged, for instance with Chicanos because they are as a group the poorest of the poor and need work more than others, leaving desperately poor individual blacks and whites without employment. By the same token large quotas of blacks or browns could be added to the Bar, waiving examinations required of other groups, so that it would be better racially balanced. The state, however, may not proceed by racial classification to force strict population equivalencies for every group in every occupation, overriding individual preferences. *The Equal Protection Clause commands the elimination of racial barriers, not their creation in order to satisfy our theory as to how society ought to be organized. The purpose of the University of Washington cannot be to produce black lawyers for blacks, Polish lawyers for Poles, Jewish lawyers for Jews, Irish lawyers for the Irish. It should be to produce good lawyers for Americans and not to place First Amendment barriers against anyone. That is the point at the heart of all our school desegregation cases* from *Brown v. Board of Education,* 347 U. S. 483, 74 S. Ct. 686, 98 L. Ed. 873, through *Swann v. Charlottee-Mecklenburg Board of Education,* 402 U. S. 1, 91 S. Ct. 1267, 28 L. Ed. 2d 554. *A segregated admissions process creates suggestions of stigma and caste no less than a segregated classroom, and in the end it may produce that result despite its contrary intentions. One other assumption must be clearly disapproved that blacks or browns cannot make it on their individual merit. That is a stamp of inferiority that a state is not permitted to place on any lawyer.*

If discrimination based on race is constitutionally permissible when those who hold the reins can come up with "compelling" reasons to justify it, then constitutional guarantees acquire an accordion like quality. Speech is closely brigaded with action when it triggers a fight, *Chaplinsky v. New Hampshire,* 315 U. S. 568, 62 S. Ct. 766, 87 L. Ed. 1031, as shouting "fire" in a crowded theatre triggers a riot. It may well be that racial strains, racial susceptibility to certain diseases, and racial sensitiveness to environmental conditions that other races do not experience may in an extreme situation justify differences in racial treatment that no fairminded person would call "invidious" discrimination. Mental ability is not in the category. All races can compete fairly at all professional levels. So far as race is concerned, any state-sponsored preference to one race over another in that competition is in my view "invidious" and violative of the equal protection clause.

The problem tendered by this case is important and crucial to the operation of our constitutional system, and educators must be given leeway. It may well be that a whole congeries of applicants in the marginal group defy known methods of selection. Conceivably, an admissions committee might conclude that a selection by lot of, perhaps, the last twenty seats is the only fair solution. Courts are not educators; their expertise is limited; and our task ends with the inquiry whether judged by the main purpose of the equal protection clause — the protection against racial discrimination — there has been an "invidious" discrimination.

Sandra L. Willett

AN OVERVIEW: CONSUMER PROTECTION IN HIGHER EDUCATION WHY? FOR WHOM? HOW?

The following presentation was originally given at the Annual Meeting of the Association of American Colleges on January 12, 1975. Ms. Willett was at that time Director of Consumer Education, Office of Consumer Affairs. Her discussion notes particularly the sources of educational consumer abuses and the likely means for their elimination.

A twenty-eight-year-old graduate student is refused readmission to his doctoral program at a large university after he failed a newly-required exam; he cannot determine his grade or take a second exam or transfer credits and two years of experience to another school.

A bright high school graduate asks a prestigious educational association about X College in the hopes of obtaining an objective assessment of the college's offerings, faculty, and reputation; no one can or will respond to her straightforward questions because to do so might lose X College a customer.

A parent calls the local consumer voluntary association, seeking help in recovering at least part of her son's tuition paid to a school which rescheduled the desired course at a time when her son's military training begins; the school has no refund policy.

College catalogs suggest sexy, successful undergraduate environments. School tuitions are increased abruptly. Top professors teach only during the day although they are advertized as leading evening classes as well. These and many more serious problems are stirring consumer awareness and general concern in the educational marketplace.

These cases are real. Also real is the increasing opportunity for students to enter postsecondary education. The Congress has

30

authorized billions of dollars to support institutions and programs. The Basic Educational Opportunity grants and the recent veterans' education increases, among others, provide direct support to the individual student. The Department of Health, Education, and Welfare has followed the lead of the Veterans Administration, Department of Labor, and other agencies in establishing broad guidelines and procedures so that federal monies now support directly and indirectly, public and private, vocational and correspondence as well as higher education study. Significant increases in the number of community colleges and free universities further widen the choice of general and specific, short-term and long-range, liberal arts and professional skills, training and education now available to a student who today might be eighteen or forty-eight years old.

However, just as there is more student aid, more flexibility, more choice available to the student, there is also more deception and more disregard of individual needs, more defaults, more fast-buck artists and in general more abuse in the educational sector.

Education, notwithstanding its real importance and patriotic appeal, is an industry. And like any other industry has its share of self-serving, insensitive, and unscrupulous operators. Until very recently, as we all know, education was considered sacred. Now with enrollments dropping 2 to 4 percent annually* and costs increasing, the student is a valuable commodity. Likewise, with more government monies available to support more students at more institutions there is more money to be had by some educational institutions. More opportunities lead to more abuses. Problems ranging from illegal advertising, abruptly changed policies and costs, loan defaults, and general disregard of the consumer plague the entire educational marketplace as they do the traditional marketplaces.

Consumer Protection: Why?

The consumer movement has its roots in history. A recent law

---

*A Department of Commerce study, among others, indicates that of the approximately 3.4 million high school seniors the percentage definitely planning to attend college dropped from 45 percent to 42 percent in 1973. The proportion planning no further schooling increased from 14 percent to 18 percent.

review article traced consumer fraud and the implied need for the consumer movement to the Old Testament where one of the prophets acknowledges marketplace exploitation, "As a nail sticketh fast between the joinings of the stone, so doth sin stick close to buying and selling."[1]

The consumer movement in more recent times has been based on the philosophical conviction that a free market economy where the market determines the price based on fair bargaining for supply and demand works fairly, and therefore best, when the supplier and purchaser come to the counter or to the bargaining table or to the classroom as respected equal participants.

The prophet's "sin" actually covers a host of exploitative evils which destroy the fair and consequently free workings of the marketplace.

The examples of real, present-day educational abuses cited earlier in this paper came to me during one day only last month. They indicate all is not well in the educational marketplace. In fact, educational complaints are rising significantly, and substantiate increasing abuses.[2]

The national press in the past year has also begun to prick the awareness of the public with discussion and documentation of educational problems. *The Boston Globe* (March 25), *New York Times* (March 31), *Saturday Review* (April 6), and *The Washington Post* (June 23) have researched educational problems ranging from weaknesses in the accreditation and eligibility processes to poor or nonexistant job placement.

Congress has held several sets of hearings this summer and fall on accreditation, student loan defaults, and general educational abuses.[3]

Other documentation comes from the federal government.

---

[1]Gilbert Geis and Herbert Edelhertz, "Criminal Law and Consumer Fraud: A Sociological View," *American Criminal Law Review*, *11*:990 (Summer 1973).

[2]Sandra L. Willett, *Who's in the Center of the Educational Marketplace?* Consumer Protection in Postsecondary Education, preconference papers (Denver Education Commission of the States, March 1974), p. 82.

[3]Representative Floyd Hicks' Special Studies Subcommittee of the Committee on Government Operations (July), and Representative James O'Hara's Special Subcommittee on Education (July), Senator Vance Hartke's Committee on Veterans Affairs, and Senator Pell's Subcommittee on Education (September).

Early in 1973 the Federal Interagency Committee on Education (FICE) established a Subcommittee on Consumer Protection in Education. This subcommittee (of which I am an enthusiastic and aggressive member) has actively sought to identify educational abuses. In January 1973 the subcommittee, drawing from the Accreditation and Eligibility staff in the U. S. Office of Education, inventoried twenty-five possible educational abuses and concerns:

(1) Degree mills.

(2) Discriminatory refund policies.

(3) Misrepresentation in selling, advertising, promotional materials, etc.

(4) Abuse of federal programs of student assistance.

(5) Lack of available jobs upon graduation.

(6) Nondelivery of items or service contracted for.

(7) Lack of provision for due process, appeal concerning injustices, etc.

(8) Arbitrariness in administrative policies and procedures.

(9) Severe and unwarranted regulation of student conduct, living arrangements, moral behavior, etc.

(10) Imposition of noneducational requirements, such as certain religious practices and customs, upon students who do not wish to fulfill them.

(11) Unrealistic academic requirements and practices, such as inaccurate grading systems, residence requirements, etc.

(12) Imposition of unwarranted and sometimes unspecified fees and other charges.

(13) Changing requirements during the life of the student's "contract" with the institution (e.g. changing degree requirements midstream).

(14) Raising tuition abruptly and without adequate notice.

(15) Excessively punitive charges for infractions such as loss of library books, lab equipment breakage, etc.

(16) Holding up transcripts, diplomas, etc., for unwarranted reasons.

(17) Lateness in obtaining qualified instructors, textbooks, equipment, classrooms, etc.

(18) A host of minor frauds, such as: poor food in dining halls,

inadequate academic or personal counseling service, inadequate student health service, listing of nonexistent faculty and courses in college catalogs, diversion of institutional resources to intercollegiate athletics and other luxuries, ineffective management of endowment and other assets, forcing faculty to subsidize education through low salaries, etc.

(19) Use of outdated or obsolete equipment, textbooks, laboratories, etc.

(20) Showing favoritism to individual or certain categories of students.

(21) Administrative tolerance of outmoded practices such as student hazing, ritualistic destruction of property, etc.

(22) Lack of adherence to promulgated standards, procedures, rules, regulations, etc.

(23) Unwarranted substitution of contracted items (such as qualified professors, dormitory rooms, etc.).

(24) Taking advantage of students because of their social status by using them as cheap labor, regularly requiring them to stand in long lines for registration, etc.

(25) Overdoing the *in loco parentis* concept by direct and illegal interference with individual freedoms and human rights.

After further research, including the results of the first National Conference on Consumer Protection in Education of March 1974, we focused our major concerns on:

(1) misleading and inaccurate advertising.

(2) indiscriminate and overly aggressive recruiting.

(3) lack of full disclosure of salient institutional characteristics useful to the consumer, such as its history, financial policies, academic standards, and other relevant information.

(4) inferior facilities, course offerings, staff.

(5) false promises of job placement.

(6) insufficient refund policies (or failure to live up to stated policies).

(7) the delivery of programs of instruction which are different from those which both the student and student funding

organization were led to expect.

(8) the use of educational funding programs for meretricious rather than educational purposes, whether through meaningless enrollment, nonattendance, default or misleading applications (e.g. use of insured loans to induce students to enroll and borrow money which is then diverted either by students or others).

(9) the award of certificates, degrees, or diplomas based on payment of fees rather than on educational accomplishment; the enrollment of foreign students for the purposes of securing residency permits and other noneducational benefits.

(10) the claim to hold a degree, certificate, or diploma which has no standing or whose name is misleading or whose standards are known to be clearly or deliberately inferior to those in common use in the United States. (Degree mills, diploma mills).

These educational abuses, serious in their direct impact on the student and indirectly on the public, provided the impetus and starting point for the FICE Subcommittee's paper on the federal role in educational consumer protection.[4]

In addition to the federal agencies, state education agencies, attorneys general, consumer offices, private educational associations, student groups and the institutions themselves increasingly tell us that abuses exist in the multibillion dollar education industry and that *therefore* consumer protection, voluntary and mandatory, is needed.

Consumer Protection: For Whom?

In the educational marketplace the student is the seeker of knowledge of skills and purchases education from a supplier to meet his needs. The student is therefore the consumer of educational services.

---

[4]*A Federal Strategy Report for Protection of the Consumer of Education*, Subcommittee on Consumer Protection, Federal Interagency Committee on Education (September 18, 1974). This report has been approved in principle. It is being forwarded to the secretaries of each member agency for review and implementation.

The student consumer invests not only his money — personal, borrowed or granted — he commits extensive time and energy and hopes. Buying education is simply not equivalent to buying a refrigerator or a stereo or a vacuum cleaner, although frequently the purchase of these products is carried out with more care and research than is the purchasing of education. Buying education or training is investing money, time, and hopes for which the consumer expects returns in the form of productive employment, social development, intellectual enrichment, or personal satisfaction.

Since the student is the consumer of educational services, he is, like the consumer in the traditional marketplace, a critical participant in the buying of education. The abuses which substantiate the need for consumer protection hit the student consumer primarily and directly.

A recent evaluation funded by the National Institute of Education[5] reveals significant dissatisfaction among graduates of both public and proprietary occupational schools. The results of this technical report are interesting because they *document* poor job placement and placement in jobs for which students did not train, discrimination in hiring and salaries against minorities and women, and general dissatisfaction among students of both public and private schools but particularly proprietary schools. The study recommends that strong consumer protection measures be carried out primarily by federal, state, and local governments, including reliable information disclosed on a timely basis to the student consumer, standards of educational effectiveness, and truthful advertising.

In addition to the direct and primary consumer (the student) the general public (the taxpayer and indirect user of the educational system) must also be protected against false claims and unethical behavior by institutions and deliberate disregard of loan repayment responsibilities by the student consumer. Senator Pell's hearings in September referenced a 1973 General Accounting Office estimate for the overall default rate on student loans as

---

[5]Wilford W. Wilms, *The Effectiveness of Public and Proprietary Occupational Training,* Center for Research and Development in Higher Education, Berkeley, University of California (October 1974).

being almost 25 percent of the loans insured by the government. When a lender does not collect from a student consumer, the debt is collected indirectly from the taxpayer. The loan, however, may have been improperly made.[6]

Government agencies which manage student aid, private and state agencies which accredit or approve schools, institutions which train students, school counselors, potential employers — all these parties need to be protected along with the student consumer. Because the abuses are great, the need for consumer protection is likewise great. In one sense the purpose of educational consumer protection is to revive in the educational marketplace the convictions of the consumer movement that the educational marketplace can operate freely and fairly only to the extent that all parties are respected in the buying and selling process, and that all parties exercise their rights and responsibilities.

Consumer Protection: How?

The very serious answer to this question is "jointly." Every party to the problem is potentially party to the solution. In fact, reform of the educational sector requires coordinated, thoughtful, vigilant action by a partnership of institutions, agencies, and individuals.

Education is an industry. Like the retailers and oil producers and food processors, many educational institutions with the agencies and individuals who surround them are guilty of some devastating abuses. This point was brought out earlier in this paper. Unlike the more "traditional" industries, however, the educational sector has been slow to recognize both the blatant and subtle exploitation within its system (some companies have been made well aware of their consumer problems for decades). A second and more positive dissimilarity, on the other hand, is that

---

[6]Remarks by Virginia H. Knauer, Special Assistant to the President for Consumer Affairs and Director of the Office of Consumer Affairs, before the Second National Conference on Consumer Protection in Postsecondary Education, November 14, 1974. The Office of Education (OE) has stressed that the overall gross default rate on the Federally Insured Student Loan Program is 23 percent, half of which is collected by OE making a net default rate of approximately 12 percent.

when confronted with its abuses the educational sector seems to be able to move more quickly than other industries to find solutions. One reason for this quick response may be the fear of government regulation, but I believe that the vast majority of schools, colleges, and universities are genuinely concerned about the educational consumer and the public trust which now more than ever are at stake.

Several events of the past year alone substantiate at least a growing awareness of the educational problems and at best some first-step solutions initiated in the educational sector.

Federal Level

Two philosophical shifts are taking place: (a) The student is defined, and more and more accepted, as the direct consumer of educational services; and (b) educational abuse is viewed as the responsibility to a large extent of the federal government, no longer exclusively of the states or of the Office of Education, but also of the Veterans Administration, the Federal Trade Commission, the Social Security Administration, the Department of Labor, the Department of Justice, the Federal Aviation Administration, and others.[7] These philosophical shifts indicate that we have passed beyond the intellectual debate over definitions and have begun to concentrate on problems and solutions.

FICE and its active subcommittee are excellent vehicles for attracting the attention and concerns of member federal agencies and for proposing active solutions. The FICE strategy report, mentioned above, describes the past areas of agency responsibility, identifies present issues and implications, and recommends the acceptance of four principles and implementation of specific action steps for future solutions to educational abuse. The full report makes interesting reading, threatening for some agencies and institutions, and innocuous for some students and consumer leaders. Hopefully the report will spawn reform in partnership at many different levels.

---

[7]Federal Interagency Committee on Education, Subcommittee on Educational Consumer Protection, *A Federal Strategy Report for Protection of the Consumer of Education,* Section II (September 18, 1974), pp. 13-30.

FICE was also responsible for funding and coordinating the first National Conference on Consumer Protection in Education last March [1974] in Denver, Colorado. Under a grant from federal agencies, the Education Commission of the States (ECS) organized a forum of 250 selected educators, federal and state education officials, private accrediting executives, congressional and state legislature officials, consumer leaders, counselors, and school administrators and students. After a full day of carefully arranged workshops, the conference participants reported in plenary session and to the public at large the major issues and abuses they (a real cross section) had identified and major recommendations urged to bring about solutions.[8] Approximately half of the participants agreed in writing to initiate reform within a specific area and report to the Second National Conference on Consumer Protection in Education funded again by the federal agencies and sponsored by ECS.

The second conference was held in Knoxville in November 1974. Its purpose this time was to develop working approaches and feasible action steps to the problems identified in Denver. A selected group of 125 people, again representing a cross section of experiences, developed very meaty recommendations in the following areas: (a) protecting the student's financial interest, (b) information needs and systems, (c) institutional responses, (d) regulations, and (e) disclosure. The conference participants recommended a Federal Tuition Insurance Corporation, policies of disclosure and refunds, prompt withdrawal of federal eligibility and financial aid for offenders, a coordinated educational complaint center with "teeth," and many other types of action some of which were discussed at the Association of American Colleges annual meeting in January.

One significant accomplishment of the second conference on educational consumer protection was living up to the subtitle of the meeting — A Federal, State, and Local Partnership.

State Level

Since much of the direct responsibility for education rests with

---

[8] *Conference Report and Recommendations,* Report Number 53, Education Commission of the States (Denver, June 1974).

the states (approval, licensing, funding, setting policy, etc.), the active participation of all states in educational reform is critical.

Many state authorities have risen to the challenge. ECS, sponsor of the two educational consumer protection conferences and the consumer-oriented model legislation developed to approve degree granting postsecondary institutions, is an important leader in educational consumer protection. Montana, Tennessee, and North Carolina have approved the model legislation.[9]

North Dakota, Wisconsin, Indiana, Ohio, Minnesota, Oregon, Washington, Florida, and California lead in consumer-oriented improvements of state licensing procedures, accountability systems, disclosure requirements, occupational information, and investigations of individual schools accused of fraudulent practices.

The administration, faculty, and students in some state universities, colleges and technical schools as well as state legislators (Senator Joseph Harder from Kansas and Representative Tom Jensen from Tennessee, among others) are encouraging consumer relations boards and more open policies at state institutions. This state impetus is needed.

State and local government consumer offices more and more bear the burden of complaint resolution. States like Wisconsin with a strong consumer protection component are using complaints as a data base to inform the public, apply pressure, and purpose corrective state legislation.

Private Level

The path to educational consumer protection branches at this point heads off in the directions of private accrediting agencies, for-profit vocational schools, nonprofit institutions (both academic and occupational), educational associations, and consumer and student groups. Without the concern and input from these groups, progress made thus far and necessary in the immediate

---

[9]*A Federal Strategy Report for Protection of the Consumer of Education,* Section III, pp.. 32-34.

future would be vague talk.

To cite briefly a few examples of awareness and initial reform, let me mention only a *partial* listing of groups and some actions they are taking to improve the educational marketplace:

Association of Independent Colleges and Schools with its developing complaint handling system;

American Association of Higher Education and its attempts to link prospective students with accurate and appropriate information;

A business college in Kentucky where the director personally canvasses and responds to student problems on a regular basis;

American Council on Consumer Interests, three of whose leading members have publicized educational problems and initiated research and reforms at their institutions;

The National Academy of Public Administration with its report on the use of private accreditation to determine institutional eligibility for federal funds and its very serious proposal that an educational Consumers Union be founded to report impartially on colleges and schools; and the

National Student Educational Fund and its Information Gap Project which is describing to policy makers what kinds of information students need.

Many educational associations are including consumer protection topics at their annual meetings in an effort to inform their speakers as well as their members about educational abuses, differing perspectives and interests, and, I hope, ways to forge a partnership to bring about reform in the educational marketplace.

Consumer Protection: More Work Required

The partnership in educational reform must move forward. There is work enough for everyone which must be accomplished in the immediate future and longer-range period. Without coordination and aggressive action the educational abuses will multiply, more students will default, and more institutions will succumb to the competitive pressures of dropping enrollments, increasing costs, slick recruiting tactics, and irresponsible treatment of educational consumers.

In the immediate future several developments underway need to be finalized and applied to other parts of the country and to other institutions. For example, a student group in Oregon has developed a computer-based system for gathering pertinent data on 95 percent of the occupations in Oregon and potential employment opportunities, thus proving the economic and technical feasibility of providing student consumers with relevant information on jobs.* The Federal Trade Commission (FTC) and the U. S. Office of Education have proposed regulations to protect consumers of proprietary, nonprofit, and public occupational and academic institutions. Although the audience and content of these sets of regulations are different, they both propose refund policies, disclosure, and other protective measures. The educational and consumer press as well as consumer organizations such as Consumers Union and the FTC are now producing articles and consumer guides to increase consumer awareness of the educational marketplace and to help consumers select the appropriate educational program. The educational complaint proposal which I am working on with FICE Subcommittee would include a standardized complaint form, a complaint and information center, and enforcement and "early warning" powers. Congress intends to hold additional hearings with an eye toward passing educational consumer protection legislation.

Other areas requiring immediate and longer-range action include: *research* to develop case studies of certain problems and a statistical base to understand the problems and costs more precisely; *technical assistance* to permit the strengthening of existing standards and development of greater consumer protection awareness and procedures; *information* to students regarding schools and potential employment, to federal agencies on institutional and student behavior, to institutions on what innovations their counterparts are undertaking, and to legal and paralegal consumer and other organizations trying to resolve complaints

---

*Career Information System located at 247 Hendricks Hall, University of Oregon, Eugene 97403. The project is funded by the Fund for the Improvement of Postsecondary Education at HEW.

and correct abusive practices; and *coordination* between the diverse but necessary partners to the solutions.

Although blatant and subtle exploitation exists, we are beginning to see some positive movement. We are becoming aware of the problems and of consumer rights and responsibilities in the educational marketplace. One nationally respected education reporter suggested to students that their predecessors used to worry about everything they always wanted to know about colleges but didn't dare ask. He advises students to *ask*.[10] I would urge that all of us ask about and respond to educational abuses and thus get on with the business of consumer protection in education.

[10]Fred M. Hechinger, *Saturday Review*, April 6, 1974.

JOAN S. STARK

THE RESPONSIBILITY OF TRUSTEES IN RELATIONSHIP TO CONSUMER PROTECTION

Professor Joan S. Stark's "The Responsibility of Trustees In Relationship to Consumer Protection" was originally presented at the Eleventh Annual Conference on the Leadership role of the Trustee. The following article was later reprinted in part in the June 1975 issue of Planning for Higher Education, *the bimonthly publication of the Society for College and University Planning published in cooperation with Educational Facilities Laboratories. Professor Stark of Syracuse University examines the impact of consumerism in postsecondary education and notes the implications of such a movement for policy-making processes at institutions of higher learning.*

There is currently a force — perhaps a social movement — which is sweeping through postsecondary education. The movement is called consumerism. You may have noticed articles in the local news media at least weekly which stress federal or state efforts to protect the consumer in postsecondary education. Letters from students appear daily in campus newspapers inquiring about the procedure for protesting a grade believed to have been given unfairly, and about the "due process" available for a student who thinks he has been misled upon admission to the institution or the victim of presumed administrative arbitrariness in one of a variety of areas from housing to class scheduling.

Perhaps the movement is due to the current buyer's market in postsecondary education and the students' recognition that they have the opportunity to be fussy about the service they receive. Perhaps the increasingly conservative students of the late seventies have taken the advice given to their predecessors that change can be most effectively brought about by "working within the system." The movement certainly owes some of its strength to the anxiety students are feeling about their employment opportunities after they leave school and the tension they and their parents feel about larger and larger tuition outlays in a time of inflation. And it may be aided and abetted by an increase in high pressure sales techniques of admissions personnel. Undoubtedly it is due, in part, to each of these causes and others.

Whatever the cause, the consumerism movement is snowballing both on the national level and within each of our institutions. It is no longer confined to institutional complaints but has reached directly into the classroom. A new faculty member at my institution reported recently that a student had inquired how she would be assured that she was getting her $300 worth out of a three-credit hour course. The new teacher wondered if this type of inquiry was characteristic of Syracuse or if such questions were being asked everywhere. The answer is that such questions are indeed being asked at institutions everywhere.

It is difficult to say to what extent the increased number of consumer complaints is due to the publicity government activities have received in the press and, in turn, to what extent governmental activity has been stimulated by student complaints. According to Virginia Knauer, Special Assistant to the President for Consumer Affairs, the volume of educational complaints received in one office at The United States Office of Education has doubled each year for the past three years.[1] Similar increases are reported by state education agencies. The complaints concern deceptive practices, violation of student rights, and deprivation of property because payment for services has not been rendered as contracted.

The complaints have been registered with government agencies for two primary reasons. First, people have learned to turn to bureaus of consumer affairs at the local, state, and national level when they need help in such matters, and secondly, many students are receiving direct government financial assistance through grants, loans, and workstudy programs. When the

---

[1]Virginia Knauer, "The Consumer's Need for Protection in the Educational Marketplace," *Preliminary Report of the Second National Conference on Consumer Protection in Postsecondary Education* (Knoxville, Tennessee, November 14-15, 1974).

citizen is using government money to purchase a major service such as education and feels he is not getting his money's worth, he may assume the government will be interested.

Indeed the government is interested. Much of the concern has been stimulated by abuses relating to provision of federal financial assistance for students attending proprietary or "profit-making" institutions. A student who receives a federally guaranteed loan to attend an institution may voluntarily drop out of the course or find that he is ill prepared or ineligible to complete it successfully. The loan money has become tuition and is already in the proprietor's pocket sometimes with little or no refund available. In such a case the student often feels little obligation to repay money from which he has received no benefit and he defaults on his government loan. The government, and thus the taxpayer, ends up paying.[2]

Although both state and federal governments are very concerned, the authority for setting standards and granting eligibility to schools for enrolling students with financial assistance is so fragmented that no agency or institution has clear responsibility for protecting the consumer of educational services. At the federal level at least twelve agencies share in this responsibility.[3] Efforts are now underway to clarify this situation.

As a variety of government agencies which receive complaints wondered where to send the complainant for satisfaction and began to discuss possible methods of centralizing authority, they discovered that all the complaints did not arise from students attending proprietary institutions. Many of the abuses that looked quite unethical in the proprietary sector of postsecondary education had been tolerated for years in nonprofit traditional collegiate institutions. As the Federal Trade Commission's proposed crackdown on proprietary schools reached the media, students in the traditional sector also began to take increased notice that this was indeed the case. As you probably know, public confidence in our educational institutions has decreased substantially in the last few years. Students and their parents no longer believe that the teacher is always right. In fact, a Harris poll has shown

---

[2]Knauer, "The Consumer's Need for Protection in the Educational Marketplace," 1974.
[3]Knauer, "The Consumer's Need for Protection in the Educational Marketplace," 1974.

that only 40 percent of Americans have a great deal of confidence in colleges as opposed to 61 percent eight years ago.[4] Students and parents are more inclined to doubt the integrity of colleges than they once were.

Proprietary schools are often engaged in interstate commerce and thus are subject to regulation by the Federal Trade Commission. Traditional collegiate instruction has long been considered a state responsibility. It has become quite clear, however, that the vehicle for regulation of abuses in the nonprofit sector does exist in the prospect of ineligibility for federal funding. For example, there are few, if any, institutions in the country which have not attempted to abide by affirmative action and civil rights legislation under the threat of ineligibility for federal funds. It seems likely that the same threat will be used to protect the consumer.

A number of recommendations have now come forth from government groups which leave little question in my mind that regulation of abuses in the proprietary sector will be quickly followed by similar regulation of the nonprofit sector — probably first the private institutions of higher education and then the public institutions. What's good for the goose is good for the gander particularly when much of the feed comes from the same bin. The Federal Interagency Commission on Education in its subcommittee report on Consumer Protection in Postsecondary Education makes the federal position quite clear:

> The Federal Government, wherever it disburses funds, directly or indirectly to support educational institutions, programs, and students, must assume responsibility as to how these funds affect the consumer of education as well as education and program objectives.[5]

In the spring of 1974, the Federal Interagency Committee, composed of representatives of twenty-nine federal agencies concerned with education, stimulated a national invitational conference on the subject of consumer protection. This was followed in November 1974 by a second such conference. At the first

---

[4]Carol Herrnstadt Shulman, "Higher Education: Public Attitudes and Federal Legislation," *Research Currents* (Washington, D. C., ERIC/AAHE, n.d.)

[5]Federal Interagency Committee on Education, Subcommittee on Educational Consumer Protection, *A Federal Strategy Report for Protection of the Consumer of Education*, draft report (Washington, D. C., September 18, 1974).

conference issues were identified and, at the second, proposals for action were initiated. At the two conferences held thus far it has been repeatedly stressed that the federal government has the responsibility to use its funds as incentives to ensure that the consumer is protected. A third meeting has been suggested to review progress.

In addition, the Fund for the Improvement of Postsecondary Education, a division of Health, Education, and Welfare, has established a national project to assist institutions in determining better methods of giving information to students making a choice of postsecondary opportunities. On February 5, bill #2786 known as the Postsecondary Education Consumer Protection Act of 1975 was introduced in the House of Representatives. A similar bill is anticipated in the Senate. Both measures would apply to all postsecondary institutions.

Advocates of state responsibility believe the states can and should retain jurisdiction over the activities of educational institutions. Federal officials seem to feel, however, that it is, at the very least, their responsibility to set up mechanisms to see that the states enforce the regulations and to use both positive and negative incentives to encourage them to do so. Even when it has been proposed that appropriate information be collected and audited by a state agency, it has also been proposed that the federal government establish standard definitions to ensure consistency among the states.

Regulatory efforts have been proposed in three distinct areas:

Access information — the type of information a student can obtain in making a choice of institution or program.

Process information — information concerning academic or classwork requirements, patterns of student interaction, student-faculty relationships, use of internal and external agencies for resolving disputes.

Outcome information — proposed outcomes of the institution, including the actual employment of the graduates of a program.[6]

---

[6]*Consumer Protection in Postsecondary Education: Conference Report and Recommendations*, Report No. 53 (Denver, Education Commission of the States, June 1974).

This, then, is the status of the consumerism movement at the present time. Some interested governmental and nongovernmental agencies are at work to develop a system of incentives for voluntary protection of the educational consumer. If voluntary efforts fail, more intense support will be gained for federal legislation.

Before proceeding to a detailed discussion of how this movement may affect our postsecondary institutions, I should like to make the basis for my interest in consumer protection in postsecondary education very clear. I do believe there is room for improvement in our communication with and accountability to the student. I see the consumer protection movement as a vehicle for positive institutional improvement. Many things we have long hoped to accomplish in our institutions can be achieved with relative rapidity when the impetus to achieve them is strong enough. But I do not insist that government should make the rules when there is substantial possibility that many facets of educational purpose and process will, as a consequence, move beyond institutional control.

In the past, institutions of higher learning have banded together in self-regulatory groups to tackle immense problems. One example is the formation of the regional accrediting agencies in the early 1900's to establish minimal standards of quality for granting degrees. About the same time a group of institutions also formed the College Entrance Examination Board to achieve some consistency in admissions standards. Even though these voluntary groups may now be less than desirably responsive to the changing times, their formation is significant because they represented self-regulation by institutions which hoped to maintain autonomy and academic freedom.

During the last few decades the federal government has greatly expanded its public welfare role, including its role in the area of education. We no longer debate whether federal control of education will follow federal support. We now typically wait to react to whatever regulation, however uninformed, comes forth from Washington. The recent adoption of the Buckley amendment, or family rights and privacy law, is a case of a needed reform but one which could have been devised by the institutions themselves in a far more workable form. If it is assumed by governmental agencies that those responsible for education at the institutional level are unable or unwilling to take steps to protect the educational consumer, we will indeed be subject to federal and state regulation to the extent that little institutional autonomy will remain. I see chaos and ineffectiveness resulting with the student, the institution, and society as ultimate losers.

In her talk to the second national invitational conference on consumer protection, Virginia Trotter, Assistant Secretary for Education, said:

> This conference marks an important and historic point in our progress toward making consumer protection in postsecondary education a reality. Just eight months ago, the first national conference on this topic was held in Denver. It was the first time representatives of the federal and state governments, institutions and consumer groups, industry, students, and the public met together to share common concerns and begin thinking about solutions.[7]

You will note that Mrs. Trotter grouped together institutions and consumer groups. I did not attend the first national conference to which she refers. In the official attendance listing twenty-nine institutions of higher education were named. Judging from the attendance at the second national conference in which I did participate, I would guess that only a few of the attendees thus included were presidents or other top administrators actually representing their institutions. None to my knowledge were members of boards of trustees who presumably represent the public stake in higher education. Rather the institutional people were professors of economics, consumer education, marketing, and other faculty concerned with higher education as a field of study, some of whom, like me, invited themselves for independent reasons. At the second conference there were, I believe, fewer than five presidents or deans from approximately 2900 traditional educational institutions throughout the country. Some representatives of major educational associations were quietly in

---

[7]Virginia Trotter, Address given to the Second National Conference on Consumer Protection. *Preliminary Report of the Second National Conference on Consumer Protection (Knoxville, Tennessee, November 14-15, 1974).*

attendance.

Were college presidents or board chairmen invited to this important and historic conference which made sweeping recommendations for national regulations and did they decline to attend? Answers to my inquiries indicate that they were not invited. This situation made the two days informative but also frightening for me. I am not yet convinced that we have reached the time when federal or state regulation is necessary without consultation with the persons at the institutional level who will finance and implement the measures. The conference proceedings continually refer to a tripartite responsibility — (1) federal, (2) state, and (3) educational and consumer agencies. Of the third group mentioned the consumer agencies were in attendance but the front-line educational contingent was sadly lacking.

Your guardianship of the public interest of postsecondary institutions, their resources and their great potential for shaping society make it important that you be aware of and consulted about an issue as broad as consumerism. It is to the credit of our Board of Regents and State Education Department personnel that they included this session on the agenda today because they felt you should be informed participants in this discussion.

I predict with some confidence that within a year or two you will be called upon to provide resources and backing to your chief executive in supplying more accurate information and better services to the customer. You may be asked to commit some resources to cooperate with similar institutions to work out solutions to these problems or alternatively, you may simply have to commit the resources in response to a federal statute you had no part in framing.

Since I see a movement which has implications for every facet of policy-making and operation of our institutions of higher learning and one which can, if we utilize its forces wisely, result in improvement in the education we provide, I will attempt to point out some common consumer complaints and to connect each with a positive mode of attack.

Many of the long lists of abuses which are reported to be perpetrated upon the student-consumer derive from the activities of diploma mills, degree frauds, and other such bogus educational enterprises. I have no intention of reviewing these lists here. New York has long been much more successful than some other states in preserving an atmosphere where such activities do not flourish. My examples will be taken from areas in which the most well-intentioned institution can improve and will be restricted to the traditional activities which institutions such as yours and mine have performed for years. Many student complaints are not new in American education. From the colonial days there were student riots and revolts centering around complaints about the curriculum, discipline, and dining hall food. In fact,

> In 1763 a group of citizens hostile to the Yale (University) administration called upon the legislature to fulfill its parental responsibility by standing as a court of last appeal for Yale undergraduates who were displeased with the college administration and its concept of discipline. It is important to note that the legislature did not act in this manner — rather it strengthened the independence of Yale, even though they were supporting it financially to some extent.[8]

The advent of universal access to postsecondary education and the establishment of broad permanent programs of federal and state financial aid have simply placed today's complaint more fully into the public arena with a somewhat different response.

Many of the current complaints about postsecondary institutions center on the recruitment and admission process. In New York State we now have a place for every student, rich or poor, bright or not so bright, career oriented or seeking to enrich the intellect. Unfortunately educators are not entirely successful in placing the pegs in the matching holes. This is true partly because we have given inadequate attention to the needs of each individual student and partly because we have entered an era of competition for bodies with test scores of 98°F. We have been less than careful about promising a student that his needs can be filled at our institution. Instead of telling him of a more suitable program at a nearby institution we often enroll him anyway in hopes that his goals will change with exposure to our particular brand of education. And sometimes they do. We certainly need to be

---

[8]Frederick Rudolph, *The American College and University: A History* (New York, Vintage, 1962).

cautious of insisting that young people make irrevocable decisions too early. We need to be equally careful, however, that we help each student to understand the reasons why he is entering postsecondary education and to become aware of the full range of opportunities open to him. We must provide better information to the student and further, we must teach him how to use it.

It has been often said of late that the increase in provision of financial aid directly to the student, from both federal and state resources, will cause the students to "vote with their feet." Some authorities believe that colleges which offer programs attractive to students will thus survive in an era of declining enrollment; those which are unattractive will fail. Unfortunately, when this proposition is examined closely in conjunction with the level of financial aid now appropriated and the need levels of families for eligibility, we find that this pedestrian vote will be exercised mainly by students from low income homes, many of whom are the first in their family to attend college, who have perhaps received the least attention from the high school guidance counselor and who lack sophistication in making institutional choices. On what basis will such purchasers make their decisions? What types of educational process can we as institutions devise to improve their effectiveness as information seekers?

If we fail to devise means of presenting more helpful information about our institutions and whom they can best serve in order to assist the student in finding his proper niche, we may initially attract many students with hard sell advertising. But we will be increasingly plagued with dropouts and dissatisfied customers, which, as any businessman knows, are the worst kind of public relations to cultivate.

It is well known that students enter college with an unrealistic idea of what college is all about. This idealism was detected by my late colleague Dr. George Stern, among other researchers, and has been aptly termed the "Freshman Myth."[9] In a very short time the new students adjust their view of the institution to be more consistent with that held by the upperclassmen and faculty. (Strangely enough, administrators commonly believe the myth,

---

[9]George Stern, "The Freshman Myth," *NEA Journal*, 55:41-43, September 1966.

too). The letdown when the student discovers that college is not all he had hoped may be severe and may, in fact, account for some of the complaints. It would be impossible to completely destroy youthful anticipation, and yet it behooves us to stop helping students to delude themselves. The problem looks a bit different too when we realize that increasing numbers of postsecondary students are not seventeen to twenty-one years old but are experienced consumers in the marketplace who are accustomed to sending a product back if it has flaws or does not fit correctly.

Current promotional materials do include student statements of what the institution is like. The statements are usually made by carefully selected students — I've never seen a college catalog which quotes a student critical of the institution or its policies. But an institution can gather data about its intellectual and social climate and make the actual profile available to prospective students. In so doing, the college is enabled to take note of its strong points and correct some weak areas which need improvement. The data can be a valuable tool for internal decision making.

We owe our students the same rigorous objectivity in examining our institution and reporting its dimensions that we expect the student to exercise in a research project or in the science lab.

Along with considerable improvement of our recruitment and admissions counseling I would include the necessity for improvement in financial aid counseling. Granted, the complicated system of financial aid is difficult to interpret to students, but we must try harder, particularly when a student is contracting for large debts which will be difficult for him to repay.

I have some "candid camera-type" tape recordings in my office, taken with the premission of the persons whose conversations were taped, at college nights around the Syracuse area. I will not release the tapes unless subpoenaed, but I would guess that some college presidents and their admissions directors, too, would be appalled if they heard the outright distortions of truth which their field representatives give students about their college and the aid available to them. One representative went so far as to respond to a mother's inquiry about the tuition fee in this way: "You've been paying taxes in New York all your life and now you're going to get it all back to educate this pretty little daughter of yours.

There is a tuition figure in this catalog but it doesn't mean anything so don't even bother with it. New York State residents are eligible for this great new Tuition Assistance Plan and your needs will all get taken care of." And, so far as I could tell — except perhaps for a quick assessment of the clothing worn by this family — the representative had no way of knowing the family income level and whether the student would be eligible for any state aid whatsoever. I hasten to add that I have, on the same tape, recordings of very careful statements being given to students and their families. We are just not all being honest enough or careful enough. There is little wonder that the student who gets only a look at the lean on the bacon is often dissatisfied when he opens the rest of the package.

Several solutions have been recommended. One suggestion is to have all advertising reviewed prior to publication by a private regulatory body which has authority to sanction its member institutions. Another suggestion is a booklet explaining student rights — much like the one that the Interstate Commerce Commission requires movers of household goods to give prospective clients. Still another suggestion is to have accountability held by a public regulatory body or a disinterested rating service.[10]

The chief danger I see in the external review agency is a failure to recognize that the types of information needed by varied students and the strengths of our many types of institutions may not be taken into account. Nor will external regulation necessarily bring about institutional assessment and improvement; it is more likely to result in searches for loopholes in the review. The very act of reviewing the goals of the institution and the examination of what students it can best serve will stimulate educational improvement. Certainly in the business world, organizations which respond to consumer complaints by upgrading their services and which communicate those efforts clearly to the public are likely to expand their clientele. Hopefully, institutions will begin efforts at self-regulation either through their accrediting agencies or through regional consortia and external reviews will be un-

---

[10]Helen E. Nelson, "Consumer Advocacy and Student Protection in Postsecondary Education," in *Consumer Protection in Postsecondary Education: Program Handbook,* (Knoxville, November 14-15, 1974).

necessary.

Let's move now to the other end of the college years and consider another potent student complaint. "The job I thought I was preparing for doesn't exist."

Many such complaints are focused on trade schools where some explicit or implicit guarantee of employment given to the student goes unfulfilled. There is considerable evidence, however, that community colleges and even liberal arts colleges are plagued with a similar problem. The Federal Trade Commission proposed regulations which would require schools offering vocational preparation to disclose the percentage of their students who actually obtained positions in the field for which they were trained. The FTC staff cites a current complaint brought by a student who enrolled for a computer course and understood that he would acquire certain skills. He later found that his skills applied only to a certain type of computer, not in very wide use. He claimed he was misled. Certainly this was a sin of omission. The student did not have the sophistication at the outset to ask specifically whether there were different skills for different computers. Was the school remiss in not bringing this to his attention? I surely think our schools do have an obligation to call such special limitations to a student's attention. It's the difference between giving selective positive information and fully disclosing all that is known which could be of assistance to the student. The principle "let the buyer beware" has no place in education.

The responsibility for providing jobs for students does not lie with the educational institution. We have, for example, no control over the economy. The responsibility of educating the students about the world of work and helping them seek an appropriate place in it does seem to me to be our responsibility.

An assumption which seemed to pervade the Knoxville Conference on Consumer Protection and the various proposed regulations emphasizing job placement, however, is that every student entering postsecondary education knows what career he wishes to pursue. We know that this is not true. At least 25 percent of entering college students have no clear career focus.

Of New York State students who took the College Board Scholastic Aptitude tests in 1973-74, 47,800 felt they needed educational and vocational counseling and would seek such assistance in college. This number of requests for assistance was exceeded only by requests for assistance in finding part-time work opportunities.

Many students look to the college to help them learn about career opportunities. The placement "track record" of an institution is indeed important if job placement is its stated purpose. More appropriate for students to know when choosing most of our institutions is the extent to which the institution makes a substantial effort to improve their ability to make a career choice and to help them plan an academic program accordingly.

It would be disturbing if government regulations should require that our liberal arts colleges report, as a measure of their effectiveness, the number of students placed in the fields of history, philosophy, and anthropology within six months after graduation. On the other hand, such institutions need to make it very clear to students that the purpose of these programs and majors is *not* to lead directly to a career.

We have long made many claims about the purposes of a liberal arts degree. They include, among others, the ability to think critically, to participate as an intelligent person in civic affairs, to appreciate the arts, to gain sufficient flexibility to be successful at many jobs and thus have a wide career choice. We have done little about demonstrating that any of these purposes are, in fact, achieved, nor have we said clearly to the students how our curricula intend to bring these ends about. The liberal arts colleges will need to devise more appropriate ways of representing their institutions to students and of demonstrating that their objectives are met.

Let me read a short portion of an unsolicited statement recently sent in the mail to superior high school students by the president of a very prestigious major university — not, I am pleased to say, in New York State. This was a statement the president had made to last year's enrolled National Merit Scholars.

It is our aim at this University to present the kind (sic) of curricula and the kind of challenges that will give you the opportunity to develop into a truly creative individual. The kind of individual that I am describing is the kind that we need in our society and the kind that we are dedicated to producing at this University. To become this kind of person you need the ability that you have shown, but in addition you must be dedicated.[11]

Throughout the entire statement the same words "kind of person needed" and "creative kind of person" are used over and over and nowhere defined beyond that stage. In the total statement of about 500 words, there were two obvious misrepresentations of the National Merit Scholars program which bright students would immediately detect, a grammatical error which you may have noted, and an attempt at charismatic appeal to the emotions rather than a clear statement of the objectives of the university. Granted there are legitimate objectives of our institutions which are not easily delineated and measured, but we have not often been honest enough to say, "We think this is what you will achieve here if you do your part and we do ours — but we can't give you a guarantee. Here is how we hope to try."

Many students today have been taught to think quite critically in high school. They read literature about systems analysis and consider inputs and outputs. Now they are asking us to relate educational outputs to inputs in a rational way. They are asking that we clearly define the goals of our institutions, tell them the method by which we expect to reach the goals and provide measures of the degree of success we are experiencing. They are saying "Demonstrate to me that I will think more critically or be a more informed citizen at the end of two or four years in your school. If you cannot, I may not be willing to buy your brand of education."

I think we should be proud of this inclination on the part of our young people. It has been said that if the educational system of a nation is good those who are educated will often find that the system itself is obsolete and will wish to negotiate new and better mechanisms.

As a result of this tendency to question the established order there are many examples of student concern which emerge between admission and graduation. Students are becoming increas-

---

[11]Printed statement by a university president, 1975. Source deliberately withheld.

ingly conscious of the academic program. They complain about the listing of courses in the college catalog that have not been taught in several years; of prestigious professors named who in fact do not actually teach. The failure to cover the material described in a course description, the concellation of classes or changing of the announced time, and the lack of appropriate grievance mechanisms are other complaints.

A balance is certainly needed in these matters between student rights and institutional stability. As student inclinations to enroll in certain courses rapidly change, institutions find it difficult to provide adequate faculty and space for one program at the same time that another declines in enrollment. Resources cannot be easily and quickly shifted from one segment of the institution to another. Students may rightfully complain, however, if they are without an assigned laboratory station, typewriter, textbooks, or other necessary equipment because of overcrowding.

It is incumbent upon us to study the methods used by other industries to handle peak loads and to maintain market flexibility. Perhaps we have not done all we can do to anticipate and respond to enrollment shifts.

Many students now want to know in advance just what type of education they will receive. They are calling for printed course objectives and clear statements of how they will be graded. These are among the hardest things for an institution to produce because faculty often see advantages to remaining flexible.

Few faculty would disagree with the proposition that their attempts to clearly delineate the objectives of a course in advance in order that both they and the students may focus the learning activities is a desirable practice. Many colleges have moved in the direction of making such objectives quite explicit for each course. It does limit flexibility, however, both for the institution and the teacher. Consequently, most institutions still retain the typical course description which consists of a few, sometimes difficult to interpret, sentences indicating what the teacher plans to cover. There is room for considerable improvement in this area.

Possibly of greatest concern to students, particularly in large universities, is the lack of responsiveness to inquiries and complaints. A clearly stated grievance procedure which provides students a fair hearing for their concerns does not seem unreasonable. A Statement of Student Rights and Freedoms, dealing mainly with the areas of student misconduct and free speech, was adopted over ten years ago by a number of educational associations. The fact that there have since emerged so few adequate grievance mechanisms is one reason that the ability of institutions to police themselves is now under question. Can we provide a mechanism within our institutions to consider student complaints, particularly in the sensitive academic realm, which continues to protect academic freedom? If not, can we provide an interinstitutional tribunal which will take on this task — a sort of fact-finding board? If we are not able or willing to do either of these things, we will find that a governmental agency, not always sensitive to the needs for academic freedom and inquiry, will provide such a mechanism.

The last specific area I would like to mention briefly is that of fees and refund policies. There are still institutions which insist upon payment of a full year's or semester's tuition in advance and which give the student no refund if he withdraws. In the business world we would not expect to receive back a deposit on a special order, but neither would we expect to pay the full amount for a product we did not accept.

Most statements of institutional fees indicate that the fees are subject to change at any time. Few of us would do business with a merchant who changed the price after we had indicated a desire for the goods. And yet, it is essential to maintain the financial viability of our institutions in the face of unanticipated rising costs. More adequate long-range planning calculated to take into account possible economic shifts, might obviate the need for frequent and abrupt raises in fees and charges. In fact, a contract between the student and the institution, which insists upon educational services at the originally agreed upon price, might spur institutions to improve their long-range planning efforts to their substantial benefit.

Some of the additional proposals for state and federal regulation which have been made include:
1. the publication of attrition rates and reasons for attrition;
2. the publication of federal loan default rates;

3. the public disclosure of full reports by accreditation agencies;
4. the publication of a prospectus about each institution similar to that used by the Securities Exchange Commission for stock offerings (the accuracy of such information would be audited by a state or federal agency);
5. establishment of a clearinghouse which would maintain comparable information about all institutions;
6. establishment of a second clearinghouse which would maintain information on complaints which have been registered against an institution (I have heard no attention given to whether complaints would be certified legitimate before being included in the data bank).

At the conclusion of the first conference on consumer protection in March 1974, Dr. Richard Millard of the Education Commission of the States reminded the conferees of the danger of simplistic solutions. He mentioned the complexity and diversity of institutions and programs and the differences between universities and colleges, community colleges and vocational schools, nonprofit and proprietary private institutions.[12] This concern emerged again, but less strongly in only one of five workshop reports at the second national conference.

In my view it is a most important point, but one which will be emphasized only if these groups of institutions with common interests will begin to set their houses in order and make it well known that they are about such a task. If uniform federal regulations which ignore these distinctions are not to be forthcoming, some haste is in order.

The Association of American Colleges held a conference in January entitled "Consumerism, Student Needs, and Liberal Learning." Information about the consumerism movement was given at the opening session. Yet, before an hour had passed, I think it not incorrect to say that the informal title of the conference had changed to "Consumerism, Institutional Survival, and Liberal Learning." This is understandable given the press for

---

[12]Richard M. Millard, "Conference Concluding Remarks," *Consumer Protection in Postsecondary Education: Conference Report and Recommendations*, Report No. 53, (Denver, Educational Commission of the States, June 1974).

survival on private institutions today. But it seems clear that institutional survival is very closely linked with responsiveness to student needs.

There are clearly some dangers in being overly responsive to student demands. This is as true now as it was when these demands were proclaimed in a different way during the late 1960's. But since colleges are institutions supported by society, and students are voting members of society, student protection and concern for student welfare in some sense belongs to you as trustees and presidents. It is your obligation to develop policies and procedures which will protect the individual member of society as well as the collective society which you represent. Somehow it seems rather obvious that, if the many individual members of society enrolled in postsecondary study are treated fairly and get their money's worth, society will too — collectively.

It is my impression that the Regents of the State of New York believe that this is your obligation too. That is, I suspect, why this topic was included on the conference agenda. In a Regents position paper published in August 1974 entitled "The Articulation of Secondary and Postsecondary Education" I find reference to many of the problems I have mentioned — from a slightly different perspective, but still concerned with meeting student needs. In each case the recommendations begin with the words "The Regents encourage postsecondary institutions to..." I hope I am correct in interpreting the Regents to share my view that this is a task best carried out by the institutions. In talking with our State Education Department officials I find that they are most aware of the differences among your institutions and the varying difficulties you will encounter. I feel they are anxious to provide whatever resources and encouragement they can to help you in a positive and profitable response to this problem. I do not sense them to be in a hurry to recommend regulatory legislation unnecessarily or prematurely.

I would like to outline some roles I see for trustees and college presidents in this context, beyond being aware that the problem exists.

First, I believe you must examine the focus of your institutions. The tendency to try to be all things to all people is probably better resisted. We seem to have an identity crisis in higher education and seldom to be sure of what our purposes should be. It is not surprising that students pick up this uncertainty.

To use a rather simple analogy, I find that the most satisfactory restaurants, and those I prefer to patronize, are those with a clear mission. If I am in a hurry and want a cheap bite to eat I go to Burger King® or Arby's® roast beef. I don't expect a feast. If, on the other hand, I want a leisurely, gourmet dinner and am not concerned about the price, I select a fine restaurant of excellent reputation. The difference between these two is clear and their intent to serve different clientele or the same clientele at different times is obvious. I find that I am most dissatisfied when I go to a restaurant whose goals are unclear. I may pay a medium price for a mediocre dinner. The problem is not with the price or the food so much as with my lack of information about what outcome to expect.

The same kind of accurate expectation concerning the nature of the educational process inside the institution and the probable consequences of attending and graduating will make satisfied student consumers, I believe. In essence the solution to the problem lies in improving communication between the buyer and the seller. I think there is little overt attempt to deceive the consumer in most of our educational institutions. There is, however, a lack of careful attempt to communicate the weaknesses as well as the advantages of the service to him. Educational institutions have a unique responsibility to do so.

Beyond establishing your institutional purposes more clearly I believe you need to delineate what you believe constitutes an ethical relationship between the consumer of education and the institution, and to give careful consideration to all policies to see if they stand up to your own "code of ethics." Policies should be periodically reviewed from this stance just as the educational program must be periodically reviewed.

I think you need to examine the access, process, and output of your institution from the point of view of the consumer as well as from the views of other constituencies you represent, primarily through systematic consultation with students and provision of ways that students can communicate with policy makers.

You need further to provide resources for identification of the kinds of information which would be most helpful in assessing program quality and for development of data collection procedures which, in turn, could be used for program self-study and improvement. In short, through undergoing the process of self-examination for the benefit of the customer you can increase your credibility and product image at the same time that you improve the product. The consumer movement is just one more stimulus toward accountability, both fiscally and educationally.

In reviewing literature on higher education with my raised consumer consciousness I have become aware that times have not changed too much. This might be interpreted to mean that our progress has been very slow. I should like to close with two quotations.

The first quotation is from Francis Wayland, the President of Brown University in 1850. President Wayland said:

> We have produced an article for which the demand is diminishing. We sell it at less than cost, and the deficiency is made up by charity. We give it away, and still the demand diminishes. Is it not time to inquire whether we cannot furnish an article for which the demand will be, at least, somewhat more remunerative?[13]

In January 1975, 125 years later, Willis W. Harman of the Stanford Research Institute spoke in a more modern vein at the Association of American Colleges meeting. He referred to consumerism as the tip of a iceberg, the iceberg itself being a challenge to social institutions, including education.

> Such a challenge to the legitimacy of a social institution or social system, by the citizenry who granted that legitimacy in the first instance, is the most potent transformation force known in human history. The issue is not whether the system will respond — if such a legitimacy challenge grows sufficiently strong, change is assured. The issue is whether the system can alter itself rapidly enough, and whether its integrating bonds will be strong enough to allow the transformation to take place in a nondestructive manner.[14]

---

[13]Rudolph, *The American College and University: A History*, 1962.
[14]Willis W. Harman, "Consumerism Legitimacy and Transformation,'"Address given at the Annual Meeting of the Association of American Colleges (Washington, D. C., January 14, 1975).

JOHN COLEMAN, JAMES GILES, TOM HEATON,
CHARLES SELDEN, and RICHARD R. ROWRAY

PROFESSIONAL AUDIT FOR ADMISSIONS' OFFICERS

The following material has been abstracted from a Professional
Audit for Admissions' Officers *prepared for the National Association of College Admissions Counselors (NACAC) by John
Coleman, James Giles, Tom Heaton, Charles Selden, and
Richard D. Rowray. Permission to reprint the following materials has been secured from NACAC, Skokie, Illinois. Such materials are often utilized by admissions personnel to ensure more
effective means for student recruitment.*

DEVELOPING AN EFFECTIVE STUDENT CONTACT PROGRAM

School-College Relations

	Yes	No	Undecided	Unknown
1. In your relationship with secondary schools and counselors, you have carefully weighed alternatives and have decided which types of recruitment and approaches are best suited to the needs and facilities of your institution?	☐	☐	☐	☐
2. Do you make a reasonable effort to provide a convenient interview opportunity if the interview is requested or required for each applicant?	☐	☐	☐	☐
3. Your institution uses sound judgment in planning the hosting and entertaining of guidance counselors?	☐	☐	☐	☐
4. Your institution establishes a workable timetable for making secondary school visits?	☐	☐	☐	☐
5. Do you encourage secondary schools to coordinate the various schedules for college night and day programs?	☐	☐	☐	☐
6. Have you been properly trained and prepared to participate in college night and college day programs?	☐	☐	☐	☐
7. In proposing a visit to high schools, do you consider the most convenient time for the counselor and the student?	☐	☐	☐	☐

BASIC PRINCIPLE: Most institutions rely heavily on an energetic and well-planned secondary school relations program to attract candidates who would be able, to utilize effectively the educational opportunities available. A college which makes no effort to inform prospective applicants and guidance counselors, candidly, about itself will experience a decline in applications from those candidates it would like most to have among its students.

PROJECTS:

(a) Do you believe college night or college day programs fill the basic need your institution has to schools, students, and counselors? Explain.

_____

_____

_____

_____

(b) Compare the relative advantage of having traveling representatives operate directly from the campus as compared to (a) full-time regional representatives or (b) the use of multicollege representatives.

_____

_____

_____

_____

(c) In what circumstances would you establish central interview stations (such as a hotel) or interview at the school or at the home of the candidate? What criteria would you use in reaching this decision?

_____

_____

_____

_____

Visits to Campus

	Yes	No	Undecided	Unknown
1. Does your institution honor requests or have a formal program for campus visitations?	☐	☐	☐	☐
2. Does your admissions office have a member of the professional staff who has the responsibility to see that campus visitations are conducted?	☐	☐	☐	☐
3. After campus tours, are individuals afforded the opportunity to have questions answered by admissions personnel?	☐	☐	☐	☐
4. Does your institution permit students, parents, and guidance counselors to visit all areas of the campus on their own?	☐	☐	☐	☐
5. Does your institution have an adequate campus map or printed guide?	☐	☐	☐	☐
6. Does your institution arrange for class visitations?	☐	☐	☐	☐

BASIC PRINCIPLE: The admissions officer should encourage and offer the opportunity to all interested parties, especially guidance personnel from both secondary schools and two-year colleges, students and their parents, for campus visitations. The admissions officer must recognize that the campus visitation is a useful tool for the individual to gain first-hand information, observations, and impressions in determining the advisability of enrolling in the institution. Thus, the visitation has to be open and directed to the interest of the individual and conducted by an individual who is knowledgeable about the campus community. The campus visitation should expose the individual not only to the physical facilities and student residential areas, but also to students, faculty, and administrative personnel whose services will be of special interest to the individual.

PROJECTS:

(a) Outline your technique for campus visitations.

_____

_____

_____

_____

(b) List campus areas, groups, and individuals that you feel should not be exposed to visitors at your school.

_____

_____

_____

_____

NOTES:

Readings:

Use Of Persons Other Than Admissions Staff

1. Is your use of students, alumni, faculty, parents, and trustees consistent with the philosophy and objectives of the institution?

Yes ☐ No ☐ Undecided ☐ Unknown ☐

2. Does your office have proper budgeting and training programs planned to obtain a maximum contribution from the use of persons other than the admissions staff?

Yes ☐ No ☐ Undecided ☐ Unknown ☐

3. Do you provide a steady flow of communications and information for these workers?

Yes ☐ No ☐ Undecided ☐ Unknown ☐

4. Have you developed techniques for measuring the effectiveness of these workers?

Yes ☐ No ☐ Undecided ☐ Unknown ☐

BASIC PRINCIPLE: The interpretation and communication of an institution's admissions policies and requirements are the responsibility of the professional admissions staff. Therefore, utilization of students, alumni, faculty, parents, and trustees must be in addition to rather than in place of the professional staff. While the selection of non-professional workers may well be made upon their communication skills, it is essential that they receive specialized training conducted by the admissions office. Included in the training should be information about the institutional admissions requirements and policies, current information about the institution, its academic program, and its student body, and counseling students from a guidance frame of reference (counseling a student in the student's own best interests).

PROJECTS:

(a) What groups do you utilize in your admissions program? Is your selection process designed to obtain quality workers or geographic distribution? Have they had an adequate training program?

_____

_____

_____

_____

(b) What techniques are you currently employing to evaluate persons serving your institution in these capacities?

_____

_____

_____

_____

(c) How will you change your program in the future?

_____

_____

_____

_____

_____

NOTES:

Readings:

Admissions Publications and Visual Aids

1. Your catalog is at least representative, if not better than, institutions similar to yours?

   Yes ☐ No ☐ Undecided ☐ Unknown ☐

2. Does your catalog clearly and accurately represent your institution?

   Yes ☐ No ☐ Undecided ☐ Unknown ☐

3. Is the quality of your publications produced for prospective students an asset in your student contact program?

   Yes ☐ No ☐ Undecided ☐ Unknown ☐

4. The admissions staff has a direct input into the content of the publications used primarily by the admissions office?

   Yes ☐ No ☐ Undecided ☐ Unknown ☐

5. You have reviewed and inspected the current classes of promotional literature that has recently been received by high school guidance counselors?

   Yes ☐ No ☐ Undecided ☐ Unknown ☐

6. Your admissions office releases to guidance counselors an objective description of your freshman class?

   Yes ☐ No ☐ Undecided ☐ Unknown ☐

7. Your objective description of the freshman class contains the following information:

   Yes ☐ No ☐ Undecided ☐ Unknown ☐

   number of applications filed, number of applicants accepted, and number who actually enrolled?

   Yes ☐ No ☐ Undecided ☐ Unknown ☐

   percentage distribution according to public and independent schools?

   Yes ☐ No ☐ Undecided ☐ Unknown ☐

	Yes	No	Undecided	Unknown
a listing by states of applicants' geographical origin?	☐	☐	☐	☐
a description of the new class's academic and career interests?	☐	☐	☐	☐
brief statistics on the academic performance of the previous year's freshman class; these should include number of drop-outs, grade-point averages, etc.	☐	☐	☐	☐
a brief account of the number of freshmen granted financial aid and the size of the awards?	☐	☐	☐	☐
comments on changes in course offerings, grading practices, new physical plant, etc.?	☐	☐	☐	☐
information on qualities most desired in students and factors that influence the admissions decision?	☐	☐	☐	☐

BASIC PRINCIPLE: The very nature of admissions requires a keen sense of interpersonal relationships as one speaks to students, parents, alumni groups, civic organizations, faculty, and others. It is important for the admissions officer to be knowledgeable and skilled in the art of communication and sensitive to the pulse of the many publics he serves. Good public relations is one of the chief areas of responsibility of an admissions officer.

BASIC PRINCIPLE: There is no single method to the promotion of interest in an institution of higher education. Most admissions officers use a wide variety of approaches and techniques of communication. Catalogs, view booklets, institutional profiles, career leaflets, slide presentations, films, and video tape releases are some of the means used to present and promote the institution. All methods of promotion should provide an accurate and clear representation of the institution.

BASIC PRINCIPLE: Each post-secondary school should issue a catalog annually or biennially to present the information needed by students, faculty, administration, and others who require a view of the educational program and goals of the institution. The catalog is usually considered the basic publication, the general reference for information and printed authority of the institution. The catalog states the institutional philosophy, objectives, and regulations which affect the student and should be readable, distinct, clear, and a quality publication.

PROJECTS:

(a) Name the one publication used by your admissions office *most* in need of revision and briefly indicate what changes you would suggest.

_____

_____

_____

_____

(b) Describe how you release to guidance counselors objective and meaningful information on your freshman class.

_____

_____

_____

_____

NOTES:

Readings:

Developing Marketing Patterns & Enrollments

	Yes	No	Undecided	Unknown
1. Does your admissions office have a formal marketing program?	☐	☐	☐	☐
2. In implementing and developing your marketing program, your institution uses services of reputable outside agencies, organizations, or individuals?	☐	☐	☐	☐
3. Are these outside services offered by agencies, organizations, and individuals whose primary functions are supportive to education, interest, and ethics?	☐	☐	☐	☐
4. If your institution has or would develop a quota system or any means of restriction for admissions action based on geographical distribution, sex, academic interest, special talent, etc., the admissions staff has been or would be involved in its development?	☐	☐	☐	☐
5. Your institution's quotas are in accord to the institution's stated philosophies, objectives, and admissions policies?	☐	☐	☐	☐
6. Your quotas or restrictions are clearly stated to the individual before he applies?	☐	☐	☐	☐

BASIC PRINCIPLE: One of the basic responsibilities of the admissions office is to help establish, meet, and maintain the desired enrollment of students for the institution. The enrollment pattern should be in accord with the principles, objectives, facilities, and services that the institution is capable of maintaining so as to insure that each student has adequate resources to pursue his educational goal. It is the responsibility of the admissions office to insure that the commitment to the enrollment pattern does not come into conflict with the established admissions policies and procedures, or lead to questionable admissions practices, or lend itself to unusual pressures directed to the applicants.

BASIC PRINCIPLE: The marketing techniques and devices that the admissions office employs to meet its enrollment obligation must be subject to constant review. Any quotas, special priorities or preference not stated in the formal admissions policy or procedures, must be clearly stated and easily obtainable to any individual seeking admissions. Future development and plans of the institution should be incorporated into the market program.

PROJECTS:

(a) List any quotas or special intent that your institution uses that are exceptions to normal admissions action.

_____

_____

_____

_____

(b) List three ways your office uses to identify and contact specific groups or categories of students.

(1)_____

_____

(2) _____

_____

(3)_____

_____

(c) Explain briefly how your professional admissions staff decides how and where it will conduct its student contact programs.

_____

_____

_____

_____

Admissions Centers, Clearing Houses

	Yes	No	Undecided	Unknown
1. You are familiar with the admissions centers currently providing students with names and/or information about a variety of colleges?	☐	☐	☐	☐
2. If your institution should use the services of an admissions center, you attempt to select those agencies that support sound, educational objectives?	☐	☐	☐	☐
3. You use with discretion any lists of prospective students obtained from admissions centers?	☐	☐	☐	☐
4. Does the professional staff in your office use sound judgment in referring students to admissions centers?	☐	☐	☐	☐

BASIC PRINCIPLE: Admissions officers should be fully informed regarding the quality and reputation of those agencies or organizations that sponsor admissions centers for the purpose of assisting prospective students with the selection of an appropriate college to which they may apply.

PROJECT:

(a) Name three reputable and reliable admissions centers and reference centers and who sponsors them.

(1)_____

_____

(2)_____

_____

(3)_____

_____

Follow-up After Admission

	Yes	No	Undecided	Unknown

1. Do you have an organized follow-up program for students admitted to your institution?

    Yes ☐ No ☐   Undecided ☐   Unknown ☐

2. Is your follow-up program primarily designed to communicate with the student in a manner which will assist in the transition to your college?

    Yes ☐ No ☐   Undecided ☐   Unknown ☐

3. Is the follow-up placed on the calendar in anticipation of the student's time, need sequence?

    Yes ☐ No ☐   Undecided ☐   Unknown ☐

BASIC PRINCIPLE: Follow-up with an admitted student, who has not yet registered, is for two purposes . . . (1) to provide for a smoother transition into the institution; (2) to make the admitted student a firm member of your student body. To serve the students, their questions, needs, and anxieties regarding attendance are anticipated by the admissions office and communications are designed to meet these requirements on a critical time, need schedule. Follow-up of admitted and prospective students is the responsibility of the admissions office.

PROJECTS:

(a) Define the most effective follow-up activities on your campus.

_____

_____

_____

(b) List anticipated needs of admitted students at your institution in time sequence.

_____

_____

_____

_____

RICHARD C. IRELAND

THE PROFESSIONAL ADMISSIONS RECRUITER POCKET PLANNER

The following material has been abstracted from The Professional Admissions-Recruiter Pocket Planner, *by Richard C. Ireland, of the Ireland Educational Organization. The* Planner *has been designed as a reference tool in student recruitment strategy.*

Here are some tips about the general characteristics of the type of admissions recruiter that prospective students like to say yes to:

A good recruiter is liked by his prospects as a person.

He has a better understanding of and is sympathetic to his prospects' problems.

He's a good conversationalist.

He's a well-rounded individual.

He's perceived as working for a dependable and student-oriented school.

He appears well trained because of his in-depth knowledge of his school, territory, prospects, and recruiting techniques.

Introduce yourself and your school in such a way that your prospects will feel it will be worthwhile to listen.

Express appreciation for being invited to make the presentation.

Reduce your anxiety by:

— reminding yourself that you can do it.

— remembering that your prospects may also feel the same tension.

— reminding yourself that you have something important to say.

Smile a genuine, sincere, warm smile. (It's amazing how many forget this simple gesture.)

When possible, refer to your prospects by name.

State the purpose of your presentation clearly and concisely.

Ask questions to verify your information or assumptions: You

79

plan to graduate in June? Your major field of interest is
_____?

Exhibit your purposefulness through your actions and statements.

Keep in mind questions that will clearly show your interest in your prospects or audience.

Be a good listener. The more your prospects talk, the more you'll learn about their problems, needs, and interests.

Make your prospects feel important.

Following are ways to help you deal effectively with objections:

Welcome objections. They give you clues as to what is on your prospects' minds.

Listen carefully before responding.

If necessary, repeat or rephrase objections.

Agree with objections, at least in part.

Probe to determine whether there are any hidden objections.

Ask "what" and "why" questions.

Test your prospects to make sure they're satisfied.

Make a list of the objections you encounter.

Action Techniques to Help You
Secure a Commitment

Assume from the outset that your prospects are set on coming to your school.

Ask your prospects to make commitments.

Summarize your key benefits.

Remind your prospects that nothing succeeds like success.

Try "yes building" by securing a series of acceptances about your location, student activities, and so on.

Use the standing-room-only approach to encourage your prospects to apply early to be sure they can get in.

Restate benefits in the form of stories or case histories.

Just before you leave, come up with a last-minute benefit.

Communicate with your prospects in such a way that they can visualize themselves in a campus situation.

Mention any trends, job opportunities, or financial aid possibilities that are likely to affect your prospects.

Keep your application forms visible at all times.

Team up with teachers, alumni, or students to help put your point across.

Offer your prospects a challenge.

Close in on objections.

Offer your prospects some alternatives, such as cooperative education, independent study, credit for experience, self-guided study, or special field work.

Maintaining Commitments

After you've secured a commitment, you will still need to follow up at regular intervals to make sure the commitment is maintained. Remember, prospects become students only when they register, and until that happens they are still anyone's prospects.

Department of Health, Education, and
Welfare, Office of Education

GUARANTEED STUDENT LOAN
PROGRAM RULES, 1975-1976*

*The following guidelines for institutions participating in the
Guaranteed Student Loan Program are excerpted from rules and
regulations promulgated for the academic year 1975-76 by the
Department of Health, Education, and Welfare, Office of Education.*

REQUIREMENTS AND STANDARDS FOR
PARTICIPATING EDUCATIONAL INSTITUTIONS

§ 177.61 Agreements Between Eligible Institutions
and the Commissioner

(a) (1) Any eligible institution seeking to participate, in any
manner, in any program covered under this part shall submit to
the commissioner for his approval, on a form provided by him, an
agreement signed by an appropriate official acknowledging the
institution's obligation to comply with all applicable laws and
all applicable regulations set forth in this part.

(2) The agreement provided for in paragraph (1) of this paragraph shall be for a term of two years and be renewable for additional terms of two years. A shorter term may, however, be
provided if the commissioner has knowledge that the institution's
accreditation or its satisfaction of other eligibility requirements,
as set forth in § 177.1, will be effective for less than two years.

(3) If a participating institution undergoes a change of controlling ownership or form of control, its agreement shall automatically expire at the time of such change. In such instance,

---

*See also H. R. 3471, introduced by Congressman James O'Hara on February 20, 1975, i.e.,
consumer aspects which compel institutions of higher education to disclose significant
cost, faculty, and program data to students.

continued participation by the institution in loan programs under this part shall require a new agreement with the commissioner and continuation of the institution's status as an eligible institution under this part.

(4) Institutions outside the States shall be required to comply with the provisions of this part only to the extent determined by the commissioner on a case-by-case basis.

(b) An institution designated as an "eligible institution" on the effective date of this regulation shall have a period of ninety days to submit the agreement described in paragraph (a) of this section in order to assure continuous participation in programs covered under this part. An institution which has not submitted such agreement by the end of this ninety day period will be subject to having its eligibility suspended or terminated pursuant to subpart G of this part.
(20 U.S.C. 1082(a) (1), 1087-1(a))

§ 177.62 Procedures, Records and Reports

(a) Each participating institution shall establish and maintain such administrative and fiscal procedures and records as may be necessary to ensure proper and efficient administration of any funds received from students who have obtained loans under this part, to assure that the rights of students established under this part are protected, to protect the United States from unreasonable risk of loss due to defaults, and to comply specifically with all applicable requirements set forth in this part.

(b) Each participating institution shall maintain records, with respect to each student who receives a loan under this part, regarding the student's admission (to the extent required for purposes of § 177.65), academic standing, periods of attendance (to the extent required for purposes of paragraph (c) of this section and § 177.63), courses taken and placement (if the institution provides a placement service and the student uses such service). Such records will also be maintained with regard to the determination of need for interest subsidies on the student's loan, receipt and disbursement of loan proceeds, receipt of tuition and fees, and refunds. The institution shall retain such records (which may be stored in microfilm or computer format) for not less than five years (unless otherwise directed by the commissioner) following the date the student graduates, withdraws, or fails to matriculate for an academic period for which he has received a loan under this part. Copies of reports submitted by the institution pursuant to this section and other forms utilized by the institution relating to loans made under this part shall also be retained for not less than five years following their completion, unless otherwise directed by the commissioner.

(c) Each participating institution shall submit such reports to the commissioner or to lenders at such times and in such manner as the commissioner may prescribe concerning the changes in enrollment status of its students who are borrowers. Such reports shall include timely completion of the Student Status Confirmation Report (OE Form 1072) and the notification to lenders, on forms provided by the commissioner for that purpose, of any change in the status of a student borrower to less than half-time enrollment.

(d) The commissioner or his designee may audit or examine the institution with respect to such matters pertaining to the institution's participation in programs covered under this part as he deems appropriate. Each participating institution shall afford access to records required by paragraphs (a) and (b) of this section and by § 177.66(d) at any reasonable time to the commissioner or his designee as needed in order to verify compliance with the regulations in this part.

(e) In the event of the closure, termination, suspension, or change of ownership of a participating institution, the institution or its retention of the records provided for in paragraph (b) of this section and for the access to such records by the commissioner as provided for in paragraph (d) of this section.

§ 177.63 Refunds

(a) Each participating institution shall establish a fair and equitable refund policy, under which it shall make a refund of unearned tuition, required fees and, where paid to the institution room and board charges to a student who receives a loan under this part and who does not matriculate or who otherwise does not complete the period of study for which the loan was advanced.

The institution shall make such policy (including the procedure for obtaining a refund) known in writing to the student prior to his initial acceptance for enrollment at the institution and prior to each academic year in which he enrolls thereafter.

(b) In determining whether a refund policy is fair and equitable, the comissioner will consider the following factors:

(1) Whether the refund policy takes into consideration the period for which tuition, and other required fees and room and board charges were paid;

(2) Whether the refund policy takes into consideration the length of time the student was enrolled at the institution;

(3) Whether the refund policy takes into consideration the kind and amount of instruction, equipment, and other services provided over the periods described in paragraphs (b) (1) and (2) of this section;

(4) Whether the refund policy produces refunds in reasonable and equitable amounts when the considerations described in paragraphs (b) (2) and (3) of this section are compared with that described in paragraph (b) (1) of this section *provided, however,* that an institution may retain reasonable fees not to exceed $100, for the period for which tuition and other fees were required, in order to cover application, enrollment, registration, and other similar charges;

(5) Whether the refund policy of the institution is mandated by state law; and

(6) Whether, in the case of an accredited institution, the commissioner has approved the refund policy requirements of the pertinent accrediting body.

(c) For purposes of this section, the date on which a student's period of enrollment shall be deemed to have ended will be:

(1) In the case of an institution of higher education, the date on which the student notifies the institution of his withdrawal or the date on which the institution determines that the student has withdrawn, whichever is earlier;

(2) In the case of a vocational school (other than a program of study by correspondence), the date on which the student notifies the institution of his withdrawal or the date of the expiration of a thirty day period during which the student does not attend any

classes or submit any assignments, whichever occurs first. An institution in this category may, however, upon a student's written request, grant a leave of absence not to exceed sixty days; if the student does not return to his classes or scheduled assignments at the expiration of such leave of absence, the date of withdrawal shall be deemed to be the first day of the approved leave of absence *provided,* however, that in determining the amount of a refund due such a student, the institution may consider the costs of any services actually provided to the student during the leave of absence. Except as approved by the commissioner, only one such leave of absence shall be granted to a student;

(3) In the case of a program of study by correspondence, sixty days after the due date of a required lesson which the student has failed to submit, unless the student, within such sixty day period, notifies the institution in writing that he is not withdrawing. For purposes of this section and § 177.46(d), each institution having a course of study by correspondence must establish a schedule of the number of lessons in the course, the intervals at which lessons are to be submitted, the date by which the course is to be completed for purposes of this part, and the period of time within which any resident training must be completed. Such a schedule must conform to the requirements set forth in § 177.1(g) (2) and must be furnished to the student prior to his enrollment.

(d) Each participating institution shall make each refund which is due under this part within forty days after the date on which the student's period of enrollment has ended *provided* that, in the case of a student whose enrollment has ended on the first day of a leave of absence, pursuant to subparagraph (c) (2) of this section, the refund shall be made within forty days of the last day of such leave of absence.

(e) In determining what portion of a refund which is due under this part shall be payable to the student, the institution shall make provision for the refund requirements of other forms of financial assistance which the student has received. In order to assure that an equitable portion of the refund is allocated to the loan made under this part, the amount of the refund attributable to such loan shall not be less than an amount which bears the same ratio to the total amount of the refund as the amount of such loan bears to the amount determined by the institution to be the cost of education for such student at such institution for the period of enrollment for which the loan was made. The net amount of the refund which is payable to the student shall be paid directly to the student after making such disbursements as may be authorized to the lender or holder of the loan by the student. The student must be given written notice of such disbursements or payments made on his behalf out of the proceeds of a refund.

(f) In the event of the closure, termination, suspension, or change of ownership of a participating institution, the institution or its successors must make provision for compliance with the requirements of this section with regard to refunds which are due or may become due for students who obtained loans under this part for periods of attendance at the institution prior to such change in status.

(20 U.S.C. 1028(a) (1), 1974-1(a))

§ 177.64 Provision of Information to a Prospective Student

Each participating institution shall make a good faith effort to present each prospective student, prior to the time the prospective student obligates himself to pay tuition or fees to the institution, with a complete and accurate statement (including printed materials) about the institution, its current academic or training programs, and its faculties and facilities, with particular emphasis on those programs in which the prospective student has expressed interest. In the case of an institution having a course or courses of study, the purpose of which is to prepare students for a particular vocation, trade, or career field, such statement shall include information regarding the employment of students enrolled in such courses, in such vocation, trade, or career field. Such information shall include data regarding the average starting salary for previously enrolled students entering positions of employment for which the courses of study offered by the institution are intended as preparation, and the percentage of such students who obtained employment in such positions. This information shall be based on the most recently available data. If the institution, after reasonable effort, cannot obtain statistically meaningful data regard-

ing its own students, it may use the most recent comparable regional or national data. Where the data the institution possesses, regarding its own students, is more than three years old and cannot be updated after reasonable effort by the institution and where there is available comparable regional or national data at least three years more recent than the institution's data, the institution shall use such regional or national data.
(20 U.S.C. 1082(a) (1), 1085(b), (c) 1087-1 (a))

§ 177.65 Admissions Criteria for a Vocational, Trade, or Career Program

Each participating institution holding itself out as preparing students for a particular vocation or career field trade, shall, prior to the time the prospective student obligates himself to pay tuition or fees to the institution, make a determination, based on an appropriate examination or other appropriate criteria, that there is a substantial and reasonable basis to conclude that such person has the ability to benefit from the instruction or training to be provided.
(20 U.S.C. 1082(a) (1), 1085(b), (c) 1087-1 (a))

TITLE IX CONSOLIDATED PROCEDURAL RULES

The following consolidated procedural compliance rules are excerpted from regulations issued by the Department of Health, Education, and Welfare. They treat the enforcement and administration of various civil rights laws and became effective July 21, 1975.

SUBPART B — COMPLIANCE INQUIRES

§ 81.4 Compliance Information

(a) *Development and maintenance of information.* Recipients shall develop and maintain data and information concerning their programs or activities which are subject to statutes to which this part applies. Such data and information shall relate to:

(1) application, admission, and assignment of students, members, or other participants;

(2) recruitment of students, faculty, staff, and other participants;

(3) financial aid administered or provided by the recipient;

(4) recruitment, selection, assignment, promotion, salary, training, demotion, and separation of employees;

(5) grievances and effectiveness of grievance procedures;

(6) disciplinary rules and application thereof; and

(7) such other matters as the director may from time to time designate.

(b) Recipients shall preserve the data and information developed and maintained pursuant to paragraph (a) of this section together with appropriate supporting materials for a period of three years provided that the three year period in the case of paragraph (a) (5) of this section will run from the time a particular grievance has been resolved or closed.

(c) *Provision of information to the director.* At the request of the director, recipients shall prepare and furnish such data and information as the director may request in connection with the performance of the duties of the director under this part.

(d) *Access to sources of information.* Each recipient shall permit access by the director during normal business hours to such of its books, records, accounts, other documents, and to its facilities, and shall permit the director to make copies of any such written information as may be pertinent to ascertain compliance with this part. Asserted considerations of privacy or confidentiality may not operate to bar the department from evaluating or seeking to enforce compliance with this part. Information of a confidential nature obtained in connection with compliance evaluation or enforcement will not be disclosed by the department except where necessary in formal enforcement proceedings or where otherwise required by law.

CHAPTER THREE

FINANCIAL AID AND THE AGE OF MAJORITY

P ASSAGE of the twenty-sixth Amendment which gave eighteen-year-olds the right to vote has had substantial impact upon state legislators and thereby has encouraged them to award majority to its citizens of the same age. The ramifications of a lowered age for adult status already has had and in the future will have serious implications for college administrators in general, and financial aid counselors, in particular.

Legal adult status at the age of eighteen years has been translated by a rapidly increasing number of students into assertions of self-supporting status for purposes of financial aid awards, notwithstanding parental income levels. At some state institutions the number of such claims has reached 50 percent.[1] A short time ago, college students who considered themselves independent did not exceed 15 percent of the total. Public institutions, of course, generally are more likely to experience claims of independence because of their more diversified student clientele, especially in terms of age and income level.

Some parents have reinforced their children's claims of independence by either refusing to provide relevant financial data upon which need is determined, or by documenting their children's emancipation in the following ways:

(1) failing to declare their children as a deduction in their federal and state income tax returns;
(2) terminating of monetary assistance and contribution to their childrens' living expenses;
(3) acknowledging their children's absence from the parents's residence for indeterminate periods of time.

Coupled with changes in contemporary lifestyles and disintegration of the family unit, self-supporting status as claimed by stu-

---

[1] *New York Times*, Monday, April 8, 1974, p. 1.

dents and parents has been given further credence. Indeed, a careful analysis of the legislative history of the Education Amendments Act of 1972 would indicate a decided shift in the qualification for aid from parent's income to individual student needs. Loan and self-help programs, cooperative education and work-study grants prefigure increasing reliance upon individual student circumstances rather than upon parental income when determining a student aid package.

Traditionally, self-supporting students were defined as primarily older students who had established their own residence, were likely to be married, and may have been veterans. Given the twenty-sixth Amendment and subsequent state legislation, a new category of self-supporting students has been created. This student comes to the university with a specific means of exchange, acutely aware of his new bargaining position with regard to financial aid. In fact, state institutions face potentially severe income losses because of judicial decisions involving students' claims of residence in order to benefit from reduced tuition rates.

In *Vlandis v. Kline,* 93 S. Ct. 2230 U. S. Supreme Court 1973, the Supreme Court ruled that out-of-state students who attend public institutions must be permitted to become bona fide residents of the state even when their primary purpose for residence was to take advantage of in-state rates at educational institutions.

The Court indicated that states could develop reasonable and rational criteria to determine in-state status such as automobile registration and license to drive, site of voter registration, locus of income, real estate tax payments, and minimums of residency periods.

Toward An Individual Financial Means Test

Determining one adult's financial needs by analysis of another adult's economic circumstances is inherently illogical and cannot be readily defended. In fact, conventional procedures of family income analysis which provide aid to the most needy students based on family income may well have prejudiced certain social and economic classes, particularly the middle class. Students whose parents earn more than arbitrary minimum incomes articulated by federal financial aid legislation may face greater deficiencies in resources to meet college costs than students whose parents fall below such minimums.

Individual qualification for aid programs avoids the homogenization of eligible college applicants. If life-long education from eighteen to eighty is to be promoted, basing an individual's financial aid on his parent's income may not only be inequitable, but also impossible. Separate identities are essential to people interested in pursuing their goals.

The contemporary college administrator should recognize individual requirements and preferences, and seek legislative changes which offer college access for individual citizens rather than groups of citizens.

CASE: RESIDENCY: CRITERIA FOR IN-STATE STATUS

John W. Vlandis, Director of Admissions, The University of Connecticut, Appellant v. *Margaret March Kline and Patricia Catapano*, 412 U.S. 441 (1973) Decided June 11, 1973.

Mr. Justice Steward delivered the opinion of the Court.

Like many other states, Connecticut requires nonresidents of the State who are enrolled in the state university system to pay tuition and other fees at higher rates than residents of the state who are so enrolled. The constitutional validity of that require-ment is not at issue in the case before us. *What is at issue here is Connecticut's statutory definition of residents and nonresidents for purposes of the above provision.*

Section 126(a) of Public Act No. 5, amending 10-329b, provides that an unmarried student shall be classified as a nonresident, or "out-of-state" student if his "legal address for any part of the one-year period immediately prior to his application for admission at a constituent unit of the state system of higher education was outside of Connecticut." With respect to married students, 126(a) (3) of the act provides that such a student, if living with his spouse, shall be classified as "out-of-state" if his "legal address at the time of his application for admission to such a unit was out-side of Connecticut." These classifications are permanent and irrebuttable for the whole time that the student remains at the university since 126(a) (5) of the act commands: *The status of a student, as established at the time of his application for admission at a constituent unit of the state system of higher education under the provisions of this section, shall be his status for the entire period of his attendance at such constituent unit. The present case concerns the constitutional validity of this conclusive and unchangeable presumption of nonresident status from the fact that, at the time of application for admission, the student, if married, was then living outside of Connecticut, or, if single, had lived outside the state at some point during the preceding year.*

The appellee, Margaret March Kline, is an undergraduate stu-dent at the University of Connecticut. In May of 1971, while attending college in California, she became engaged to Peter Kline, a life-long Connecticut resident. Because the Klines wished to reside in Connecticut after their marriage, Mrs. Kline applied to the University of Connecticut from California. In late May, she was accepted and informed by the university that she would be considered an in-state student. On June 26, 1971, the appellee and Peter Kline were married in California, and soon thereafter took up residence in Storrs, Connecticut, where they have established a permanent home. Mrs. Kline has a Connecticut driver's license, her car is registered in Connecticut, and she is registered as a Connecticut voter. In July 1971, Public Act. No. 5 went into effect. Accordingly, the appellant, Director of Admissions at the University of Connecticut, irreversibly classified Mrs. Kline as an out-of-state student, pursuant to 126(a) (3) of that act. As a consequence, she was required to pay $150 tuition and $200 nonresident fee for the first semester, whereas a student classified as a Connecticut resident paid no tuition; and upon registration for the second semester, she was required to pay $425 tuition plus another $200 nonresident fee, while a student classified as a Connecticut resident paid only $175 tuition.

The other appellee, Patricia Catapano, is an unmarried graduate student at the same University. She applied for admission from Ohio in January 1971, and was accepted in February of that year. In August 1971, she moved her residence from Ohio to Connecticut and registered as a full-time student at the University. Like Mrs. Kline, she has a Connecticut driver's license, her car is registered in Connecticut, and she is registered as a Connecticut voter. Pursuant to 126(a) (2) of the 1971 Act, the appellant classified her permanently as an out-of-state student. Consequently, she, too, was required to pay $150 tuition and a $200 nonresident fee for her first semester, and $425 tuition plus a $200 nonresident fee for her second semester.

Appellees then brought suit in the District Court pursuant to the Civil Rights Acts, 42 U. S. C. 1983, contending that they were bona fide residents of Connecticut, and that 126 of Public Act No. 5, under which they were classified as nonresidents for purposes of their tuition and fees, infringed their rights to due process of law and equal protection of the laws, guaranteed by the Fourteenth Amendment to the Constitution. After the convening of a three-judge District Court, that court unanimously held 126(a)

(2), (a) (3), and (a) (5) unconstitutional, as violative of the Fourteenth Amendment, and enjoined the appellant from enforcing those sections. D.C., 346 F. Supp. 526 (1972). The court also found that before the commencement of the spring semester in 1972, each appellee was a bona fide resident of Connecticut; and it accordingly ordered that the appellant refund to each of them the amount of tuition and fees paid in excess of the amount paid by resident students for that semester. On December 4, 1972, we noted probable jurisdiction of this appeal. 409 U. S. 1036, 93 S. Ct. 521, 34 L. Ed. 2d 485.

The appellees do not challenge, nor did the District Court invalidate, the option of the state to classify students as resident and nonresident students, thereby obligating nonresident students to pay higher tuition and fees than do bona fide residents. The state's right to make such a classification is unquestioned here. Rather, the appellees attack Connecticut's irreversible and irrebuttable statutory presumption that because a student's legal address was outside the state at the time of his application for admission or at some point during the preceding year, he remains a nonresident for as long as he is a student there. This conclusive presumption, they say, is invalid in that it allows the state to classify as "out-of-state students" those who are, in fact, bona fide residents of the state. The appellees claim that they have a constitutional right to controvert that presumption of nonresidence by presenting evidence that they are bona fide residents of Connecticut. The District Court agreed, "Assuming that it is permissible for the state to impose a heavier burden of tuition and fees on nonresident than on resident students, the state may not classify as 'out-of-state students' those who do not belong in that class." 346 F. Supp., at 528. We affirm the judgment of the District Court.

Statutes creating permanent irrebuttable presumptions have long been disfavored under the due process clause of the Fifth and Fourteenth Amendments. In *Heiner v. Donnan*, 285 U. S. 312, 52 S. Ct. 358, 76 L. Ed. 772 (1932), the Court was faced with a constitutional challenge to a federal statute that created a conclusive presumption that gifts made within two years prior to the donor's death were made in contemplation of death, thus requiring payment by his estate of a higher tax. In holding that this irrefutable assumption was so arbitrary and unreasonable as to deprive the taxpayer of his property without due process of law, the Court stated that it had "held more than once that a statute creating a presumption which operates to deny a fair opportunity to rebut it violates the due process clause of the Fourteenth Amendment.

The state proffers three reasons to justify that permanent irrebuttable presumption. The first is that the state has a valid interest in equalizing the cost of public higher education between Connecticut residents and nonresidents, and that by freezing a student's residential status as of the time he applies, the state ensures that its bona fide in-state students will receive their full subsidy. The state's objective of cost equalization between bona fide residents and nonresidents may well be legitimate, but basing the bona fides of residency solely on where a student lived when he applied for admission to the university is a criterion wholly unrelated to that objective. As is evident from the situation of the appellees, a student may be a bona fide resident of Connecticut even though he applied to the university from out of state. Thus, Connecticut's conclusive presumption of nonresidence, instead of ensuring that only its bona fide residents receive their full subsidy, ensures that certain of its bona fide residents, such as the appellees, do not receive their full subsidy, and can never do so while they remain students.

Second, the state argues that even if a student who applied to the University from out of state may at some point become a bona fide resident of Connecticut, the state can nonetheless reasonably decide to favor with the lower rates only its established residents, whose past tax contributions to the state have been higher. According to the state, the fact that established residents or their parents have supported the state in the past justifies the conclusion that applicants from out of state — who are presumed not to be such established residents — may be denied the lower rates, even if they have become bona fide residents.

The third ground advanced to justify 126(a) (3) of Public Act No. 5 is that it provides a degree of administrative certainty. The state points to its interest in preventing out-of-state students from coming to Connecticut solely to obtain an education and then claiming Connecticut residence in order to secure the lower tuition and fees. The irrebuttable presumption, the state contends, makes it easier to separate out students who come to the state solely for its educational facilities from true Connecticut residents, by eliminating the need for an individual determination of the *bona fides* of a person who lived out of state at the time of his application. Such an individual determination, it is said, would not only be an expensive administrative burden, but would also be very difficult to make, since it is hard to evaluate when bona fide residency exists. Without the conclusive presumption, the state argues, it would be almost impossible to prevent out-of-state students from claiming a Connecticut residence merely to obtain the lower rates.

In sum, since Connecticut purports to be concerned with residency in allocating the rates for tuition and fees at its university system, it is forbidden by the due process clause to deny an individual the resident rates on the basis of a permanent and irrebuttable presumption of nonresidence, when that presumption is not necessarily or universally true in fact, and when the state has reasonable alternative means of making the crucial determination. Rather, standards of due process require that the state allow such an individual the opportunity to present evidence showing that he is a bona fide resident entitled to the in-state rates. Since 126 (a) of the 1971 act precluded the appellees from ever rebutting the presumption that they were nonresidents of Connecticut, that statute operated to deprive them of a significant amount of their money without due process of law.

We are aware, of course, of the special problems involved in determining the bona fide residence of college students who come from out of state to attend that state's public university. Our holding today should in no wise be taken to mean that Connecticut must classify the students in its university system as residents, for purposes of tuition and fees, just because they go to school there. Nor should our decision be construed to deny a state the right to impose on a student, as one element in demonstrating bona fide residence, a reasonable durational residency requirement, which can be met while in student status. We fully recognize that a state has a legitimate interest in protecting and preserving the quality of its colleges and universities and the right to its own bona fide residents to attend such institutions on a preferential tuition basis.

We hold only that a permanent irrebuttable presumption of nonresidence — the means adopted by Connecticut to preserve that legitimate interest — is violative of the due process clause, because it provides no opportunity for students who applied from out of state to demonstrate that they have become bona fide Connecticut residents. The state can establish such reasonable criteria for in-state status as to make virtually certain that students who are not, in fact, bona fide residents of the state, but who have come there solely for educational purposes, cannot take advantage of the in-state rates.

ROBERT AND ELEANOR LAUDICINA

FINANCING PRIVATE HIGHER EDUCATION: FOUNDATIONS FOR A NEW PUBLIC COMMITMENT

The following article, "Financing Private Higher Education: Foundations for a New Public Commitment," by Robert and Eleanor Laudicina is from the Winter, 1971 issue of the Fairleigh Dickinson University Business Review. *The authors of Fairleigh Dickinson University and Kean College, respectively, discuss the advantages of educational vouchers financed by a national trust fund. Permission to reprint has been granted by the* Fairleigh Dickinson University Business Review.

Education is an important source in a knowledge-based society and should be considered a national investment. Inordinate emphasis has been placed on the development of natural resources, too little on the question of human development. If a highly technological society is to avoid loss of direction, its human component must develop sufficient awareness, expertise, and consciousness to guide successfully the course of technology. The obvious necessity to increase the pool of informed, competent, and aware citizens can be realized only by improving opportunities for higher education, and by redirecting higher education to the changing needs of the future.

The problem of access to higher education is no longer merely the concern of professionals in the field, but a subject enmeshed with those vital issues revolving around the direction of higher education within its surrounding social, political, and economic environment. Despite the dramatic growth of public institutions during the last decade and a concomitant increase in student populations at both public and private institutions, opportunities for the rich still outnumber those for the poor.[1] Yet the push towards higher education now involves all social classes, ethnic groups, and economic strata. The needs of our complex social and economic structure, furthermore, require a continued enlargement of a skilled, professional work force. Education, therefore, becomes an absolute requirement not only for upward mobility and personal and occupational integration, but also for progressive expansion of economic and social potentialities.

Public v. Private Financing

Historically, universities have derived the greatest part of their financial backing from those institutions for whose functional requisites graduates were most necessary. Prior to 1910, the private sector both supported and derived the greatest benefit from university output:

> ...for the period 1893-1916 gifts to all forms of education amounted to over $1 billion; this figure is equal to more than 70 percent of the total income of higher education during these years, and while the exact portion of these gifts to colleges and universities is unknown, it was undoubtedly substantial.[2]

Since World War I, a system of parallel support emerged as private and state-supported institutions cohabitated the educational arena. A relatively clear division of function between private and public institutions, nevertheless, persisted until at least World War II. Private institutions prepared their students for high-level positions within the economic, professional, and social elite. State-supported institutions primarily devoted their efforts to training in subordinate vocational and technical positions in the private sphere and for limited public needs, such as teaching.

---

[1]Alice M. Rivlin and Jeffery H. Weiss, "Social Goals and Federal Support of Higher Education — The Implications of Various Strategies," *The Economics and Financing of Higher Education in the United States* (Washington, U. S. Government Printing Office, 1969) p. 544.

[2]Hayden W. Smith, "Prospects For Voluntary Support," in Robert H. Connery (ed.), *The Corporation and The Campus*, (New York, Academy of Political Science, Columbia University, 1970) p. 121.

With the end of World War II, however, federal support of higher education increased enormously in both the amount of money distributed and the breadth of distribution. The sudden and massive increase in federal support to higher education reflected a broad contemporary trend towards the blurring of the distinction between private and public academic endeavor. For example, students at private institutions increasingly are recruited for public service and government-related vocations; the intellectual and institutional resources of private institutions are increasingly at the disposal of governmentally defined priorities. Public education, furthermore, has broadened its perspective to include training in many fields directly linked to what had been traditionally private endeavor, i.e. schools or business, law, dentistry, and medicine.

Increasing Federal Assistance

Given the blurring of the distinction between private and public education, and awareness of education as a national resource, a number of proposals already have been initiated to increase the level and scope of federal assistance to private and public institutions. Currently, the Congress is investigating ways in which federal grants could go directly to colleges and universities on a "no strings basis."[3] Previously, federal aid has been geared to specific programs or particular kinds of capital construction, and not to the number of students attending a particular college or university. The Congress also is considering adjusted scales of aid favorable to those institutions which have an equal distribution of men and women, and have large numbers of students from low-income families. Aid to institution programs, however, no matter how beneficial to and supportive of higher education it may be, tends to erode the difference between private and public institutions, and does little to encourage the particular values of private higher education.

It may be asked, is there in fact a unique contribution that private education offers? One of the great values of private education historically has been its capacity for flexibility, innovation,

---

[3] *The New York Times*, October 1, 1971, p. 20.

creativity, and autonomy in its activities. Nevertheless, private education is now jeopardized by increasing costs and a narrowing financial base. Indeed, the current financial crisis of private education threatens to obliterate the distinction between public and private education through public takeover of debt-ridden private institutions. Given the clear need for increased access to higher education, not only for college-age citizens, but other sectors of the population, what alternatives can be devised which best fit the needs of personal and national priorities, and, at the same time, preserve the unique contributions of private education?

Benefits of Education Vouchers

One promising proposal offered by the Educational Policy Institute at Syracuse University would establish the legal right of every citizen to fifteen years of federally supported education, financed by the Social Security system. Citizens, by request, could receive educational vouchers which would be used at any institution where they were accepted. Citizens would be able to use such vouchers at any point in their lives, and, thereby, be able to chart their own educational program. A student, then, would be able to move in and out of the educational system with much more freedom and flexibility. Indeed, the dramatically changing needs of a technological society may require many citizens to be retrained in their middle years. Women, too, would benefit from an educational system which promotes access at different times in an individual's life.

A voucher system of the kind described above would tend to maintain a healthy competition between private and public institutions. Curricula probably would tend to be responsive to the needs of students and would likely match the requirements of the country's economic and social advancement. Such a system also may encourage good teaching and the development of new learning forms.

Logic and experience indicate that federal and not state government should accept substantial responsibility for funding higher education in the future. The greater financial resources available in the federal treasury obviously favor this argument. But a number of other factors are equally important. Uniformity among regions, states, and localities is possible only through a national program. Those states with the greatest needs, moreover, are frequently those with the fewest resources to finance those needs. The spectre of governmental control and subsequent loss of autonomy is far more likely to arise at the state rather than at the national level. The fears of private college administrators that educational issues may become political tools are more frequently realized at the state and local levels when proximity and publicity can present an explosive combination.

Public support, through the voucher system described above, would provide a substantial proportion of needed funds for higher education, but this is not to say that voluntary support from foundations, corporations, and individuals would no longer be valuable to private institutions. There is little doubt that the specific needs of certain subgroups within the population can be served best by the continued support of such groups as a means of maintaining educational diversity.

Institutions of higher learning must retain the kind of adaptability and responsiveness which can meet the needs of a speeding technological environment. It is important for educators in particular but for all citizens in general to promote an educational system which would encourage access for more citizens over a longer period of time. The dynamic interplay of both private and public institutions would seem to be the most effective means of fulfilling the greatest potential and highest promise of both private and public education in the United States.

ALEXANDER G. SIDAR, JR.

THE SELF-SUPPORTING STUDENT — ISSUES AND PREMISES

The following article, "The Self-Supporting Student — Issues and Premises," by Alexander G. Sidar, Jr. of College Scholarship Services describes some of the problems of self-supporting students who are applying for postsecondary financial aid.

Self-supporting students are here to stay, and their numbers are increasing rapidly. The problems characteristic of self-supporting students continue to be raised at meetings and conferences of financial aid administrators whether presented as a formal program topic or as the subject of informal "corridor discussions." Interest centers on several aspects of the issue, and these may be divided into three general areas — definition of the self-supporting student, procedures used in evaluating expected contributions, and methods used in determining budgets and living costs.

Defining the Self-Supporting Student

Universally acceptable definitions of self-supporting students do not now exist, although it is possible to establish clear categories for their identification. The federal Division of Student Assistance criteria for qualification as self-supporting are the most widely used because they are mandated for eligibility in federal student aid programs.*

However, these criteria should be the subject of review because they are extremely demanding and virtually hold students in a

---

*The criteria are: (1) A student cannot have been claimed as a tax dependent by anyone other than a spouse for the calendar year preceding the academic year in which public funds are requested; and (2) the student shall not have received financial support from parent(s) in money or kind, including education expenses, in excess of $200 for the preceding calendar year.

dependency thrall unless the continuing pattern of education is broken. In addition they have not been fully satisfactory because they serve the purpose of determining eligibility for public student aid funds rather than identifying categories of self-supporting students. It is important and necessary to identify, as clearly as possible, generally standardized and widely acceptable characteristics of self-supporting students. Once these categories have been established, then sound eligibility criteria can be applied to the categories.

For purposes of this discussion, we can identify as self-supporting students those who fall into the following four categories:

(1) the returning veteran,
(2) the working student (single, married, or married with family) who has established his own residence,
(3) the older returning married student,
(4) the ward of the state.

For any of these categories, it would be possible to ascertain that for the *forthcoming year* for which the student is applying for aid, financial support in a prescribed amount *will not* be available from the parents and tax dependency *will not* be claimed. An acceptable procedure in such cases could be the requirement of an affidavit signed by the parents or guardian attesting to these conditions. This document could contain, as a deterrent, a statement describing penalties for falsification of information in applications for public student aid funds.

Two other kinds of self-supporting students should be mentioned. The "voluntary" student who wishes to relieve the family of the burden of financial support presents a special problem to the institution. An even greater dilemma exists in treating fairly the one who has been summarily dismissed from the family, probably because of differences in lifestyle philosophies. These students cannot qualify for federal aid funds under existing criteria. Most aid administrators would agree that the voluntary student should not receive consideration. The student dismissed by his family may be considered eligible for institutional aid at some postsecondary institutions. Because any consideration given to these two kinds of students is basically an institutional responsibility, there is less reason to consider them at this time. The issues of identification and qualification for funds are of primary importance as they relate to the larger group of self-supporting students.

PREMISE. These four readily identifiable kinds of self-supporting students should be officially acknowledged and recognized as standard categories.

PREMISE. Those students who fall in these categories should not be excluded from eligibility for public student aid funds on the basis of historical information but should be judged on the basis of their tax and financial dependency status as they begin an academic year or begin study for a clearly identifiable time interval.

Procedures in Evaluating Expected Contributions — Students', Parents' and Spouses' Income and Assets

After standardized criteria are established for the identification of self-supporting students, procedures must be adopted for evaluating potential contributions from different sources.

Assets: Assets held by the student or student's spouse are a source of funds for educational costs. Need assessment rationale for dependent students has long recognized the greater financial strength of the family that has assets in comparison to the family at the same income level without assets. This dependent student rational is equally applicable to the self-supporting student. However, the method in which assets are evaluated should reflect the reality of different characteristics among the categories of self-supporting students. The present procedure is to prorate all student assets over the remaining years in college. This may be an equitable procedure among single undergraduate or graduate students who are between the ages of eighteen and thirty because they are involved in an educational investment in themselves for the future. However, it is questionable when applied to older family units who have broader economic responsibilities.

Expectations from net assets should be based on marital status, number of dependents, and age. The single self-supporting student, aged twenty, with assets, should be expected to use these as an investment in his future. The widowed mother, aged forty with several children of school age, should have a protected asset base below which no income supplement or financial contribution is expected.

PREMISE. A progressive rate or index of expectations from net assets should be established to apply from the higher to the lower age levels for married student families in order to establish better equity in asset treatment.

Income: Income from salaries, wages, and other sources must also be evaluated on the basis of a student's age, marital status, and family size. The distinctive differences among self-supporting students that require recognition in the treatment of assets also demand differing evaluation regarding the ability to contribute to educational costs from income sources. The wages of a fifty-year-old father who has a wife, several children, and home to sustain are subjected to a wider variety of expenditure demands than are the wages of a twenty-five-year-old graduate student living in university housing.

PREMISE. Expected contributions from the income of self-supporting students must continue to be a primary source of funding educational costs. However, income, age levels, and family responsibilities should be considered in establishing a contribution rate schedule for self-supporting married students that is distinct from the income expectation procedure for single, self-supporting students.

Contributions from parents: Parental contributions are expected for clearly identifiable self-supporting students by some institutions. This is usually in instances where a history of family affluence exists. Also, the College Scholarship Services (CSS) rationale in the student's financial statement includes an expected contribution from parental discretionary income.

However, part of the federal criteria for a self-supporting student is based on the absence of, or very minimal, financial support from parents regardless of family circumstances.

PREMISE. If the applicant meets the generally standardized criteria for classification as self-supporting, potential parental contributions should not be expected.

Spouses' contributions: The working spouse of a student classified as self-supporting has an obligation to contribute to the financing of the student's education just as the parents of a dependent student have this responsibility. The education of the husband or the wife in a family benefits the student and the spouse more directly than a dependent student's education benefits the family. The educational process produces direct benefits to husband, wife, and children, and therefore a contribution from the spouse's income and assets is a family investment with visible short and long-range returns. (The evaluation of potential contributions should be in accord with the premises proposed in the asset and income sections of this paper.)

PREMISE. The spouse should be expected to contribute to the educational costs incurred by the student (husband or wife) from income and assets based on expected contribution levels determined by age, family size, income levels, and net assets.

Budgets and Living Costs

There is a distinct difference between the student who receives no support from his family and the student who has a family to support. Subsistence costs can and do vary dramatically. In most instances, institutions are not able to fill the complete need gap of either category of these students. If full need cannot be met, the self-supporting student is often left with a problem that must be solved in some other way. Many financial aid administrators are concerned about their inability to aid these students fully. However, the aid administrator should not attempt to solve the problem through the construction of inadequate budgets.

The construction of realistic institutional budgets is of importance in the equitable evaluation of the financial need of self-supporting students. All costs attendant to postsecondary education should be included. Realistic living costs for families of different sizes should be included in the total cost of education. An allowance for summer living expenses is necessary when the student is in attendance for nine months of the year. Institutions should be prepared to support, with hard statistics, the budgets and living costs for self-supporting students.

Basic living costs include
(1) food,
(2) housing,
(3) clothing,
(4) medical and dental expenses,
(5) family personal expenses,
(6) emergency and miscellaneous expenses.
In addition, education costs should be added for
(1) tuition and fees,
(2) books and supplies.
PREMISE. The self-supporting student's need should be determined through consideration of realistic basic living costs for the student or the family and the addition of educational costs in comparison to all income and net asset resources regardless of the capability of the institution to meet all of the student's funding requirements.

Conclusion

Financial aid administrators should actively participate in the design of a rationale to identify and evaluate self-supporting students. The self-supporting student issue contains many problem areas wherein differentiations must be made, basic premises examined, and recommendations proposed. In addition to firm definitive categories, evaluative procedures for expected contributions, and proper methods of determining budgets and living costs, judgment must still play an important role in the entire process of dealing with the self-supporting student. It is the task of the financial aid administrator to exercise that judgment responsibly.

This paper identifies some of the issues that need full discussion. The CSS wishes to receive the recommendations of financial aid administrators regarding proposals for identifying and evaluating the self-supporting student. These will be presented to an *ad hoc* committee for review and to the Committee on Need Assessment Procedures for approval as recommended procedures in the financial aid assessment process.

Richard L. Tombaugh

THE INDEPENDENT STUDENT — FISH, FOWL, OR OTHER?

The following article, "The Independent Student — Fish, Fowl, or Other?" by Richard L. Tombaugh of George Washington University was presented to the Special Conference on New York State Financial Aid, Syracuse University, July, 1973. Mr. Tombaugh discussed the inherent difficulties of identifying and properly funding the independent student.

As a group, student financial aid officers are not very prolific writers of professional papers, however, of the professional writings that are available, no topic is more frequently addressed than student emancipation, or the independent, self-supporting student. That this topic attracts so much attention is ample evidence of the divided opinion about what self-supporting students are and how they should be handled. The aid community must stir itself and bring about a satisfactory resolution, or someone less familiar with the problem and its ramifications will dictate the decision, probably in a way not in the best interests of the students.

The number of independent students is growing with each passing day. Not only is postsecondary education extending its program beyond the traditional dependent eighteen to twenty-two-year-old student to encompass a much broader constituency, consisting of older, obviously emancipated individuals, but there is also at work an increasing attitude on the part of parents and offspring alike that education beyond high school is a right rather than a privilege, and that the society, rather than the family, should provide the resources to aid the student.

The declining concept of family responsibility for postsecondary educational costs is being hastened by the recent advent of legislation lowering the age of majority for many purposes from twenty-one years to eighteen years. Many parents and students alike are asking, understandably, why students should remain tied to parental financial apron strings once they are considered adults for purposes of voting, drinking, holding property, entering into legal contracts, etc. This is not an easy question to answer, and it is complicated by the fact that the aid community has traditionally tied, for ease of explanations, responsibility of the family to the age of majority concept. The concept of family support for postsecondary education is a more basic philosophical matter, reflecting a responsibility of parents to provide the means for the self-sufficiency of their offspring, at the level determined by the family to be desired for each particular individual member. Yet there exists the convenient "out" of justifying the expected parental contribution with the less debatable legalistic framework of age of majority. Now that rationale has disintegrated, leaving two alternatives. One either sticks with age of majority and consequently emancipates almost all postsecondary students from parental support; or one adopts a new rationale (or begins to utilize the one society should have been using all along) based upon parental responsibility for the costs of preparation for life. The first alternative has some very obvious cost implications for all of postsecondary education. Even under the traditional rationale of parental responsibility, in which over half of the cost of postsecondary education is borne by parents, society falls short of having sufficient resources to adequately supplement those parental contributions. It does not require a great deal of imagination to picture the "need gap" which would be generated by a public policy that excused parents from financial support of offspring at the age of eighteen years. While there would be a significant amount of voluntary support extended beyond the age of majority, just as there is now, there would be a great many parents who would be glad to be relieved of such responsibilities, and likewise many students eager to be relieved of the accompanying parental control. If the society, through its governmental units, were ready to assume the resultant loss of parental support, there might be less cause for concern. However, the growing reluctance of the voting public to approve elementary and secondary school bond issues and similar measures where public support has traditionally been accepted suggests that society is not ready to accept postsecondary education as a purely societal responsibility. The net result would be a drastic decline in access to postsecondary educational opportunity.

For this reason, society must choose the second alternative, espousing a philosophy of family responsibility for the financial support of offspring to the extent necessary to maximize the full potential of the individual and bring about self-sufficiency. Obviously, such a philosophy would continue to incorporate the limitation of responsibility to the reasonable ability of the family resources to provide such support. This rationale would have to stand on its own merits, without the legal "crutch" of age of majority. It would require a uniform acceptance and adherence on the part of the educational community in order to remain operative. While there are other options falling between the two extremes presented here, the most viable ones will approximate the philosophical approach rather than the legal one.

Thus far the preservation of the dependent student has been addressed, which is a prerequisite to any consideration of the independent student. Otherwise, the distinction between the two becomes obsolete and unnecessary. Some financial aid officers deny the existence of any distinction currently, but maintain that all students are dependent. Such a position may be philosophically based or motivated by a more practical concern, such as the rationing of scarce resources, but seems to lack a recognition of a very real situation in which many young people find themselves. The remainder of this paper will concern itself with two distinct and separable elements of the independent student question, the identification of the legitimately self-supporting individual, and the establishment of financial need for the self-supporting student.

Identifying the Self-Supporting Student

Assuming that one can accept the existence of the independent student as a reality the challenge then becomes one of identifying the truly emancipated individual so that he or she can be treated accordingly, at the same time sorting out those individuals who should not be so treated. The alternatives can best be identified by characterizing the two extremes. On the one hand, independent status can be defined in a very arbitrary manner, with either/or criterion and few, if any, exceptions. This approach is best exemplified by the U. S. Office of Education (USOE) definitions of the independent student. This approach is objective, likely to be consistent case by case, and is relatively easy to administer. Most aid officers probably feel comfortable using this approach, which explains, along with the impractical nature of utilizing different methods for federal and other funds, why the USOE approach is almost solely utilized. Yet any such absolute approach has the very real disadvantage of excluding individuals who should be included and accepting some who have no business being considered independent.

On the other hand, independent status could be conferred on the basis of subjective judgment on the part of the financial aid officer. Although this would be "professional" judgment, such an approach would have obvious drawbacks. It would lack consistency, not only between institutions, but probably within institutions. It would subject the aid officers to much more "heat" from students and parents. The student would be subjected to uncertainty of what was required to be considered independent, and unfortunately, he would encounter a good deal of capriciousness because of the varied philosophical orientations of those making the determinations. The author favors a compromise of these two extremes, consisting of a set of objective criteria easily identified by all, but with the provision of exceptions when warranted.

Since it is very difficult to disallow independent status when a nondeserving applicant meets the technical criteria, those measures should be sufficiently demanding to minimize abuses to the system. While one might argue that $200 (or $600) of support is the wrong amount, or that residing with parents for varying periods of time should not disqualify one from being considered self-supporting, one could resolve these points if one additional element were added to the decision process — the authority of the aid officer to exempt the prior year test in exceptional circumstances. There seems to be a basic agreement in the aid community that the tax deduction, support, and residency tests for the year in which aid is being requested are a reasonable approach. The prior year-current year criteria present little problem for the clearly independent and obviously dependent students, but they do provide a stumbling block to the individual who is in transition and whose circumstances have changed significantly since the prior calendar year. Such events as the transition from single to married, from undergraduate to graduate, from commuter to resident, while not in and of themselves justifying independent status, frequently work in combination with other factors to make reference to the prior calendar year inappropriate. USOE has recognized the concept of changed circumstances in allowing for exclusion of the prior year test in the event that both parents become deceased, but there are other changes that deserve latitude for judgment on the part of the aid officer. It would not be unreasonable to define some parameters of discretion, or to require documentation for making the exception; but it should be available.

The consideration of the definitional problem may be closed with one word of caution. It is very important to seek a common definition of the independent student for use with all student aid programs which normally expect a parental contribution. There is little, if any, rationale for treating a student as independent for some aid programs and dependent for other forms of assistance. Although there is an understandable reluctance to open gift aid sources to independent students and their frequently greater financial needs, there are, however, better ways to control undesired drain upon gift aid in the need determination and packaging policies to be utilized later in the process than "juggling" the emancipation criteria.

Establishing the Need of the Independent Student and Providing For Those Needs

Once an aid applicant has been determined to be independent, the aid officer must establish the financial need or eligibility for assistance. *Estimating* the need (the process is not an exact science) of an independent student is not really different than for the dependent student. It remains a comparison of the applicant's resources against his or her costs of attendance. Some of the elements of both resources and costs are unique to the independent student, but the process is the same. First there must be established a time frame for the analysis. Some need analysis systems and aid officer methods automatically assume a twelve-month period for all independent students, unless they are to terminate their student status in a shorter time. The author prefers to utilize a nine-month analysis as a base (except when termination is sooner) and then supplement with a three-month analysis if the student will in fact be enrolled for the summer term. His rationale rests with a theory that a student who does not enroll in the summer session should be able to at least support himself (and his family, if married) when not enrolled and should not require subsidy during periods of nonenrollment. At the same time, he may require all his current income to sustain himself during that period and will be unable to save funds for the next enrollment period. However, if that were the case he should be encouraged to continue his enrollment in order to complete his degree sooner. At the same time, some students need that time off to maintain their emotional stability even though their financial status is not improved by it.

Once the time frame is established, one proceeds to evaluate the resources and costs of the applicant. Some of the analysis methods now in use and under development attempt to separate the resources and costs of the married independent student from those of his family. With the single student, this is no problem; but there is little rationale for attempting to divide the costs and resources of a family unit. The student does not budget in that manner and dividing his own costs and resources from those of his family makes no sense to him. No one normally budgets his own financial affairs on a split basis, and to do so creates a very artificial and misleading situation. Once again, the motivation of those in a position to render financial aid seems to be a fear that the independent student will receive a disproportionate share of the gift aid resources because of his larger budget requirements. However, there are more logical ways to alleviate this problem than constructing an artificial analysis of costs and resources. In establishing the budget, all reasonable expenses of the family unit should be included. Institutional norms are helpful in evaluating the reasonableness of the student's own estimates, but sufficient flexibility should be provided to reflect the unique expenses and prior obligations of the applicants, no two of whom are exactly alike. It does no good to provide assistance based upon an artificial budget that covers current expenses but ignores prior debts which must be paid if the student is to remain in school. Just as is done with parents of dependent students, the independent student must be taken in his current state of financial affairs.

In the assessment of resources, one must evaluate current income, accumulated assets, and any educational benefits available to the student and his family unit. Just as some methods attempt to divide costs, they try to separate resources. However, if all costs are taken together there is no need to divide resources between the student and his family. The author prefers to utilize all current income of the family unit in the analysis, assuming all costs are included. Likewise, all educational benefits should be used on a current basis. The treatment of assets is somewhat more complex, and should vary according to marital status, number of dependents, age of head of household, and the number of years of education remaining for the student and spouse (educational needs of dependent children are allowed for in the protection of assets on account of family size). The variables to be utilized in the assessment of assets are too detailed to describe here, but will be available separately.

The need figure derived from this comparison of resources and costs might be labeled "gross need" for assistance of all types. It is at this stage that a protection of gift aid resources should be interjected into the process. If one is concerned about the disproportionate distribution of gift dollars to independent students, at least three mechanisms are available to promote equity. One is to limit gift aid to the purely educational expenses encountered by all students, i.e. tuition, fees, books, and supplies. Another means is to use the institutional single dependent budget norm for comparison with the independent student's resources for purposes of gift aid eligibility. A third means would be to use an appropriate independent student budget norm that ignores the unusual expenses for gift aid purposes, which puts all independent applicants on the same plane in gift aid decisions. In all three options, however, the individualized family budget would be used for establishing self-help eligibility.

Some have expected more specific "how to do it" recommendations from this paper, but there must be better agreement on the basic concepts inherent in the independent student situation before arriving at the desired operational specifics. Hopefully, these thoughts will help to bring about that needed consensus.

APPENDIX: SELF-SUPPORTING STUDENT DEFINITIONS

(States with Comprehensive Programs, 1973-74*)

CALIFORNIA. The definition of a self-supporting student requires twelve month California residence, and one of the following: twenty-three years old by 9/1 of academic year; honorable discharge from armed services with minimum one year service; ward of the court, orphan; residence with neither parent since junior year of high school and not tax dependent for twelve months by parents (part of extremely adverse home situation documented by school or responsible community personnel where student has received no support from family for preceding twelve months, or a "generally unacceptable family situation," e.g. frequent mergings and separations of family due to frequent remarriage, or a family on the state public assistance program); not claimed as tax exemption other than by self or spouse.

CONNECTICUT. State Scholarship and College Continuation Grant Programs define a self-supporting student as financially independent of his parents or legal guardians. Restricted Educational Achievement Grants define that a self-supporting student must come from a poverty background and due to circumstances be forced to be self-supporting.

FLORIDA. Student Assistance Grants define a self-supporting student as one not claimed as dependent for income tax, not living with parents, and not receiving more than $600 from parents.

ILLINOIS. In Illinois, a self-supporting student is defined as living in the state six months other than as full-time student and not having lived with or been claimed on federal income tax forms by parents for the calendar year prior to applying, the year applying, and the year of the award.

IOWA. A self-supporting student is one not claimed by parents or guardian as an income tax exemption for prior to the year in which the award is to be used and will not be so claimed for the award year, and who has not lived in a parent's home for twelve months prior to application (unless reasonable room and board are paid) and has not received any financial aid from his parents

---

*States not reporting: Alaska, Indiana, Kansas (Scholarship Program), Missouri, Oregon.

for this period.

KANSAS. The Tuition Grant Program's definition of a self-supporting student is identical to the one used with federal programs.

MAINE. A student either married or eighteen years old who has not been dependent on his parents for the last income reporting year is defined as self-supporting.

MARYLAND. A student who files a Student Confidential Statement instead of a Parents Confidential Statement is self-supporting.

MASSACHUSETTS. Single self-supporting students under twenty-five years of age must not be claimed as tax exemption by their parents for the previous two consecutive years.

MICHIGAN. Self-supporting students have not been claimed by parents as an exemption on previous year's federal income tax return; they must have maintained separate residence apart from parents for the previous twelve months; and they must not have received more than $500 in support from parents during the previous twelve months.

MINNESOTA. The definition follows federal guidelines.

NEW JERSEY. The Educational Opportunity Fund defines a self-supporting student as one who has not resided with a parent or guardian and has not nor will be claimed as an exemption (excluding spouse), and has not nor will receive financial assistance of more than $200 per year (food, clothing, shelter) in the calendar year in which aid is received or the calendar year prior. All other New Jersey programs define the self-supporting student as being age twenty-three or older, not claimed as a dependent on the previous year's tax return, not living at home or receiving contributions to educational expenses from parents. (This means that the student must show how he supported himself during the past year.) This self-supporting definition currently is being reviewed.

NEW YORK. A self-supporting student must have had an interruption in education of at least one year prior to the term for which he seeks an award, during which time he has not lived with or received support from parents.

NORTH DAKOTA. To be classified as a self-supporting student, one must not have been claimed by parents for the last tax year, nor have received more than $200 from parents in cash or kind in the last twelve months.

OHIO. A self-supporting student must have twelve month financial independent status in terms of financial support, federal income tax purposes, and residency.

PENNSYLVANIA. Veterans of U. S. Armed Forces and married students out of high school six years or more are considered self-supporting. Nonveterans not out of high school six years or not married are considered on individual circumstances within policy guidelines.

RHODE ISLAND. A self-supporting student is one who is not declared as a tax dependent by his parents.

SOUTH CAROLINA. A self-supporting student is one who is not claimed on parents' income tax form(s) as dependent, did not receive more than $600 support last year from parents, and did not live with a parent or guardian in the last year.

TENNESSEE. United States Office of Education guidelines serve as the definition for a self-supporting student.

TEXAS. The definition is the same as for the Federal Insured Loan Program.

VERMONT. A self-supporting student has not been claimed or will not be claimed as an exemption for federal income tax purposes by either parent or any other person (except spouse) for either the calendar year in which aid is received or the two *prior* calendar years; he has not received or will not receive financial assistance of more than $200 including room and board of any kind from one or both parents or from persons acting *in loco parentis* in either the calendar year in which aid is received or the two *prior* calendar years. A student is considered to have received more than $200 in assistance if he or she has resided with his or her parents for a period of one month or longer. A student whose parents or others acting *in loco parentis* have died within the period discussed above is eligible for consideration as a self-supporting student even if the tests are not met. Two specified kinds of documentation for self-supporting student status are required.

WASHINGTON. A self-supporting student is one who is not claimed by parents as dependent on their last filed income tax form and who has not resided with parents for one calendar year or received more than $200 in cash or kind from parents for one calendar year preceding receipt of the Need Grant.

WEST VIRGINIA. A self-supporting student has not been or will not be claimed as exemption by parents or guardians. He has not received or will not receive financial assistance of more than $600 from parents or guardians; he has not or will not maintain residence with parents except during vacation periods.

WISCONSIN. The Tuition Grant Program maintains that if a student and/or spouse provided the majority of his own support in preceding calendar year, he or she is a self-supporting student. Other Wisconsin programs maintain that a self-supporting student is one not claimed by parents as tax exemption in previous calendar year.

CHAPTER FOUR

CONFIDENTIALITY AND
THE COLLEGE STUDENT

PRIVACY OF RECORDS

WITH intensified technologically based record-keeping, college students as well as private citizens today are systematically subject to an imposing and awesome storage of statistical data about themselves and those with whom they associate. The release of such statistical data, particularly commentary on one's personal activities, often has occurred without appropriate institutional controls, including the securing of the affected individual's consent.

As a means to ensure proper and uniform institutional control and provide legitimate access to educational records, the Ninety-Third Congress passed the Family Educational Rights and Privacy Act of 1974, more commonly known as the Buckley Amendment.

At first little noticed, the Buckley Amendment rapidly became a subject of heated controversy between educational administrators and governmental officials — as well as within the groups themselves. Senator James Buckley's initial and apparent intent was to restore the rights of parents with regard to the availability of their children's educational records. The Buckley Amendment further ensured the individual student's rights of privacy.

An inadvertent consequence of Senator Buckley's concern for school children and their parents was the creation of access legislation for the adult student having potentially serious impact upon postsecondary institutions. Colleges and universities were concerned that Senator Buckley's original legislation, particularly as it related to student access of information, would cause breaches of confidentially and probable demise of meaningful and informative faculty recommendations. Subsequent legislative amendment and interpretative rules, however, largely resolved early reservations held by administrators relating to the Buckley Amendment's provisions for student inspection and review of university-maintained records.

CRITERIA FOR INSTITUTIONAL RECORDKEEPING

If a college's first responsibility is to help students grow personally and intellectually, institutional records which, in fact, belong to the student should be used primarily as an advising and counseling device. Unfortunately, however, a plethora of recordkeeping by all college departments and offices with which a student may have contact has often led to an indiscriminate decentralization of records without appropriate and protective means of control. Photocopy devices now in abundance at colleges and universities have made possible the storage of complete student data inventories rather than the relevant portions essential to a particular office's requirements. In effect, the request for a student's college entrance examination scores by one department can readily cause the release of irrelevant data such as a student's relationship with his high school counselor noted on the same computer printout sheet.

Confidentiality can be defined as relying upon another's secrecy and fidelity, and the term denotes trust. For students, the institution is the repository for personal and academic materials, and as such the institution has the affirmative obligation to assure reasonable secrecy. The storage and release of student information by a college, therefore, should satisfy at least three fundamental criteria:

(1) Information recorded should be based on the absolute needs of the institution.
(2) Recorded data should be utilized in ways which will promote intellectual and social growth. The functional mode of such data should be consultative rather than punitive.
(3) The release of student data should be limited to legitimate inquiries conforming to the Family Educational Rights and Privacy Act of 1974.

College administrators should recognize that problems of confidentiality can only exist when information requested has been recorded. No problem of improper storage or disclosure adversely affecting a student's personal or professional life can occur when damaging information has not been stored. The release of information to outside agencies may, in fact, be secondary in importance to a student's right to know with respect to his own files. While possible inconvenience or embarrassment to a university may occur because of the availability of recorded information to a student, nevertheless, such administrative disturbance is outweighed by a student's constitutional, statutory, and personal prerogatives. A student's ability to appropriately respond to adverse information contained in his records can only be improved when file materials and documents are made available to him.

In state institutions, particularly, there is an additional basis upon which a student may have access to his personal file and records. Such basis is predicated upon the so-called right-to-know statutes which apply to public documents. There statutes also include policies and procedures for inspection and reproduction.

CONFIDENTIAL COMMUNICATIONS

The legal parameters of guaranteed confidence are predicated upon two principles of law:
(1) privileged communications, and
(2) an individual's constitutional right to privacy.
The term *privileged communications* is used to designate any information which one person derives from another by reason of a confidential relationship. If it were not for this relationship, private information would not have been released or communicated. This concept of privileged communication offers some support for limiting the uses that can be made of student records.

There are two general kinds of privilege: absolute and qualified. An absolute privilege may be described as one where the recipient cannot disclose the information obtained to anyone. State legislatures have conferred this privilege in different ways depending upon jurisdiction. Usually based upon the grounds of public policy, the party to whom private information was disclosed is made incompetent by law to testify in civil, criminal, and legislative hearings. Some of these relationships are attorney-client, clergyman-penitent, physician-patient, certified psychologist-patient, husband-wife, and newspaperman-source. Within the context of a university environment, not all of such relationships are of equal importance. It should be noted, furthermore, that the communication itself is not incompetent, but the recipient is an incompetent witness. Third parties who obtain privileged information, however, might be compelled and able to testify.

Some characteristics concerning these privileges may be generalized in the following manner.

(1) The privileged relationship must exist between the parties with reference to the material involved. The mere fact that an individual may be a priest does not *ipso facto* confer the immunity of the privilege upon a conversation he may be having informally with a student concerning a problem.

(2) The protected party need not receive any pledge of secrecy in order to receive this protection.

(3) The privilege belongs solely to the protected party and his personal representative.

(4) The communication to be covered by the privilege is information conferred either orally or by writings exhibited.

(5) The protected party may at his option waive the privilege during his lifetime.

(6) No privilege is conferred upon information given in the presence of a third party.

(7) The communication must not be pursuant to a consultation for unlawful purposes.

Even though the appropriate relationship may exist, not all communications between parties are necessarily to be considered confidential and entitled to the privilege of confidentiality.

Qualified privilege permits the disclosure of information in certain instances without the protected party's permission. For example, even though certain information contained in a student's file cannot be released to the public, a substantial number of individuals could possibly have access to it on a "need-to-know basis." Public officials, teachers, administrators, parents, and prospective employers are generally considered to have proper bases for requesting confidential or private information which may, in fact, rest outside the parameters of the Family Educational Rights and Privacy Act. Responsible educators have increasingly honored such requests only where this "need to know" is firmly established or where the student directly or indirectly has authorized the release of private information.

THE FAMILY EDUCATIONAL RIGHTS AND PRIVACY ACT

The Family Educational Rights and Privacy Act of 1974 has added considerably to the privacy of the records of college and university students. The protection of this act applies to a student's parents and to the student himself when he reaches eighteen years of age. Adult students who are defined as dependent according to Internal Revenue Service (IRS) definitions, however, share the prerogatives of this legislation with their parents.

Since the greatest majority of college students have attained adult status, this federal act is an extremely important piece of legislation for guiding the college and university administrator. The Family Educational Rights and Privacy Act of 1974 affords substantial protection and control to the college student over his records, files, and personal data. Upon the penalty of having federal funding terminate, educational institutions (including virtually all private colleges and universities since federal monies in one way or another are received in support of various programs by a very large number of those institutions) are restrained from releasing information from student records and files without the express written consent of the student involved. In addition, the student has the right to inspect his records and to challenge their accuracy at a formal hearing.

College and university administrators should closely review Department of Health, Education, and Welfare (HEW) regulatory guidelines interpreting (1) the nature of educational records, and (2) student access and nonconsensual access to the records. Most of the definitions contained in HEW guidelines generally repeat statutory language. Educational records include "those records, files, documents, and other materials which...contain information directly related to a student..., are maintained by an educational... institution... or its agents." Not included are records privately maintained by institutional personnel for their own use; records and documents maintained for law enforcement purposes only, employment records made in the regular course of business, and professional or paraprofessional histories of treatment. Such histories may be reviewed, however, by a physician or other professional designated by the student.

Institutions including colleges or universities which maintain educational records or information personally identifying students must permit access to the following categories of request:

(1) *Students:* Currently or formerly enrolled who have not signed a waiver of their rights under this act;

(2) *Parents:* Of currently or formerly enrolled students who are dependent per section 152 of the IRS code of 1954 at the time of the request;

(3) *Agencies and Organizations:* Which require student data not personally identifiable for the purposes of test validation and development, and institutional accreditation;

(4) *Educational officers and institutions:* Which have a legitimate educational interest such as teachers, financial aid officers, admission and transfer counselors, among others;

(5) *Governmental and Judicial Petition:* Release of student data whether personally identifiable or not must be made to authorized federal agencies for purposes of the act's enforcement. Requests for data relating to students' health and safety also must be respected. Information required by state statute adopted prior to November 19, 1974 must be furnished to the appropriate state or local agencies seeking such information. Judicial orders including subpoenae and other court-related requests for data fall within this category of release.

Compliance with Buckley Amendment guidelines also requires that educational administrators establish procedures for notification to students and parents of records maintained, the methods by which such records may be copied and secured, recourse available for challenging record content, and for institutional nondisclosure of data requested.*

---

*Notification to students and their parents of their rights and of institutional procedures under the Buckley Amendment must be accomplished annually and "by such means as are reasonably likely to inform" protected individuals. Department of Health, Education, and Welfare rules published in the June 17, 1976 issue of the *Federal Register* also note that guarantees of access to educational records by students and former students does not include those records collected for alumni. In addition, recent rules do not provide records access to individuals who have not yet been admitted to a particular institution.

The right of access to private information may be further limited by an individual's constitutional right to privacy. There is legal recognition that an individual has certain prerogatives to safeguard certain facets of his personal life from the scrutiny of others. The courts in honoring these basic rights can prohibit incursions as well as award compensatory or punitive damages. Courts have not up to this time issued definitive guidelines with regard to the right of privacy, but the capacity of electronic devices to pierce the cloak of one's private life and conversations makes it likely that further judicial commentary and guidance will be forthcoming.

SUGGESTED ACCESS REQUEST FORM

ACCESS REQUEST - EDUCATIONAL RECORDS

(For examination in person)

Instructions: Complete Part One of the form and give it to the office. After examination, complete Part Two and return it to the office.

PART ONE

Name:_____   Soc. Sec. No._____

Address_____   Date of Birth_____

City, State_____   Today's Date_____

Campus M____, R____, T____   Active?____ Inactive?____

Undergraduate College?____: Graduate School?____

REQUEST: Subject to the rules of XYZ University and in compliance with the Buckley Amendment, Educational Rights and Privacy Act, I wish to make a request for an in-person examination of my official university records.

_____
signature

Please Note - Individuals who request copies of records by mail must furnish in addition to the information requested above a notarized signature. If not within the state of New Jersey, such notarization must be exemplified.

PART TWO

CERTIFICATION: I certify that I have examined in the presence of a university witness my official university records (as inventoried on reverse side) and found them to be in order or have commented to the contrary.

Date_____   Student_____

Date_____   Witness_____

Comments: if any _____

_____

_____

Date of Appointment if any_____   For
                                                  Office
Payment received for copies, if any_____   Use

RECORD OF ACCESS

Name_____ Soc. Sec. No._____

Date of	Requested By	Purpose of Request	Action Taken
_____	_____	_____	_____
_____	_____	_____	_____
_____	_____	_____	_____
_____	_____	_____	_____
_____	_____	_____	_____
_____	_____	_____	_____
_____	_____	_____	_____
_____	_____	_____	_____
_____	_____	_____	_____
_____	_____	_____	_____
_____	_____	_____	_____
_____	_____	_____	_____
_____	_____	_____	_____

RULES — PRIVACY RIGHTS OF PARENTS AND STUDENTS*

Sec. 438. (a) (1) (A) No funds shall be made available under any applicable program to any educational agency or institution which has a policy of denying, or which effectively prevents, the parents of students who are or have been in attendance at a school of such agency or at such institution, as the case may be, the right to inspect and review the education records of their children. If any material or document in the education record of a student includes information on more than one student, the parents of one of such students shall have the right to inspect and review only such part of such material or document as relates to such student or to be informed of the specific information contained in such part of such material. Each educational agency or institution shall establish appropriate procedures for the granting of a request by parents for access to the education records of their children within a reasonable period of time, but in no case more than forty-five days after the request has been made.

(B) The first sentence of subparagraph (A) shall not operate to make available to students in institutions of postsecondary education the following materials:

(i) financial records of the parents of the student or any information contained therein;

(ii) confidential letters and statements of recommendation, which were placed in the education records prior to Janaury 1, 1975, if such letters or statements are not used for purposes other than those for which they were specifically intended;

(iii) if the student has signed a waiver of the student's right of access under this subsection in accordance with subparagraph (C), confidential recommendations —

(I) respecting admission to any educational agency or institution,

---

*See *Federal Register*, March 2, 1976, pages 9062-9064 for subsequent revisions. Currently implemented regulations include due process definitions for hearings called to challenge record contents, and precise conditions for disclosure in health and safety emergencies. Essentially, colleges and universities are now required to act in good faith relative to student record challenges and to permit legal counsel at hearings if requested by students or their parents. In addition, health and safety emergencies are described as ones which seriously threaten an individual and/or where time is of the essence.

(II) respecting an application for employment, and

(III) respecting the receipt of an honor or honorary recognition.

(C) A student or a person applying for admission may waive his right of access to confidential statements described in clause (iii) of subparagraph (B), except that such waiver shall apply to recommendations only if (i) the student is, upon request, notified of the names of all persons making confidential recommendations and (ii) such recommendations are used solely for the purpose for which they were specifically intended. Such waivers may not be recurred [sic] as a condition for admission to, receipt of financial aid from, or receipt of any other services or benefits from such agency or institution.

(2) No funds shall be made available under any applicable program to any educational agency or institution unless the parents of students who are or have been in attendance at a school of such agency or at such institution are provided an opportunity for a hearing by such agency or institution, in accordance with regulations of the secretary, to challenge the content of such student's education records, in order to insure that the records are not inaccurate, misleading, or otherwise in violation of the privacy or other rights of students, and to provide an opportunity for the correction or deletion of any such inaccurate, misleading, or otherwise inappropriate data contained therein and to insert into such records a written explanation of the parents respecting the content of such records.

(3) For the purposes of this section the term "educational agency" or "institution" means any public or private agency or institution which is the recipient of funds under any applicable program.

(4) (A) For the purposes of this section, the term "education records" means, except as may be provided otherwise in subparagraph (B), those records, files, documents, and other materials which —

(i) contain information directly related to a student; and

(ii) are maintained by an educational agency or institution, or by a person acting for such agency or institution.

(B) The term "education records" does not include —

(i) records of institutional, supervisory, and administrative personnel and educational personnel ancillary thereto which are in the sole possession of the maker thereof and which are not accessible or revealed to any other person except a substitute;

(ii) if the personnel of a law enforcement unit do not have access to education records under subsection (b) (1), the records and documents of such law enforcement unit which (I) are kept apart from records described in subparagraph (A), (II) are maintained solely for law enforcement purposes, and (III) are not made available to persons other than law enforcement officials of the same jurisdiction;

(iii) in the case of persons who are employed by an educational agency or institution but who are not in attendance at such agency or institution, records made and maintained in the normal course of business which relate exclusively to such person in that person's capacity as an employee and are not available for use for any other purpose; or

(iv) records on a student who is eighteen years of age or older, or is attending an institution of postsecondary education, which are created or maintained by a physician, psychiatrist, psychologist, or other recognized professional or paraprofessional acting in his professional or paraprofessional capacity, or assisting in that capacity, and which are created, maintained, or used only in connection with the provision of treatment to the student, and are not available to anyone other than persons providing such treatment; provided, however, that such records can be personally reviewed by a physician or other appropriate professional of the student's choice.

(5) (A) For the purposes of this section the term "directory information" relating to a student includes the following: the student's name, address, telephone listing, date and place of birth, major field of study, participation in officially recognized activities and sports, weight and height of members of athletic teams, dates of attendance, degrees and awards received, and the most recent previous educational agency or institution attended by the student.

(B) Any educational agency or institution making public directory information shall give public notice of the categories of information which it has designated as such information with respect to each student attending the institution or agency and shall allow a reasonable period of time after such notice has been given for a parent to inform the institution or agency that any or all of the information designated should not be released without the parent's prior consent.

(6) For the purposes of this section, the term "student" includes any person with respect to whom an educational agency or institution maintains education records or personally identifiable information, but does not include a person who has not been in attendance at such agency or institution.

(b) (1) No funds shall be made available under any applicable program to any educational agency or institution which has a policy or practice of permitting the release of education records (or personally identifiable information contained therein other than directory information, as defined in paragraph (5) of subsection (a)) of students without the written consent of their parents to any individual agency, or organization, other than to the following —

(A) other school officials, including teachers within the educational institution or local educational agency who have been determined by such agency or institution to have legitimate educational interests;

(B) officials of other schools or school systems in which the student seeks or, intends to enroll, upon condition that the student's parents be notified of the transfer, receive a copy of the record if desired, and have an opportunity for a hearing to challenge the content of the record;

(C) authorized representatives of (i) the Comptroller General of the United States, (ii) the secretary, (iii) an administrative head of an education agency (as defined in section 408 (c) of this act), or (iv) state educational authorities, under the conditions set forth in paragraph (3) of this subsection; and

(D) in connection with a student's applications for, or receipt of, financial aid;

(E) state and local officials or authorities to which such information is specifically required to be reported or disclosed pursuant to state statute adopted prior to November 19, 1974;

(F) organizations conducting studies for, or on behalf of, educational agencies or institutions for the purpose of developing, validating, or administering predictive tests, administering student aid programs, and improving instruction, if such studies are conducted in such a manner as will not permit the personal identification of students and their parents by persons other than representatives of such organizations and such information will be destroyed when no longer needed for the purpose for which it is conducted;

(G) accrediting organizations in order to carry out their accrediting functions;

(H) parents of a dependent student of such parents, as defined in section 152 of the Internal Revenue Code of 1954; and

(I) subject to regulations of the secretary in connection with an emergency, appropriate persons if the knowledge of such information is necessary to protect the health or safety of the student or other persons.

(2) No funds shall be made available under any applicable program to any education agency or institution which has a policy or practice of releasing, or providing access to, any personally identifiable information in education records other than directory information, or as is permitted under paragraph (1) of this subsection unless —

(A) there is written consent from the student's parents specifying records to be released, the reasons for such release, and to whom, and with a copy of the records to be released to the student's parents and the student if desired by the parents, or

(B) such information is furnished in compliance with judicial order, or pursuant to any lawfully issued subpoena, upon condition that parents and the students are notified of all such orders or subpoena in advance of the compliance therewith by the educational institution or agency.

(3) Nothing contained in this section shall preclude authorized representatives of (A) the Comptroller General of the United States, (B) the secretary, (C) an administrative head of an education agency or (D) state educational authorities from having access to student or other records which may be necessary in connection with the audit and evaluation of federally supported education programs, or in connection with the enforcement of the federal legal requirements which relate to such programs, *provided* that, except when collection of personally identifiable in-

formation is specifically authorized by federal law, any data collected by such officials shall be protected in a manner which will not permit the personal identification of students and their parents by other than those officials, and such personally identifiable data shall be destroyed when no longer needed for such audit, evaluation, and enforcement of federal legal requirements.

(4) (A) Each educational agency or institution shall maintain a record, kept with the education records of each student, which will indicate all individuals (other than those specified in paragraph (1) (A) of this subsection), agencies, or organizations which have requested or obtained access to a student's education records maintained by such educational agency or institution, and which will indicate specifically the legitimate interest that each such person, agency, or organization has in obtaining this information. Such record of access shall be available only to parents, to the school official and his assistants who are responsible for the custody of such records, and to persons or organizations authorized in, and under the conditions of, clauses (A) and (C) of paragraph (1) as a means of auditing the operation of the system.

(B) With respect to this subsection, personal information shall only be transferred to a third party on the condition that such party will not permit any other party to have access to such information without the written consent of the parents of the student.

(c) The secretary shall adopt appropriate regulations to protect the rights of privacy of students and their families in connection with any surveys or data-gathering activities conducted, assisted, or authorized by the secretary or an administrative head of an education agency. Regulations established under this subsection shall include provisions controlling the use, dissemination, and protection of such data. No survey or data-gathering activities shall be conducted by the secretary, or an administrative head of an education agency under an applicable program, unless such activities are authorized by law.

(d) For the purposes of this section, whenever a student has attained eighteen years of age, or is attending an institution of postsecondary education the permission or consent required of and the rights accorded to the parents of the student shall thereafter only be required of and accorded to the student.

(e) No funds shall be made available under any applicable program to any educational agency or institution unless such agency or institution informs the parents of students, or the students, if they are eighteen years of age or older, or are attending an institution of postsecondary education, of the rights accorded them by this section.

(f) The secretary, or an administrative head of an education agency, shall take appropriate actions to enforce provisions of this section and to deal with violations of this section, according to the provisions of this act, except that action to terminate assistance may be taken only if the secretary finds there has been a failure to comply with the provisions of this section, and he has determined that compliance cannot be secured by voluntary means.

(g) The secretary shall establish or designate an office and review board within the Department of Health, Education, and Welfare for the purpose of investigating, processing, reviewing, and adjudicating violations of the provisions of this section and complaints which may be filed concerning alleged violations of this section. Except for the conduct of hearings, none of the functions of the secretary under this section shall be carried out in any of the regional offices of such department.

CASE: PRIVACY — ACCESSIBILITY
OF STUDENT RECORDS

Chester R. Morris, Appellant, v. Joseph R. Smiley et al., Appellees, Court of Civil Appeals of Texas, April 8, 1964, 378 S. W. 2d 149.

Justice Hughes.

Chester R. Morris, appellant, sued Joseph R. Smiley, President of the University of Texas, Arno Nowotny, Dean of Student Life at the University of Texas, and Pat Bailey, Assistant Attorney General of the State of Texas, appellees, in which he sought issuance of a writ of mandamus requiring appellees to produce a permit for inspection, copying, and photographing of certain records maintained by the University of Texas relating to appellant.*

The appellees filed an answer consisting of special exceptions and a general denial. This answer was subject to an unsworn plea in abatement which pleaded that this was a suit brought against the state without its consent and that the appellant had not exhausted his legal remedies. These remedies were alleged to be a discovery suit then pending in this court, being our cause no. 11,109, and a discovery action pending in the Seventy-Third Judicial District Court of Bexar County, being cause no. F-150,-020.

The trial court sustained this plea in abatement and dismissed the appellant's suit.

We hold that the appellees' plea in abatement should not have been sustained and that it was error to dismiss this suit.

The appellant filed a motion for summary judgment, which motion the court denied. In such motion, the appellant stated, under oath, that he went to the University of Texas Health Building and requested to see his health records. This request was denied. A similar request was made of Dr. Paul White who denied the request. The appellant also stated that he called on Dean Nowotny and requested permission to inspect such records as he had pertaining to the appellant. Some such records were shown to him, but the appellant had heard rumors that the file shown him was not complete.

---

*In this case, C. Morris, a student, successfully secured copies of his health records albeit through strained judicial reasoning.

The appellant made Mr. Bailey a party to this suit because Dean Nowotny testified, according to the appellant, that Mr. Bailey had the records, pertaining to the appellant which had been previously shown him by the Dean.

This motion shows no cause of action against Mr. Bailey and the dismissal as to him is correct. If Mr. Bailey has the records mentioned, they are presumably held as attorney for Dean Nowotny. Mr. Bailey undoubtedly will comply with any order regarding such records which may be made.

There are two questions remaining to be determined. Are the records sought to be inspected and copied public records? Who is the legal custodian of such records?

"A public record has been defined as a written memorial made by a public officer, and as a record of an officer made in the discharge of his official duties by doing an act he is empowered by law to do." 49 Tex. Jur. 2d p. 326. See *Dallas Coffee & Tea Co. v. Williams*, 45 S. W. 2d 724, Dallas Civ. App., writ dism.

A more comprehensive definition is given in 45 Am. Jur., p. 420, which we quote:

> It is said that a public record is one required by law to be kept, or necessary to be kept, in the discharge of a duty imposed by law, or directed by law to serve as a memorial and evidence of something written, said, or done. In all instances where by law or regulation a document is filed in a public office and required to be kept there, it is of a public nature, but this is not quite inclusive of all that may properly be considered public records. For whenever a written record of the transactions of a public officer in his office is a convenient and appropriate mode of discharging the duties of his office, it is not only his right, but his duty, to keep that memorial whether expressly required so to do or not; and when kept it becomes a public document which belongs to the office rather than to the officer. What is a public record is a question of law.

We are not cited to any statute or rule of the University of Texas requiring the keeping of records by an officer or employee.

We direct attention to Art. 259, Vernon's Ann. Civ. St., which provides in part, that the "librarian of the University of Texas and the archivist of the Department of History of said university are hereby authorized to make certified copies of all public records in the custody of the university..."

We also direct attention to Art. 3731a, V.A.C.S., regarding the admissibility in evidence of copies of records "... made by an officer of this state or of any governmental subdivision thereof, or by his deputy, or person or employee under his supervision, in the performance of the functions of his office and employment..."

We do not find the motion for summary judgment to be conclusive in establishing that the records sought to be inspected and copied are public records or, if so, who is the legal custodian of them.

If the records which the appellant desired to inspect and copy come within the definitions of public records contained in this opinion, then the appellant is entitled to inspect and copy them and the lawful custodian of those records is under a legal duty to comply with all reasonable requests to this end.

We overrule the appellant's motion to bar the attorney general from representing all appellees in this case. See our opinion in *Morris v. Hoerster,* Tex. Civ. App., 377 S. W. 2d 841.

We affirm the judgment of the trial court in dismissing Mr. Bailey, otherwise the cause is reversed and remanded.

Affirmed in part and reversed and remanded in part.

CASE: PRIVACY — CONSTITUTIONAL GUARANTEES

Estelle T. Griswold et al., Appellants, v. State of Connecticut,
Argued March 29, 1965, Decided June 7, 1965, 381 U.S. 479 (1965)
    Mr. Justice Douglas.

Appellant Griswold is executive director of the Planned Parenthood League of Connecticut. Appellant Buxton is a licensed physician and a professor at the Yale Medical School who served as medical director for the league at its center in New Haven — a center open and operating from November 1 to November 10, 1961, when appellants were arrested.

They gave information, instruction, and medical advice to married persons as the means of preventing conception. They examined the wife and prescribed the best contraceptive device or material for her use. Fees were usually charged, although some couples were serviced free.

The statutes whose constitutionality is involved in this appeal are 53-32 and 54-196 of the General Statutes of Connecticut (1958 rev.). The former provides:

> Any person who uses any drug, medicinal article, or instrument for the purpose of preventing conception shall be fined not less than fifty dollars or imprisoned not less than sixty days nor more than one year or be both fined and imprisoned.

Section 54-196 provides:

> Any person who assists, abets, counsels, causes, hires, or commands another to commit any offense may be prosecuted and punished as if he were the principal offender.

The appellants were found guilty as accessories and fined $100 each, against the claim that the accessory statute as so applied violated the Fourteenth Amendment. The Appellate Division of the Circuit Court affirmed. The Supreme Court of Errors affirmed that judgment. We noted probable jurisdiction.

We think that appellants have standing to raise the constitutional rights of the married people with whom they had a professional relationship. *Tileston v. Ullman,* 318 U.S. 44, 63 S. Ct. 493, 87 L. Ed. 693, is different, for there the plaintiff seeking to represent others asked for a declaratory judgment. In that situation we thought that the requirements of standing should be strict, lest the standards of "case or controversy" in Article III of the Constitution become blurred. Here those doubts are removed by reason of a criminal conviction for serving married couples in violation of an aiding-and-abetting statute. Certainly the accessory should have standing to assert that the offense which he is charged with assisting is not, or cannot constitutionally be a crime.

This case is more akin to *Truax v. Raich*, 239 U. S. 33, where an employee was permitted to assert the rights of his employer; to *Pierce v. Society of Sisters*, 268 U. S. 510, where the owners of private schools were entitled to assert the rights of potential pupils and their parents; and to *Barrows v. Jackson*, 346 U. S. 249, where a White defendant, party to a racially restrictive covenant, who was being sued for damages by the covenators because she had conveyed her property to Negroes, was allowed to raise the issue that enforcement of the covenant violated the rights of prospective Negro purchasers to equal protection, although no Negro was a party to the suit. The rights of husband and wife, pressed here, are likely to be diluted or adversely affected unless those rights are considered in a suit involving those who have this kind of confidential relation to them.

Coming to the merits, we are met with a wide range of questions that implicate the due process clause of the Fourteenth Amendment. We do not sit as a super-legislature to determine the wisdom, need, and 'propriety of laws that touch economic problems, business affairs, or social conditions. This law, however, operates directly on an intimate relation of husband and wife and their physician's role in one aspect of that relation.

The association of people is not mentioned in the Constitution nor in the Bill of Rights. The right to educate a child in a school of the parents' choice — whether public or private or parochial — is also not mentioned. Nor is the right to study any particular subject or any foreign language. Yet the First Amendment has been construed to include certain of those rights.

By *Pierce v. Society of Sisters*, supra, the right to educate one's children as one chooses is made applicable to the states by the force of the First and Fourteenth Amendments. By *Meyer v. State of Nebraska*, supra, the same dignity is given the right to study the German language in a private school. In other words, the state may not, consistently with the spirit of the First Amendment, contract the spectrum of available knowledge. The right of freedom of speech and press includes not only the right to utter or to print, but the right to distribute, the right to receive, the right to read, and freedom of inquiry, freedom of thought, and freedom to teach — indeed the freedom of the entire university community.

In *NAACP v. State of Alabama*, 357 U. S. 449, 462, we protected the "freedom to associate and privacy in one's associations," noting that freedom of association was a peripheral First Amendment right. Disclosure of membership lists of a constitutionally valid association, we held, was invalid "as entailing the likelihood of a substantial restraint upon the exercise by petitioner's members of their right to freedom of association." (*Ibid.*) *In other words, the first Amendment has a penumbra where privacy is protected from governmental intrusion. In like context, we have protected forms of "association" that are not political in the customary sense but pertain to the social, legal, and economic benefit of the members.*

The foregoing cases suggest that specific guarantees in the Bill of Rights have penumbras, formed by emanations from those guarantees that help give them life and substance. *Various guarantees create zones of privacy. The right to association contained in the penumbra of the First Amendment is one, as we have seen. The Third Amendment in its prohibition against the quartering of soldiers "in any house" in time of peace without the consent of the owner is another facet of that privacy. The Fourth Amendment explicitly affirms the "right of the people to be secure in their persons, houses, papers, and affects, against unreasonable searches and seizures." The Fifth Amendment in its self-incrimination clause enables the citizen to create a zone of privacy which government may not force him to surrender to his detriment. The Ninth Amendment provides, "The enumeration in the Constitution, of certain rights, shall not be construed to deny or disparage others retained by the people."*

The Fourth and Fifth Amendments were described in *Boyd v. United States* as protection against all governmental invasions "of the sanctity of a man's home and the privacies of life."

We recently referred in *Mapp v. Ohio* to the Fourth Amendment as creating a "right to privacy, no less important than any other right carefully and particularly reserved to the people."

The present case, then, concerns a relationship lying within the zone of privacy created by several fundamental constitutional guarantees. And it concerns a law which, in forbidding the use of contraceptives rather than regulating their manufacture or sale, seeks to achieve its goals by means having a maximum destructive impact upon that relationship. Such a law cannot stand in light of the familiar principle, so often applied by this Court, that a "governmental purpose to control or prevent activities constitutionally subject to state regulation may not be achieved by means which sweep unnecessarily broadly and thereby invade the area of protected freedoms." Would we allow the police to search the sacred precincts of marital bedrooms for telltale signs of the use of contraceptives? The very idea is repulsive to the notions of privacy surrounding the marriage relationship.

We deal with a right of privacy older than the Bill of Rights — older than our political parties, older than our school system. *Marriage is a coming together for better or for worse, hopefully enduring, and intimate to the degree of being sacred. It is an association that promotes a way of life, not causes; a harmony in living, not political faiths; a bilateral loyalty, not commercial or social projects.* Yet it is an association for as noble a purpose as any involved in our prior decisions.

Reversed.

CASE: PRIVACY — PERSONAL BELONGINGS

The People v. John Lanthier, 97 Cal. Rptr. 297 (1971)
Justice Mosk.

Summary

A university employee, in carrying out his superiors' orders to locate the source of an unpleasant odor in the locker room, opened all the lockers in the room, found the source of the odor in a brief case in the defendant-student's locker, opened the case, saw numerous transparent packets therein, and turned the case and packets over to his superiors. The superiors asked a university police officer if he recognized the contents of the packets and he identified the material as marijuana. The defendant was charged with possession of marijuana for sale, his motion to suppress on the ground of illegal search and seizure was denied, he pleaded guilty, and was placed on probation on condition of service of a county jail term. (Superior Court of Santa Clara County, John S. McInerny, Judge.)

On the defendant's appeal from the order granting probation, the Supreme Court affirmed, rejecting the contention that the marijuana was taken in an illegal search. The Court held that the search came within the "emergency" exception to the warrant requirement, that the initial search was reasonable and that the superiors acted reasonably thereafter in seeking identification of material that was "in plain sight." (Opinion by Mosk, expressing the unanimous view of the Court.)

Opinion

Justice Moske — The defendant was charged with possession of marijuana for sale. His motions to dismiss the information and to suppress the evidence on the ground of illegal search and seizure were denied, and he entered a plea of guilty. The court placed him on probation for a period of three years on the condition that he serve sixty days in the county jail. The defendant appeals from the order denying the motion to suppress the evidence and from the order granting probation.

The motions were submitted on the transcript of the preliminary examination. The defendant, a student at Stanford University, had been assigned a "carrel" — i.e. a desk with attached bookcase and small locker — in a study hall in a university library building. On the morning of Monday, January 13, 1969, Joseph Riley, supervisor of maintenance services and security guards at the library, received a complaint of a noxious odor emanating from somewhere in the study hall. He was informed that "it smelled as if someone had vomited in the room," and it had been necessary to prop the doors open to air out the room throughout the previous day. That remedy had not cured the situation, however, and Riley was asked to check the room "and see if there was something causing the smell coming from the lockers." To Riley, the odor resembled that of sweet apples; he was not able to determine its source by smelling the outside of the lockers, however, it "permeated the room so strongly that you could smell any locker and think it was coming from any locker." Using his master key, he therefore began opening each of the lockers in turn, "looking for anything that would put off the smell that was complained about in the area."

When Riley opened the locker used by the defendant — the last of forty-two in the room — the odor grew noticeably stronger. A briefcase occupied virtually the entire inside space. Riley removed it in order to examine the rest of the locker, and then realized the odor was emanating directly from the briefcase. On the basis of that smell, Riley testified, "I thought it was bad food that was in the briefcase... So I opened the briefcase to see if it was bad food and then I saw all these small packets of material there." The contents were thirty-eight packets of marijuana, each in a transparent plastic wrapping of the size of a sandwich bag; the odor, also described in the transcript as resembling that of sour wine, apparently came from a preservative added to the marijuana.

Although he did not know what marijuana looked or smelled like, Riley "suspected it might be something like marijuana." He informed the director of the undergraduate library, Mr. Golter, that he had found the substance which had been causing the smell, and was told to bring it to the latter's office. There he opened the briefcase and showed its contents to Golter, who said, "We'll have to find out what it is." Other Stanford officials were consulted, during which time the briefcase was held in the basement because "It was giving off a very strong odor." Finally it was turned over to a university police officer, who contacted the Santa Clara Sheriff's Department.

Deputy Richard Saldivar responded to the call. He testified he was advised there was "a possible narcotics violation" and that "a briefcase was found in a locker at Meyers Library at Stanford University and that a strong odor was emanating from this briefcase. It was turned over ... by the officials at the university, and they asked me to inspect it to determine if I could identify the contents." The university police officer unfastened the catch on the briefcase, opened it, and exposed its contents; Deputy Saldivar removed one of the packets, and by sight and smell recognized the material to be marijuana. The defendant was subsequently arrested when he returned to his locker to reclaim the briefcase.

In overruling the defendant's objections to the evidence on the ground of illegal search and seizure, the magistrate at the preliminary examination made two findings: First, he found that "the initial search by Mr. Riley in this case was a reasonable search. Mr. Riley was merely seeking to locate the source of an unpleasant odor in a part of the library that was under his control and supervision. He was not looking for contraband or illicit or stolen property or any form of evidence of guilt of any crime or other offense and, under the law, such a search is not unreasonable and it did not become unreasonable even when Mr. Riley opened the briefcase from which that odor apparently was emanating." Secondly, the magistrate ruled that governmental involvement in the operations of Stanford University was not so pervasive as to render that institution subject to the limitations placed upon "state action" by the Fourteenth Amendment.

We need not reach the latter issue. Even if Stanford University were a "public" rather than a "private" institution, the search here challenged would be reasonable within the meaning of the Fourth Amendment. (1) It is true the search was conducted without a warrant, and the burden therefore rested upon the People to show justification. (2a) But that burden was sustained in the case at bar by a compelling showing of facts bringing the search within the "emergency" exception to the warrant requirement.

In *Camara v. Municipal Court*, 387 U. S. 523 (1967), the United States Supreme Court held that routine administrative searches of private property for violations of local health or safety codes must be made with a warrant; among other objections, the Court dismissed the claim that the delay attendant upon obtaining a warrant would frustrate the governmental purpose behind the search. But in authorizing such warrants to be based on area-wide conditions rather than on probable cause to believe that a particular dwelling contains code violations, the Court recognized that "the public interest demands that all dangerous conditions be prevented or abated." Finally, the Court was careful to emphasize, "Since our holding emphasizes the controlling standard of reasonableness, nothing we say today is intended to foreclose prompt inspections, even without a warrant, that the law has traditionally upheld in emergency situations. *The Court distinguished the routine administrative searches before it as presenting "no compelling urgency," and concluded that "warrants should normally be sought only after entry is refused unless there has been a citizen complaint or there is other satisfactory reason for securing immediate entry."*

In the case at bar such a "compelling urgency" was clearly shown. There had indeed been a "citizen complaint" about the malodorous smell permeating the entire study hall, and the smell was no less noticeable to Riley when he arrived to investigate. It was therefore reasonable for him to undertake, in his capacity of maintenance supervisor, a "prompt inspection" of the carrel area for the purpose of discovering and abating the nuisance. And inasmuch as the students entitled to use the room had already been disturbed by this offensive odor throughout the preceding day, further delay in suppressing it would not have been justifiable.

It is true that upon opening the briefcase Riley did not immediately recognize the contents, although he suspected it was marijuana. But it remained a reasonable course of action for the university officials to seek to identify the substance thus exposed to view. If, for example, the substance has presented an immediate health hazard, its summary destruction might well have been justified; on the other hand, if the substance had been wholly innocuous apart from its odor it would have been proper to return it to the owner, albeit with directions to store it in a different location. Such a decision could be made only with knowledge of the precise nature of the material involved.

In their effort to identify the contents of the defendant's briefcase, finally, it was reasonable for the university officials to secure professional advice by enlisting the aid of campus and local police. A single consultation by such officials with a police expert on narcotics falls far short, for example, of a general police-instigated exploratory search of student housing or belongings in the hope of turning up contraband. Rather, the officials' conduct in the case at bar is analogous to that of "the landlord or bailee who innocently discovers the suspicious circumstances, and seeks expert advice as to the nature of the use to which his premises or facilities are being appropriated. The latter would be no more than an extension of the plainsight rule, by augmenting the observations of the layman with the expertise of the police."

Viewed in this light, the question of who opened or closed the defendant's briefcase pales into insignificance. What matters here is that until Deputy Saldivar was asked to examine the briefcase, its contents remained a mystery to the officials who bore the responsibility of properly disposing of it. The deputy's inspection therefore does not require justification over and above that of the continuing emergency which authorized the original warrantless search of defendant's locker.

(2b) *We conclude there was substantial evidence to support the trial court's ruling that the contraband here in issue was not the product of an illegal search and seizure.*

The appeal from the order denying the motion to suppress the evidence is dismissed as nonappealable, and the order granting probation is affirmed.

PRIVACY OF RESIDENCE

Search and Seizure

The Fourth Amendment states:

> The right of the people to be secure in their persons, houses, papers, and effects, against unreasonable searches and seizures, shall not be violated, and no Warrants shall issue, but upon probable cause, supported by Oath or affirmation, and particularly describing the place to be searched, and the persons or things to be seized.

In *Boyd v. U. S.*, 116 U. S. 616, (1883), Justice Bradley noted that the breaking of doors and the rummaging through personal possessions does not in and of itself violate the protections inherent in The Fourth Amendment, but rather its protections are abused in the incursion upon one's nonforfeitable rights of security including those of liberty and private possessions.

The Supreme Court in the years after *Boyd v. U. S.* intentionally never developed fixed criteria which would lead to a clear and consistent model for viable searches. The Court, however, preferred the standard of reasonableness which could be utilized on a *sui generis* or case-by-case basis. Consequently, two cases which might have great similarity could lead to different judicial determinations because of slightly different fact patterns. Such a standard takes into account all the factors in a given situation.

In *Elkins v. U. S.*, 364 U. S. 206, (1960), the Supreme Court departed from the standard of reasonableness in order to create a greater consistency and more equitable judicial environment, at least in federal trials. The Court held that all evidence introduced at a federal trial, whether secured by state or federal officers, would have to comply with federal rules of evidence.

In what has become a landmark decision, the Supreme Court, in *Mapp v. Ohio*, 367 U. S. 643, (1961), not only reinforced but extended the *Elkins* decision, and decided that all evidence secured in searches which violate the Fourth Amendment is inadmissible in state as well as in federal court. The *Mapp* case pointedly did not include searches by private parties who do not act in a representative capacity for either state or federal governments.

College officials must now recognize the traditional freedom with which they may have inspected student lockers, dormitories, and living quarters has been circumscribed by judicial *desiderata* as discussed previously. Students who reside in off-campus facilities, of course, possess customary landlord-tenant rights and obligations. Such students clearly retain the protections against unlawful searches and seizures guaranteed by the Fourth Amendment, and are considered, in point of law, no different than any private citizen in his own home.

Historically, searches conducted by private college administrators have not been said to violate Fourth Amendment guarantees so long as evidence obtained is not utilized in a state or federal criminal procedure. This is so because the shield of Fourth Amendment protections extends to searches and seizures conducted only by governmental officers and agents. State and federal financial support of private college facilities, activities, and programs, however, may well erode the distinction between a private and public institution for purposes of this constitutional limitation.

Public colleges and universities are not insulated in any way from Fourth Amendment rights. In fact, public college officers may not enter the living quarters of resident students without having secured a warrant only issued upon probable cause that a crime has been committed. Public school administrators should be aware that all evidence secured through unauthorized searches or searches which go beyond the limitations of the warrant issued, or which were made without a warrant, cannot be introduced in either state or federal proceedings, or possibly even school tribunals.

In *Smyth and Smith v. Lubbers,* 398 F. Supp. 777 U. S. District Court, W. D. of Michigan 1975, public school officials were prohibited from searching a student's room without a warrant even though he previously had waived objections to reasonable searches in signing his housing contract. The court stated that although no criminal proceedings were initiated, the "state could not condition attendance at Grand Valley State College on a waiver of constitutional rights."

Contractual agreements between students and institutions which include waivers of constitutional guarantees are clearly proscribed by the *Smyth* case, particularly in public educational facilities and to a more limited extent in private schools. In those cases where personal prerogatives not constitutional in nature are limited by contractual agreement, some courts may be unwilling to enforce such limitations where they are arbitrarily formulated.

CASE: PRIVACY — RESIDENCE

Frank Piazzola v. John Watkins, 442 F. 2d 284, United States Court of Appeals, Fifth Circuit, April 27, 1971.

The district court condensed the transcript of testimony into the following findings of fact:

> On the morning of February 28, 1968, the Dean of Men of Troy State University was called to the office of the Chief of Police of Troy, Alabama, to discuss "the drug problem" at the University. Two state narcotic agents and two student informers from Troy State University were also present. Later on that same day, the Dean of Men was called to the city police station for another meeting; at this time he was informed by the officers that they had sufficient evidence that marijuana was in the dormitory rooms of certain Troy State students and that they desired the cooperation of university officials in searching these rooms. The police officers were advised by the Dean of Men that they would receive the full cooperation of the university officials in searching for the marijuana. The informers, whose identities have not yet been disclosed, provided the police officers with names of students whose rooms were to be searched. Still later on that same day (which was during the week and was to be followed by a week-long holiday) the law enforcement officers, accompanied by some of the university officials, searched six or seven dormitory rooms located in two separate residence halls. The rooms of both Piazzola and Marinshaw were searched without search warrants and without their consent. Present during the search of the room occupied by Marinshaw were two state narcotic agents, the university security officer, and a counselor of the residence hall where Marinshaw's room was located. Piazzola's room was searched twice. Present during the first search were two state narcotic agents and a university official; no evidence was found at this time. The second search of Piazzola's room, which disclosed the incriminating evidence, was conducted solely by the state and city police officials.
>
> At the time of the seizure the university had in effect the following regulation:
>
> "The college reserves the right to enter rooms for inspection purposes. If the administration deems it necessary, the room may be searched and the occupant required to open his per-

sonal baggage and any other personal material which is sealed."

Each of the petitioners was familiar with this regulation. After the search of the petitioners' rooms and the discovery of the marijuana, they were arrested, and the state criminal prosecutions and convictions ensued.

Validity of Search and Seizure

The Fourth Amendment protects "the right of the *people* to be secure in their persons, houses, papers, and effects against *unreasonable* searches and seizures" (emphasis added). The question is whether in the light of all of the facts and circumstances, including the university regulation, the search which disclosed the marijuana was an unreasonable search. The district judge made reasonableness the touchstone of his opinion as to the validity of the search. We (this court) find ourselves in agreement with his view that this search was unreasonable.

In a case where the facts were similar, *People v. Cohen,* 61 Misc. 2d 858, 306 N. Y. S. 2d 788, Judge Burstein said:

> The police and the Hofstra University officials admitted that they entered the room in order to make an arrest, if an arrest was warranted. This was, in essence, a fishing expedition calculated to discover narcotics. It offends reason and logic to suppose that a student will consent to an entry into his room designed to establish grounds upon which to arrest him. Certainly, there can be no rational claim that a student will self-consciously waive his constitutional right to a lawful search and seizure. Finally, even if the doctrine of implied consent were imported into this case, the consent is given, not to police officials, but to the university and the latter cannot fragmentize, share, or delegate it.

Another case somewhat in point on the facts is *Commonwealth v. McCloskey, Appellant,* 1970, 217 Pa. Super. 432, 272 A2d. 271. There the court reversed a student's marijuana conviction because the policemen who entered his dormitory room to execute a search warrant did not knock or announce their presence and purpose before entering. In part, Judge Cercone speaking for the majority of the court said:

It was the Commonwealth's position that the Fourth Amendment protections do not apply to a search of a college dormitory room. The test to be used in determining the applicability of the Fourth Amendment protections is whether or not the particular locale is one "... in which there was a reasonable expectation of freedom from governmental intrusion." A dormitory room is analogous to an apartment or a hotel room. It certainly offers its occupant a more reasonable expectation of freedom from governmental intrusion than does a public telephone booth. The defendant rented the dormitory room for a certain period of time, agreeing to abide by the rules established by his lessor, the university. As in most rental situations, the lessor, Bucknell University, reserved the right to check the room for damages, wear, and unauthorized appliances. Such right of the lessor, however, does not mean McCloskey was not entitled to have a "reasonable expectation of freedom from governmental intrusion" or that he gave consent to the police search, or gave the university authority to consent to such search.

In the case of *Katz v. United States*, 1967, 389 U. S. 347, 88 S. Ct. 507, 19 L. Ed. 2d 576, to which Judge Cercone referred, the Court commented at some length on the concept of "constitutionally protected areas":

> The petitioner has strenuously argued that the booth was a "constitutionally protected area." The Government has maintained with equal vigor that it was not. But this effort to decide whether or not a given "area," viewed in the abstract, is "constitutionally protected" deflects attention from the problem presented by this case. For the Fourth Amendment protects people, not places. What a person knowingly exposes to the public, even in his own home or office, is not a subject of Fourth Amendment protection. But what he seeks to preserve as private, even in an area accessible to the public, may be constitutionally protected.

We must conclude that a student who occupies a college dormitory room enjoys the protection of the Fourth Amendment. True the university retains broad supervisory powers which permit it to adopt the regulation heretofore quoted, provided that regulation is reasonably construed and is limited in its application to further the university's function as an educational institution. The regu-

lation cannot be construed or applied so as to give consent to a search for evidence for the primary purpose of a criminal prosecution. Otherwise, the regulation itself would constitute an unconstitutional attempt to require a student to waive his protection from unreasonable searches and seizures as a condition to his occupancy of a college dormitory room. Compare *Tinker v. Des Moines Independent Community School District,* 1969, 393 U. S. 503, 506, 89 S. Ct. 733, 21 L. Ed. 2d 731. Clearly the university had no authority to consent to or join in a police search for evidence of crime.

The right to privacy is "no less important than any other right carefully and particularly reserved to the people." Mapp v. Ohio, 161, 367 U. S. 643, 657, 81 S. Ct. 1684, 1692, 6 L. Ed. 2d 1081. *The results of the search do not prove its reasonableness. This search was an unconstitutional invasion of the privacy both of these appellees and of the students in whose rooms no evidence of marijuana was found. The warrantless search of these students' dormitory rooms cannot be justified. The judgment is therefore affirmed.*

CHAPTER FIVE

STUDENT SERVICE CONTRACTS

FOR the first time in the history of higher education, the great majority of students will assume, by their attendance at a college or university, a contractual relationship. Education institutions should now recognize that failure to provide services to the extent of promises could result in a legal breach of contract. A student's failure to honor a bona fide agreement with the university also may result in a breach of contract.

Residence and food service contracts, as well as health service and insurance agreements between students and institution, previously unenforceable by the university, now take on a new dimension. Universities in many states can legally enforce legitimate claims against student residents based upon contractual agreements. A student also will be on firm legal ground in refusing to agree to penalty clauses, unconscionable reservation and deposit fees, and nonrelated university surcharges. University requirements that students maintain campus residence must be supported not by arbitrary classifications of age or sex, but by careful relationship between living on campus and the learning process.

University regulations involving the use of its facilities or amenities, including dormitory usage and contracted food and health services, generally are not subject to judicial prying. Nevertheless, where there has been an abuse of discretion or evidence of arbitrary conduct in the administration of such regulations, the courts in a given controversy will provide judicial relief. Regulations in and of themselves, however, will not customarily be reviewed by the courts. Even though relevant regulations may have been agreed upon by both college administrators and the student body, because of the fundamental inequality of such bargaining processes, the courts will question such agreements to ensure fairness.

Although colleges may legally require students to live in

campus residence facilities, such requirements may not be made by selective technique, that is, certain selected students on the basis of age, race, or sex cannot be asked to maintain residence or compelled to pay special fees or assessments. In *Molliere v. Southeastern Louisiana College,* 304 F. Supp. 826 (1969), the court held that a rule requiring unmarried women students under twenty-one years of age to live in college dormitories was impermissible under the equal protection clause of the Fourteenth Amendment. The court reasoned that although colleges may require all or only some students to live on campus, such requirements must be based on educational benefits and not merely upon the income requirements necessary to support campus facilities.* It is well to note that Title IX of the Education Amendments Act of 1972 which prohibits discrimination on the basis of sex to all recipients of federal aid may well be used to upset college regulations which categorize students according to sex.

The maintenance of separate housing facilities for students who happen to be black or who may belong to a social group having membership provisions which preclude students on the basis of either race or sex is vulnerable to judicial attack and inconsistent with Title VI of the Civil Rights Act of 1964 and of Title IX of the Education Amendments Act of 1972.†

Public college administrators should be aware that requiring the use of food service facilities by students is subject to judicial review unless such use is tied to a living learning concept. Special fees for health service and insurance also should be directly related to institutional objective, that is, the personal welfare of students. College and university assessments which bear no relationship to the educational process or the student's personal well-being and which are grounded only in the need to satisfy dormitory amortization or to fulfill numerical quotas, generally, will not withstand the test of litigation.

LEGAL MEMORANDA — STUDENT SERVICE CONTRACTS

Within recent years, student-institutional controversies have

---

*See *Cooper v. Nix,* 496 F. Supp. 2d. 1285 (1974).
†See Chapter Seven for annotated materials on Title IX.

extended from traditional areas of conflict to what can be categorized as commercial disputes. That is to say, those controversies do not speak of the customary claims for freedom of speech and expression, or for the right to counsel, but of the more prosaic but equally important allegations of breach of contract for not only academic services but those that deal with student life. These include student service contracts involving housing, food, medical facilities, and the like.

The advent of state legislation which conferred legal majority on the eighteen-year-old in most of the United States, coupled with a trend among colleges and universities toward outside entrepreneurial contractors because of financial retrenchments, has provided the material for new sources of conflict between student and institution. Institutions that promise certain services must either perform them or be liable to suits for breach of contract. Conversely, the adult student is equally bound. In all cases, the equity of provisions involving deposit fees, refunds, and penalties will be under judicial examination. No longer can a perhaps legally naive administrator fix financial and other penalties by his own personal standards and discretion. To do so in today's society can bring legal and public relations repercussions that even the most intrepid administrator would find disconcerting, if not professionally suicidal.

It has become judicially axiomatic that colleges eager to satisfy their newly found partners in business cannot compel their students to use these contracted services in order to encourage the cooperation of such vendors or even to ensure them a financial profit. In all cases adjudicated on this point, the courts, even with an eye on the financial plight of today's educational institutions, have required that such outside contacts be consistent with sound educational policies and not solely a device for raising revenue. Representative judicial decisions include: *Pratz v. Louisiana Polytechnic Institute,* 316 F. Supp. 872 (1970) and *Poynter v. Drevdahl,* file no. m-31-71CA, U. S. District Court, W. D., Michigan, N. D., (1972).

In both cases college policies requiring residence in university dormitories were contested. The courts stated that the regulations were reasonably constructed and nondiscriminatory, and legitimately tied to a sound educational mission. The living/learning concepts upon which such regulations were based were given credence by the courts. The court in the *Pratz* case took notice of the university need for revenue for dormitory rental to retire bond indebtedness.

The student-university contractual relationship applies equally to both public and private institutions, with a notable exception that procedural and substantive due process is not guaranteed students in the private college or university. See *Soglin v. Kauffman*, 418 F. 2d 163 (1969) and *Esteban v. Central Missouri State College*, 415 F. 2d 1077 (1969). In private universities, however, agreements could be struck down on the premise that such agreements were "unconscionable" in ignoring student rights. This general contract law philosophy gained major importance in the leading case of *Henningsen v. Bloomfield Motors, Inc.*, 32 NJ 358 (1960), and the philosophy has been reinforced by a multitude of decisions in virtually every state in the country. There have been some minor attempts to restrict this concept to purely commercial situations and not to student-university litigation. In *Anser v. Cornell University*, 337 NY Supp. 2d 878 (1972), the court sustained such an inequitable agreement in the absence of fraud or mistake. It is highly unlikely that the *Anser* case will represent a majority of judicial opinion in forthcoming litigation since it is uncompromisingly narrow in its interpretation, and contrary to the growing need to protect all of the public against unfair agreements which offend public policy. See, generally, *Williams v. Walker-Thomas Furniture Co.*, 350 F. 2d 445 (1965), and *Frostifresh Corp. v. Peynoss*, 274 NY 2d 757 (1966). Also persuasive in arguing that this policy of unconscionability can be utilized in student-university agreements is the increasing use of commercial contractors to furnish services required by students.

A contract may be implied, according to judicial construction, by virtue of the student's membership in the university community. The courts, in *Greene v. Howard University*, 271 F. Supp. 609 (1967), and *Anderson v. Regents of U.C.L.A.*, 22 Cal. Supp. 3d 763 (1972), inferred such contracts from the legal principle that an individual's actions can constitute the acceptance of an offer even though no specific contract document was signed. However, it is more likely that, at least in student service relationships, more formality of agreement will be required. Dormitory food and health service contracts in written form, when specifically agreed upon, would then be binding on the student whether or not he understood them to be so, as long as such agreements complied with the legal requirements of a contract and the equitable standards of fairness. It should be noted, however, that the courts would probably apply a different degree of scrutiny to terms in student service contacts than to other such litigation involving grading and advising. In the latter cases, courts have generally enforced the university position, if based on reasonable discretion. See *Paynter v. New York University,* 319 NY Supp. 2d 893 (1971). Since the university, however, maintains exclusive control in creating a commercial type as opposed to an academic agreement, the logic which applies the theory of "contracts of adhesion" could be utilized. In such contracts the courts have universally construed questionable terms and provisions against the developer of the contract. See Kessler, *Contracts of Adhesion,* 43 Colum. L. Rev. 629 (1943).

In these commercial relationships of student-university-outside vendor courts would clearly require all parties to determine actual monetary loss and would not accept the university statement of loss in such contacts as controlling unless it was not possible to fix the money loss in litigation due to the speculative nature of the subject matter, or market conditions, etc. In these cases, if the liquidated claim reflected a reasonable expectation of damage, such contractual provisions would be upheld. But mere percentage penalty clauses based simply on the number of weeks of a student's attendance would not be sustained. See *Uniform Commercial Code,* section 2-718, subsection 2.

In conclusion, it is clear that general contract principles apply most readily to student service agreements. The college or university as well as the student may attempt to legally enforce them. The student, however, if not on an elevated position as a consumer of commercial services, will be at least on an equal position in the bargaining and enforcement processes. This is an appreciable improvement over his status prior to the reduction of the majority age from twenty-one to eighteen.

Jonathan Flagg Buchter

CONTRACT LAW AND THE
STUDENT-UNIVERSITY RELATIONSHIP

"Contract Law and the Student-University Relationship," by Jonathan Flagg Buchter, was originally prepared for the Winter, 1973 issue of the Indiana Law Journal.* *Buchter, an attorney, examines the application of general contract principles to students and the university, and argues for increased legal awareness on the part of students who may unknowingly be bound by college catalogue provisions. Permission to reprint has been granted by Fred B. Rothman and Co., South Hackensack, New Jersey, publishers.*

The relationship between universities and their students has been analyzed by courts under many different legal doctrines. The most enduring and pervasive of these has been the theory that there exists an implied contract between the student and the institution. Over the years, a patchwork of holdings has created a common law of contract governing the student-university relationship. Principles espoused by these holdings merit more careful consideration than that provided in recent literature on the subject. In addition the common law resulting from such decisions deserves comparison with the general law of contract.

Evolution of Student-University Contract Doctrine

Until the early 1900's, the relationship between the student and the institution was expressly stated in a written enrollment contract, which was essentially a business agreement between the parent of the student and the institution. Among other things, the agreement provided that the university assume the parental, supervisory role over the child. The doctrine of *in loco parentis* was developed in order to reflect the legal incidents of this relationship. Since this theory viewed the institution as standing "in place of the parent," the school had the right to control and

---

*48 Indiana Law Journal 253 (1973).

discipline the child. *In loco parentis* proved to be of limited usefulness as a legal framework in many situations. Thus, courts began to rely on the actual written contract for guidance. When no written contract existed, the courts found it useful to use an implied contract theory to delineate the relationship of the parties.

During the early part of this century, the contract approach became the dominant theory under which student-university cases were litigated. Other concepts of the relationship were occasionally used to supplement implied contract law. One such theory was that the student was granted the privilege of attendance by the university, allowing courts to uphold any university action since students had no rights under such a relationship. Another theory used to sustain institutional judgment was that the student was the beneficiary in a trust relationship.

This theoretical mixture was applied in student-university litigation until *Dixon v. Alabama State Board of Education* was decided in 1961. *Dixon* held, generally, that a public university's actions were state actions and therefore subject to constitutional restraints and, more particularly, that a student must be afforded procedural due process prior to expulsion.

However, the state action doctrine in *Dixon* has not replaced the implied contract theory. Courts still view the student-university relationship as one of contract with certain constitutional protections required if the institution is public. Thus, there may currently be some limits on what the public university may demand from the student. For example, a public university may not be able to deny a student certain First Amendment rights. However, since the *Dixon* holding is limited to public institutions, a private university may be able to contract in such a way as to limit these constitutional rights.

Many litigants have attempted to extend the *Dixon* holding to private institutions on the grounds that state action is involved in funding, tax exemptions and grant programs. These attempts have been almost universally unsuccessful. Thus, contract considerations remain the prevalent judicial tools used to settle disputes between a private university and its students, and to judge public university litigation not involving constitutional claims.

The Implied Student-University Contract

Courts still approach student-university implied contracts by using essentially traditional, early twentieth century contract doctrines. Under such an approach, there is the implication that the institution had obligated itself — subject, of course, to changes in plan, curriculum, and the like — to permit a student in good standing to continue the particular course for which he has entered upon payment of the necessary fees and compliance with other reasonable requirements. Fees, student conduct and discipline, academic matters, and even the continued existence of the college have all been found to be covered by this implied contract.

In general, if no specific contract document is signed at the time of application, admission, or registration, entry of the student onto the university campus, or into university life is regarded as the point of formation of the student-university contract. This construction is consistent with the contract principle that acceptance of an offer may be inferred from the parties' actions. Moreover, even if the student has not yet arrived at the university, some courts have held that advance payment and acceptance of tuition may create binding obligations on both parties. Therefore, although the student notifies the university in writing of his intention not to attend, the school may not be obligated to refund his tuition. If there is a catalogue provision stating that tuition is not refundable, the student is bound by his implied contract with the university. For the same reason, the university cannot increase its charges to the student after accepting payment of full tuition.

The implied contract is considered to be between the individual student and the university as a corporate body. Although students have attempted to join faculty members, administrative officers, and trustees in suits, courts have usually dismissed such defendants on the grounds that they were not parties to the contract.

In the older cases, the parent was often considered one of the parties to the contract. More recently, a parent sued to enjoin a college from implementing new liberal parietal hours. The court found that the setting of students' hours was within the college's authority, but, in finding no breach of contract, the decision implied that parents were still considered parties to university contracts involving their children.

In attempting to determine the terms of the implied contract, the courts have usually looked to the documents which are familiar to the student in the university setting. Generally, the university catalogue or bulletin is considered the primary document in the relationship. Statements made in other documents have also been held to constitute terms of the bargain. Thus, dormitory contracts, registration cards, admission applications, catalogue supplements, as well as oral statements have all been found to contain contract terms. Such terms are binding on the parties, independent of whether the university so intended, and regardless of whether the student knew of them or understood them to be a part of the contract.

Courts apply varying degrees of scrutiny to different categories of contract terms. In litigation over fees, the rule is that the courts will enforce whatever the university's published statements prescribe. In disputes over grading or curricula, courts have usually avoided any action on their part which might be construed as judicial interference with academic judgments, unless arbitrary or unreasonable conduct can be shown. However, student reliance on misrepresented academic standards may estop the university from later changing its agreements. In disagreements concerning student conduct, courts have generally favored the university's interpretation of the contract.

The remedies granted for breach of the student-university contract are of three types: damages, injunction, and specific performance. Money damages may be sought by either side in fee disputes, but cases contesting fees are rare. Recent cases have also raised the question of availability of consequential damages for failure of the university to provide promised academic services. Plaintiffs in these cases requested damages to replace earnings which were alleged to have been lost as a result of university acts or inadequacies. While none of these cases reached the damage issue, such claims may become more prevalent in the future as the courts increasingly recognize the income value of education.

Injunctive relief is usually sought in expulsion-reinstatement disputes. The relief prayed for is an injunction barring the institution from denying the student the use of university facilities or attempting to hamper his education by disciplining him for previous misconduct. Such injunctions have been granted by trial courts which have found a contract breach by the university, but these have not been enforced because of appellate reversals on the other grounds.

Specific performance has been held to be a possible remedy in disputes which involve academic services. Since the courts are reluctant to review the professional judgment of university academicians, specific performance has been limited to those cases in which the professional requirements have apparently been satisfied, and there remains only university action of a clerical or administrative nature.

The Contrast Between Student-University Contract Law and the General Law of Contract

The view that the student-university relationship was one of implied contract grew out of the necessity for a description that adequately depicted the nature of the relationship and the kinds of litigation it was generating. Originally, contract theory in this area provided results which reflected the parties' expectations. It reinforced general nineteenth century notions of freedom of contract and equality of parties. Today, however, many of these theories have been modified or abandoned by courts which have recognized that contract principles developed to adjudicate disputes between commercial interests may not be appropriate in consumer affairs and other relationships where lay individuals are parties.

In the area of fees, courts have reviewed the contract between the student and the university as a commercial relationship, in which specific prices are agreed upon and paid. This approach appears to coincide with the intentions of the parties. Both the student and the university desire certainty in their financial obligations and are likely to view the published statement of fees as binding. However, courts' decisions upholding refund schedules have not adhered to current commercial contract law. Under the Uniform Commercial Code, an aggrieved seller is unable to retain the full contract price after breach if that amount exceeds his damages. The mechanical university catalogue rules relating weeks of attendance to percentage refunds, do not accurately reflect the costs to the university as they actually exist over the semester. Thus, under the commercial model, a court faced with litigation concerning such a schedule would have to determine the actual monetary loss and would not accept the university's specification of damages as controlling.

In the area of academic services, the courts' approach has been similar to that used with contracts conditioned upon the satisfaction of one party. The university requires that the student's academic performance be satisfactory to the university in its honest judgment. Absent a showing of bad faith on the part of the university or a professor, the court will not interfere. The good faith judgment model both maximizes academic freedom and provides an acceptable approximation of the educational expectations of the parties.

In the area of student conduct and discipline, the courts' view of the contract which governs the student-university relationship has not followed contract law trends. Two areas of divergence are notable.

First, courts have upheld waiver clauses and other catalogue provisions even though there was no finding that they had been read or understood as binding by a reasonable student. Contract law has adopted a different approach in similar situations. The courts will not bind a party to terms of a document, such as a catalogue, unless the facts present a case where the person receiving the paper should as a reasonable man understand that it contained terms of the contract which he must read at his peril, and regard as part of the proposed agreement. The student is not likely to expect that the catalogue contains such binding terms regulating conduct.

Although this absence of a knowledge requirement is found in the areas of fees and academic services, the considerations which make such action justifiable in those areas are not valid in the discipline situation. Viewing the catalogue as the contract document does not accurately reflect the apparent expectation of either party as to its role in conduct regulation. The student, in attempting to decide which university to attend, is most likely to make comparisons on the basis of the academic program and tuition of each institution, and will look to the catalogue for this information. Differences among universities as to conduct regulations and discipline powers, on the other hand, are probably not considered by the student. In addition, the very nature of a catalogue does not suggest that binding conduct rules are contained therein. The majority of a catalogue is devoted to the listing of academic offerings. Conduct clauses are usually found in miscellaneous sections, often surrounded by idyllic descriptions of student life and campus ambiance.

The second major divergence from general contract law occurs when there are either no written provisions governing discipline or else the provisions are unclear or ambiguous. In these situations, courts have required the student to prove that the university's unilateral action was not within the terms of his agreement, as interpreted by the university. Here again, the normal expectations of the student seem to conflict with the court's interpretation of the contract and its terms. A student is not likely to view the university campus as an area requiring a standard of conduct any different from that provided for any other public or private area by the state's criminal law. The university administration is similarly viewed as having no special insight as the propriety of a student's nonacademic conduct. A student will expect that his interpretation of a term requiring reasonable conduct will not differ from the standard applied by the university. And when a disagreement over meaning occurs, the student has no reason to expect that his interpretation will be given any less credence than that of the institution. Thus, a student may well be surprised when a regulation which states that the university will be allowed to discharge a student for grounds it deems reasonable is held to mean that the student must prove his expulsion unreasonable and that the court will accept, without scrutiny, the university's interpretation.

Contract law has dealt with analogous situations with different results. Two methods of interpreting the student-university contract may be derived from courts' experience with these situations. First, since the institution maintains exclusive control over the drafting of the contract terms, the logic applied to contracts of adhesion could be employed. In viewing such agreements, the courts have construed ambiguous terms of the contract against the party who wrote them, reasoning that the drafter's advantage in being able to write the agreement should have resulted in a contract which clearly expressed his position. If such an analysis were applied to the student-university contract, students could not be expelled unless the university had, prior to the violation, either spelled out as prohibited the specific conduct of the student or declared clearly and openly that it did not consider itself bound by a standard of reasonableness in matters concerning student conduct.

An alternative and less severe method of resolving a dispute over interpretation of any provision is simply to find no agreement on the type of conduct in question. A decision that there was no meeting of the minds would allow the court to imply a term which it felt to be reasonable in the context of the parties' relationship. Under this view, the university can still discipline without specific rules if it is willing to risk an unfavorable, independent determination of reasonableness by a reviewing court.

Application of Contract Doctrine to the Private University

Much recent litigation has sought to extend constitutional protections to students at private universities. These efforts have relied upon characterization of private university discipline as state action because of governmental involvement in funding and taxation. This constitutional focus has neglected the possibility of achieving many of the same results through the law of the implied student-university contract which constitutes the basic legal relationship in both public and private universities.

General contract law, through its protection of expectations and intents, often produces outcomes which parallel those obtained through constitutional analysis. For example, students in public universities have sought reinstatement after expulsion on the ground that the rules allegedly violated were unconstitutionally vague. Contract law doctrine provides a method of resolving the same types of disputes by construing ambiguous terms against the drafting party. Where constitutional law prohibits implication of a waiver of rights by conduct without clear manifestation of intent, contract law provides that agreement to terms will be implied only when it is reasonable to believe such assent was intended.

Contract theory also has the potential to establish in the private university many of the substantive rights which are protected by the state action theory in the public university. When a court finds that there has been no meeting of the minds as to university rules or powers in these areas, either because there is nothing written or because the meaning of what is written is unclear, the court may imply a term which reflects an accommodation of the parties' reasonable expectations.

It is unlikely that a student will perceive any rationale for differences in conduct regulation based on the private-public distinction unless there is something special about the character of the particular private institution which would draw this distinction to his attention. Therefore, in most cases he will expect the same freedoms on the private campus as he would enjoy at a public university. As for the university's expectations, one noted commentator has suggested a reasonable perspective:

> Historically private colleges and universities have allowed more freedom to their students than has been true at public institutions, and, in the turbulent atmosphere on today's campuses, it seems to me unthinkable that the faculty and administration of any private institution would consider recognizing fewer rights in their students than the minimum the Constitution exacts of the state universities.

Thus a court, in defining a term based on the parties' expectations, could find that the substantive protections afforded students in the public university would have been adopted as an expression of their agreement.

Contract law cannot assure private university students all the protections enjoyed by their counterparts in public institutions. For example, many of the elements of procedural due process, such as preexpulsion notice and hearing, are not provided under traditional contract analysis. All that can be established by contract law is that after a university has acted, the decision will be reviewed by a court which has no preconceived notion of the correctness of the action, and that the burden of proof will be on the university.

In addition, traditional contract law, based on the expectations of the parties, cannot prevent the private university from requiring terms which would be considered unconstitutional waivers of rights in the public university. It would, however, insure that the university make these conditions both specific and obvious so that both parties, as well as others outside the relationship, are aware of what is being done.

Conclusion

Application of these general contract principles should not bind students to any terms unless the catalogue provisions are presented in such a way that the student can reasonably be expected to read them and understand them to be part of a binding contract with the university. If the university desires to enforce any rule or waiver clause against the student, it should be required to bring these provisions to the attention of the student before he enrolls. Contract law upholds the value of private agreements and diversity, what Judge Friendly has called:

> the very possibility of doing something different than government can do, of creating an institution free to make choices government cannot — even seemingly arbitrary ones — without having to provide a justification that will be examined in a court of law.

At the same time, the application of contract law can protect the student by making sure that this "something different" is well known to him and something he intended to do.

DAVID HILL

CONTRACT SERVICES: A NEW ROLE FOR THE STUDENT PERSONNEL ADMINISTRATOR

In "Contract Services: A New Role for the Student Personnel Administrator," David Hill, Director of Residence, Fairleigh Dickinson University, notes the advantages and disadvantages of outside contracted services, and the momentum of campus constituencies toward contractual rather than collegiate bonds.

Effective student affairs programs constantly anticipate the changing moods and needs of campus communities. New legal and budgetary pressures on campuses presage a new role for the student affairs dean.

Higher education in 1976 is in fiscal despair. Administrators of colleges and universities are evaluating programs at their campuses with eyes focused on the budget and enrollment trends.

At the same time, the relationship between student and institution is quickly changing, often to the chagrin of students, faculty, and deans schooled in collegiate notions which are becoming less operable. Educational decision makers no longer assume the role of surrogate parent. As *in loco parentis* died, a new student-institutional relationship emerged. The uncertain sixties caused most educators to rethink their positions on student rights and to consider the student voice in the design of his education. With unadmitted tinges of authority still vested, a counseling approach replaced the role of surrogate.

But while institutions and students are growing accustomed to this counseling framework, a still different administrative mode is emerging. Colleagues in counseling-learning relationships are becoming cooperative members of educational partnerships. Contractual commitments between students and their universities are replacing the remnants of the student-surrogate model, and even the now prevalent counselor-educator model.

A student's relationship with his college or university has been placed on an adjusted legal footing. The Educational Amendments Act of 1972 and the widespread unionization of faculties and other campus constituencies such as professional administrators and service staffs have altered the notion of collegiality, be it surrogate or counselor.

The intense budgetary stresses facing institutions of higher education, together with this altered affinity between student and university, portend still further changes in institutional structure and operation.

The campus environment is changing from one of collegiate cooperation to one of contractual commitment between campus constituencies. Changes will come in the areas of residence, food, and health services. Campus administrators are evaluating the efficacy of these programs from both fiscal and educational standpoints. In an atmosphere of financial pressure and with the altered legal relationship between student and university, auxiliary educational services will be leased to corporations and enterprises in the surrounding community.

The change from campus-operated residence halls, food services, and infirmaries present appealing cost reduction incentives to administrators with enrollment-driven budgets and rapidly rising operational costs.

Both at large and small campuses, student life programs are developed to integrate instructional and living-learning activities. Institutional objectives are broadly defined and include residential life experiences as key elements of the educational offering of the college or university. Administrators committed to providing a living-learning campus environment are confronted with a dilemma when budgetary strains demand cost reductions and contractual services seem to offer sustained relief.

Many educators wonder if such fiscal imperatives and educational objectives can coexist. The new environment at many campuses suggests that most, if not all, campus constituencies will soon be bound by contractual rather than collegiate bonds. Yet, this does not spell doom for living-learning programs designed to promote student growth.

Contracted maintenance services are already common at many campuses. Food service programs are more and more frequently operated by catering concerns under contract with the university. Campus security is not infrequently provided by trained security professionals. Less common, but likely, candidates for further contractual commitment are residence halls, infirmaries, bookstores, and counseling centers.

The advantages of contracted services can be both fiscally and educationally seductive. However, each service under consideration must be carefully evaluated. Will there be real fiscal and educational advantages? Moreover, administrators must sensitively balance budgetary and educational priorities in view of institutional goals before service contractors are invited to submit operational proposals.

The use of contractual services for catering or medical care is not new to industry or business where such operations are only supportive. However, such services, which are becoming increasingly utilized by colleges and universities, have as their primary goal the personal and intellectual well-being of students.

A student life program that includes counseling and medical centers, residence hall programs that are supportive of student development, financial assistance plans, and cafeteria services becomes more successful because it is concerned with all aspects of student growth and learning. The programs offered in each of these areas are integrated under the direction of a dean of students or other chief student personnel officer. The combination of services makes a viable student life program.

A central drawback to contracted services is the possible isolation of the various student affairs units. For example, an infirmary independently operated by a community medical center will often lack administrative linkage to other campus service units such as dormitories. Cooperation between residence hall counseling staffs and health care specialists is a significant aspect of an effective student life program. Close staff communication promotes the development of a system of educational services that encourages student growth. Without an integrated network of programs where personnel are in close contact and working collectively with students and student groups, the growth of living-learning environments is curtailed.

Student problems and activities are multifaceted. Therefore, a cooperative approach by all personnel responsible for working with students and developing activities is essential. Moreover, such a cooperative approach enables the student personnel staff to view student and campus needs in wider perspective. The dean of students catalyzes the services offered by each unit of his division.

A related disadvantage to outside services is that independent contractors are specialized. Their concern for operating a residence hall or infirmary may not be consistent with the institutional objective of promoting a campus living-learning environment. Indeed, in an era of inflated operating costs a contractor will be especially concerned with his budget, and it is certain that he will be far less disturbed by the cost versus quality educational services dilemma.

Disadvantages in Focus

An alternative to the university-operated residence hall is the leasing of housing facilities to independent management concerns, who operate them in turn on a rental basis to students. This plan is especially appealing to campus administrators with apartment-type dormitories.

Many campuses already utilize a rental agreement where the student enters into a housing contract with the university. The use of such an instrument is reflective of the changing legal atmosphere on campuses.

However, a complete changeover to the management leasing system presents problems. Students often receive financial aid packages from the university which provide housing allowances. To accommodate such students, close coordination is required between the university and the housing management. A more complex problem concerns the staffing of leased facilities. Are they isolated apartment enclaves or are they part of the greater campus community? Who is responsible for dealing with objectionable tenents — landlord or campus administrator?

Campus food services programs are often operated by catering firms. Again, without close coordination with students and the campus administration, catered food services can become an isolated operating unit, insensitive to student needs. This insensitivity is compounded at residential campuses where students have no alternative but to dine at the cafeteria.

In the health care area the disadvantages to leased services are two-fold. At large residential campuses, or at smaller campuses situated in rural or suburban areas the distance to a community health clinic can present transportation problems for students. Also, as the population of some campuses is considerably greater than that of the surrounding community, emergency circumstances present a burden to local ambulance and first-aid squads. This requires careful evaluation of local political sentiment should a contractual health care program be considered.

An advantage of the campus-operated infirmary, not usually present in a contracted service, concerns the role played by the campus health care staff. Campus nurses, physicians, and first-aid workers are often engaged in educative as well as health care delivery programs. Furthermore, medical personnel are often involved with first-level personal counseling for students. Personal and academic problems often manifest themselves in illness. Once again, it is essential that health care personnel work closely with other units in the student affairs division. It is equally important that student life programs continue to provide health information and personnel trained to conduct seminars in such areas as hygiene, birth control, and venereal disease. A local medical center is not oriented in this fashion.

The general disadvantages of contracted student services are several fold. First, the campus administration may lose control of these essential areas. Consequently, it is difficult to insure that the services provided are consistent with institutional objectives. Second, contracted services are inherently insulated from one another. The resulting loss of communication between units drastically reduces the effectiveness of the student affairs program.

Advantages

Despite the problems of contracted services they are appealing because of the cost reductions that can result from their use. Compensation and operational expenses can be reduced. Administrative costs can be decreased. Food service programs which drain the campus treasury can become profit-making concerns. The benefits accruing to the university help to defray fixed overhead and amortization costs. The same is true of residence halls and health centers.

These are irresistible temptations to campus administrators strapped by rising costs and stable or declining enrollments.

Together with a total environment that is conducive to contractual relationships between campus constituencies, outside services are a most appealing alternative. However, the move to contractual services must be considered in view of broader institutional and educational objectives.

The Role of the Student Service Administrator

New contractual commitments between campus constituencies will require that administrators, and particularly student affairs officers, develop new administrative modes. The surrogate mode is deceased and the counselor mode is now constantly under pressure from the changing character of the campus environment. Educators readily acknowledge the value of the counseling framework, and understandably it will not be easy to alter the orientation. Yet it is most important that a new working administrative model be developed that will accommodate both a counseling framework and the fiscal lure of contracted service. The dean must meld these potentially antagonistic forces and generate a working educational climate despite the insulation of constituencies and the inherent loss of close coordination between the units of his division.

The new role of the dean will be that of convener and arbiter. Purely collegiate relationships will give way to legal compacts between members of the campus community. The dean must assure that service contractors remain as constituents of this community. Where the student service dean previously directed a staff of cooperating assistants and directors, he must now assume a firm posture as the convener of student, faculty, and contractor groups. He must focus their tripartite needs and demands with broader institutional goals in mind. At the same time, he must continually emphasize the educative purpose belying each area and promote coordination and cooperation between them.

Student government constitutions must provide a committee system for each of the areas under contract. The faculty governance body must also provide committee representation for each area. Finally, the contractor must be prepared to meet with these constituencies on a regular basis. This provisory should be included in the service contract. The dean of students convenes and chairs these meetings. As an institutional representative, the dean articulates objectives and seeks to resolve differences between groups. It is essential to remember that each group is bound by contractual, rather than collegiate, commitments. As such, the dean of students must be particularly objective and firm. His position as arbiter is the key to successfully integrating onetime collegiate constituencies, while maintaining institutional integrity.

Financial pressure and new legal considerations demand that the role of the dean change. Moreover, all student personnel workers must retool their approaches with these factors in mind.

Collegiate orientations are growing dysfunctional in an age of contracts, arbitration, and an adjusted legal operating framework. For many, denying the viability of collegiality is painful. Nevertheless, current affairs require that university administrators acknowledge the weakened status of collegiality, and move to develop new administrative modes that conform to the modified needs of today's campus.

APPENDIX: SPECIMEN CONTRACTS

The following specimen contracts, including student-institutional agreements (housing and food service), and institutional-vendor agreements (food service and bookstore), are contractual forms that are commonly used on many college and university campuses.

Residence Hall Rental Agreement

This agreement is entered into by the parties signing below.

Mr.
Ms._____
              First   Middle   Last

Address_____
              Street   City   State   Zip Code

Class Year: Fr.____ Soph.____ Jr.____ Sr.____ Date of Birth_____

The university and the student mutually agree to the terms and conditions appearing on this page and on Schedule A and B and C attached, which are incorporated herein and made a part hereof:

1. *Term*

That the term of this contract shall extend for one academic year consisting of two semesters, specifically:

_____Fall and Spring semesters_____
                                      (Academic Year)
_____Spring Semester only_____
                                      (Year)

The Thanksgiving, Christmas, intersession, and spring recess periods are excluded from the term of this agreement.

2. *Rent and deposits (See Schedule A attached)*

Rent for the contract term is payable to the bursar in two equal installments. See Schedule A attached for amount of rent and dates for payment.

A reservation deposit of $50.00, to be credited toward the first rent installment is payable with this signed agreement. This deposit is nonrefundable.

A damage deposit of $50.00 is payable one time only.

The $50.00 damage deposit will be refunded upon the tenant's withdrawal from the residence halls, such refund to be conditioned upon the surrender of the premises in as good condition as the reasonable use thereof will permit. Assessments will be made by the director of residence when damages occur. This clause does not constitute a waiver of any other remedy for damage to the premises during the tenant's occupancy nor does it constitute a liquidation of damages.

In the event of nonpayment of rent as the times provided, the university may re-let the premises, and all rights of the student-tenant to possession of the premises under this agreement will be forfeited.

The university reserves the right to make reasonable changes in rent and food plan fees under this contract when necessitated by unusual circumstances in the general economy.

3. Food plan (See Schedule B attached)

Participation in the university food plan is required as stated in Schedule B attached. See Schedule B for amount of the food plan fee and dates for payment.

4. Rent refunds (See Schedule C attached)

Rent refunds will be in order (1) when the student takes an official leave of absence from the university, (2) when the student officially withdraws from the university, (3) when the student receives an honorable transfer from the university, (4) in case of necessity as determined and approved by the university.

Refunds are computed on a pro rata basis reflected in Schedule C attached.

5. Room changes

No room changes may be made except with the written permission of the director of residence.

6. Rules and regulations, laws and ordinances

The tenant shall observe all rules and regulations regarding the premises set forth in this agreement as well as any other reasonable rules and regulations which have been or shall be made by the university. The tenant shall also observe and comply with all laws, ordinances, rules, and regulations of the federal, state, and municipal authorities.

7. Condition of premises

Tenant will not make any alterations, additions, or improvements to said premises without the written permission of the director of residence. Tenant further agrees to keep said premises in a clean and sanitary condition and free from trash, inflammable material, or other objectionable matter.

8. Cooking on premises

The use of cooking appliances in the residence halls, except for specially designated areas, is expressly prohibited.

9. Pets

The keeping of pets in the residence halls, or on university grounds is expressly prohibited.

10. Right to enter and inspect

The director of residence or his designates shall have the right to enter the demised premises at reasonable hours in the day or night to examine the same, or to make such repairs, additions, or alteration as they shall deem necessary. In addition, the director of residence or his designates shall have the right to enter the premises at any time, upon reasonable cause, to take those precautions which he finds necessary to protect the health and safety of the occupants or other persons therein.

11. Subletting and assignment

The tenant may not sublet the demised premises nor any part thereof, nor may this lease be assigned by the tenant without the prior written consent of the director of residence.

12. Liability

The student will hold the university harmless from any suit, action at law, or other claim whatsoever resulting from or arising out of any injury to the student's person or property while an occupant of a residence hall under this contract. The tenant agrees to indemnify and hold the university harmless from all claims and liability for losses of or damage to property, or for injuries to persons occurring in or about the demised premises, which losses, damage, or injuries are caused by the acts, omissions, or negligence of the tenant.

13. Tripled occupancy

Occupancy is normally based on two occupants per bedroom with the exception of the old infirmary wing of Twombly Hall, on which each room is occupied by three people. However, the university reserves the right to place one additional occupant in the demised premises when, in the determination of the director of residence, exigent circumstances make such action necessary. In such cases, the rent for each occupant of the room involved will be reduced (by one third for bedrooms in Twombly Halls and in Dormitory Village, and by one fourth for bedrooms in the Infirmary wing of Twombly Hall) for the period during which the tripled occupancy continues.

This instrument constitutes the full and complete agreement between the tenant and the university, and may not be modified in any way without the express written consent of both the tenant and the director of residence.

For office use only:

Bursar:

residence assignment_____

_____ _____
Student's Signature   Date

_____ _____
Parent or Guardian (if stu-   Date
dent is under 18 years of
age)

_____ _____
Director of Residence for   Date
the University

SCHEDULE A: RENT AND DATES PAYABLE

A. Residence in Dormitory Village (suites) and Old Infirmary Wing
    (air-conditioned rooms in Twombly Hall):

    1. Rent: $686 per year
    2. Installments:
        fall semester - $50 deposit payable with signed rental agreement.
                        $293 balance payable August 1, 1974.
                        $343 total fall semester

        spring semester - $343 payable January 15, 1974.

B. Residence in Twombly Hall (except Old Infirmary Wing):

    1. Rent: $673 per year
    2. Installments:
        fall semester - $50 deposit payable with signed rental agreement.
                        $287 balance payable August 1, 1974.
                        $337 total fall semester

        spring semester - $337 payable January 15, 1975.

SCHEDULE B: FOOD PLAN FEE AND DATES PAYABLE

Participation in the university food plan is required of:

    (a) All students residing in Twombly Hall, including the Old Infirmary Wing.
    (b) All freshman resident students.
    (c) All advanced standing transfer students assigned to Twombly Hall.

Note: Advanced standing transfer students are normally assigned to Twombly
Hall. Requests for placement in the Dormitory Village residence area will be
honored as space permits.

Any student who so wishes may *elect* to participate in the university food plan
by returning the completed food plan application with the signed rental agreement.

A student participating in the food plan during any semester may not terminate
his participation during that semester even if a change in residence area is
made.

Food plan fee and dates payable: (proposed subject to final adoption by student government and the university administration).

Fee - $790 per year

    fall semester - $395 payable August 1, 1974.
    spring semester - $395 payable January 15, 1975.

Note: Prices are subject to modification in line with changes in the wholesale
price index.

SCHEDULE C: RENT REFUND SCHEDULE

FALL SEMESTER - 1974		SPRING SEMESTER - 1975	
Withdrawal between	*Refund*	*Withdrawal between*	*Refund*
before - 9/14	$280	before - 2/1	$280
9/15 - 9/21	264	2/2 - 2/8	264
9/22 - 9/28	242	2/9 - 2/15	242
9/29 - 10/5	220	2/16 - 2/22	220
10/6 - 10/12	198	2/23 - 3/1	198
10/13 - 10/19	176	3/2 - 3/8	176
after - 10/19	no refunds	after - 3/16	no refunds

AGREEMENT

Agreement made this _____ day of _____
between Automatic Foods, Inc., a New York Corporation, hereinafter referred to as Automatic Foods, Inc. and Floham Falls
University, Florham Falls, New Jersey, hereinafter called the
University.

Whereas Automatic Foods, Inc. is engaged in the business of
supplying and operating food services in schools and colleges,
and whereas the University if willing to permit Automatic Foods,
Inc. to operate a food service program for the students, faculty,
staff, and guests of said University upon the terms and conditions
herein below set forth, the parties therefore agree as follows:

1. Facilities, Equipment, and Inventory

The University will provide within the institution space facilities, and all necessary cafeteria and kitchen equipment. Automatic Foods, Inc. will keep all of said property in proper
condition and will replace all loss and breakage other than loss or
damage by fire, explosion, water, or an act of God. The University, however, shall maintain ownership and control of such
space and equipment. The University reserves the right to use the
dining areas from time to time for such purposes as registration of
students, testing, dances, meetings, etc. The director of physical
facilities and campus services of the University shall have full
right of access to all portions of the food service at any and all
times. The University will also provide at its cost and expense the
necessary water, heat, light, gas, and electric current for the operation of said food service. A maximum of $250 will apply to any
repair by Automatic Foods, Inc. except that any repair caused by
the negligence of Automatic Foods, Inc. or its employees would
be the financial responsibility of Automatic Foods, Inc.

2. Operating Specifications

In the operation of the University food service program,
Automatic Foods, Inc. will be responsible to:

(A) Order, receive, and pay for all food and supplies used in the
University's food operation.

(B) Hire, direct, and supervise all food service personnel. All employees will be employees of Automatic Foods Inc. The food service director and other management personnel will be assigned to the University upon approval by the director of physical facilities and campus services for the Madison Campus.

(C) Maintain all bookkeeping, accounting, and food service records required within the food service operation.

(D) Automatic Foods, Inc. shall provide, furnish, and serve whatever food and beverage may be required by the University for receptions, banquets, conferences, symposiums, seminars, luncheons, dinners, teas, etc. The consideration for such functions is stated in the addendum.

(E) Operate the food and refreshment service in keeping with the highest quality of service. The meals will be varied and nutritionally planned. In addition to expertly prepared foods, special recognition will be made of season and holiday motifs.

(F) Provide all of the food service manuals and technical staff services required. These include operation, purchasing, engineering, auditing, and accounting department, as well as such other supervisory, administrative and/or special functions as may be necessary from time to time.

(G) Accept the direction and policies of the University at all times. This is not intended to preclude Automatic Foods, Inc. responsibility to advise and recommend changes and adjustments in service that are thought to be in the best interests of the University.

3. Food Service Director

It is agreed that the food service director will be responsible for departmental planning organization and administration, and will have complete on-location responsibility for the food service, including all phases of food production and serving, and will maintain an active and effective development program. The food service director:

prepares employee work and time schedules;

attends staff meetings called by the dean of students or director of physical facilities and campus services acquainting him with the needs, objectives, and accomplishments of the department;

participates in the formalization and application of continuous and intensive orientation, training, and supervisory
program for employees;

is responsible for establishing and maintaining sanitation
standards throughout the food service facility covered by this
contract;

maintains the standards of quality in food purchased and
served;

assures economic use of labor and food;

directs the training of an efficient working force;

instructs employees in maintenance and care of equipment;

supervises activities of work areas, including kitchen and
cafeteria;

maintains refrigerator inventories;

supervises the receiving of all deliveries;

caters special functions;

prepares efficiency ratings of employees;

interviews students for menu preferences;

formulates, directs, and participates in staff development and
in-service training of food service employees;

plans and directs all activities of the units for which he is responsible;

supervises the use of standardized recipes.

4. Food Preparation and Standards

All food will be prepared on campus in the kitchen area.
Automatic Foods, Inc. will not use convenience foods. The
quality of the food items used in the preparation of meals will be
excellent.

The following minimum standards of quality for purchases
will be maintained:

meats (raw)	USDA inspected — Choice
meats (processed)	USDA inspected only
poultry	USDA Inspected — Grade A
dairy products	Grade A
canned fruits and vegetables	USDA Grade A
fresh produce	highest available quality
fish and shellfish	Government inspected top

	quality fresh and frozen
frozen fruits and vegetables	best available
butter	93 score

Merchandise received will be verified for quality and cost and appropriately stored.

Invoices recorded by the resident manager will be verified by district supervision and central accounting as well.

5. Prices

The price structure now in effect at the University will be adopted and maintained without changes for a minimum of two semesters.

6. Hours and Periods of Operation

Automatic Foods, Inc. will operate a food service program throughout the calendar year at all periods requested by the University. Cafeteria service will be available each day from 7:00 AM to 7:00 PM. It is agreed that during these hours the snack bar facilities will be closed unless the management responsibility for same is awarded to Automatic Foods, Inc.

7. Serving Lines

During meal times one serving line will be open for complete dinners. Two hot entrees will be available at each meal. At each serving a daily special, consisting of a complete meal, will be offered at a package price that will be lower than the total charge for similar à la carte items.

A second line will be used to serve short order or grill items.

8. Food Committee — Menus

Menus will be prepared in advance with the assistance of University representatives. A student food committee will be selected and scheduled to meet with the general manager, the vice president, and the resident manager of Automatic Foods, Inc. on a regular basis.

9. Buffet Night — Unlimited Food

Twice each month a buffet dinner will be prepared and offered at a single price. Students will be allowed to eat all they wish at that meal for the one price.

10. Special Evening Menus

Periodically, special evening dinners will be presented featuring menus associated with a specific country. These evenings will be planned and scheduled by the student food committee.

11. Purchase of Present Food and Supplies

Automatic Foods, Inc. is willing to purchase at cost from the University the present food and supplies inventory.

12. Maintenance and Sanitation

Automatic Foods, Inc. will be responsible for keeping neat and clean all areas and equipment within the kitchen, serving locations, and cafeteria tables. The University shall maintain at its own expense adequate service for the disposal of waste materials resulting from the operation of the food service program. However, separation and accumulation of such waste materials shall be the responsibility of Automatic Foods, Inc.

13. Present Personnel

All food service personnel shall be compensated by Automatic Foods, Inc. in its own name and at its own expense. Automatic Foods, Inc. will review the qualifications and skills of present food service employees at the University and where deemed appropriate by Automatic Foods, Inc. employment will be offered. It is recognized that the food service is an integral part of the operation of the total educational facilities of the University. For that reason, the wages, hours of work, fringe benefits, and general conditions of employment of food service employees must be established and maintained in a manner consistent with the employee relations policies, practices, and conditions established by the University with respect to other campus employees. Therefore, Automatic Foods, Inc. may not, without prior consultation and agreement with the University, change in any general or substantial way the wages, fringe benefits, or working conditions of nonmanagement food service employees.

14. Equal Opportunity

It is Automatic Foods, Inc.'s policy to maintain the highest ethical relationships with its customers, employees, suppliers, and competitors. In maintaining such relationships, Automatic Foods, Inc. will not discriminate in any of its activities because of race, creed, color, national origin, ancestry, age, sex, marital status, or because of liability for service in the armed forces of the United States.

15. Insurance

Automatic Foods, Inc. will obtain and keep in force during the term of the agreement public liability and products liability insurance, each in the sum of $300,000/$500,000 in a company satisfactory to the University. The University shall be named as additional insured on these policies. The policies shall contain a convenant by the company issuing the same that the policies shall not be cancelled by the insuring company unless a thirty (30) day written notice of cancellation first be given to the University. Copies of the policy or policies representing the same shall be delivered to the University for its records. All premiums upon said policies shall be paid by Automatic Foods, Inc.

Automatic Foods, Inc. will also obtain and keep in force according to the terms stated above a $2,000,000 excess liability policy.

Automatic Foods, Inc. will provide certificates of insurance to the University on workmen's compensation and on comprehensive automobile insurance in the sum of $300,000/$500,000, including property damage in the sum of $50,000. The University will be advised in writing immediately of any and all valid or nonvalid claims arriving out of food operations either on the premises or elsewhere.

Employees of Automatic Foods, Inc. are to be examined for communicable diseases seasonally and prior to commencement of operation. All new employees are to be examined prior to the start of employment. Certificates of health are to be filed with the director of physical facilities and campus services.

In the event that Automatic Foods, Inc. fails to maintain and keep in force products liability insurance, public liability insurance, and workmen's compensation insurance, the University shall have the right to cancel and terminate this agreement forthwith and without notice.

16. Claims, Suits, or Proceedings

Automatic Foods, Inc. shall indemnify and forever hold harmless the University against any and all claims, causes of action, suits, or proceedings, including all damages, costs, and expenses in connection therewith, arising out of the performance of this agreement by Automatic Foods, Inc. or any of its agents or employees, including without limiting the generality of the foregoing and all claims, causes of action, suits, or proceedings arising out of the death or injury of any person or persons resulting from the acts or omissions of Automatic Foods, Inc., its agents or employees in connection with the operation of said food service whether such food or beverages are made or prepared by Automatic Foods, Inc. or are purchased from others.

17. Permits and Licenses

Automatic Foods, Inc. shall obtain at its own expense all necessary permits and licenses required by any federal, state, or municipal law for the operation of said food service, and shall pay direct to the proper authorities any federal, state, county, or local taxes which may be assessed against its property or business while in or upon the University's premises. Automatic Foods, Inc. shall comply with all rules and regulations of any federal, state, county, or municipal government bureau or department applicable to said food service.

18. Financial

In order to provide the University with full knowledge of all income and expenses registered in the operation of the University food service program, Automatic Foods, Inc. will initiate a known cost agreement with the University that will disclose in detail income and expenses. In addition to regularly scheduled quarterly reports, records will be submitted to the campus business manager for review by the University.

Automatic Foods, Inc. assumes full responsibility for all costs related to labor, food, and insurance. In addition, Automatic Foods, Inc. will return to the University all profits before taxes earned over and above 5 percent during any one year with a guaranteed minimum return of $5,000 payable on or before July 31.

19. Term and Termination

This agreement shall continue for a period of ten months from its effective date of September 1, 1972, and thereafter from year to year, provided, however, that either party may at any time during the life of this agreement or any extension thereof terminate this agreement by giving a full semester's notice in writing to the other party of its intention to terminate this agreement.

This agreement may not be assigned by Automatic Foods, Inc. in whole or in part without the consent in writing of the University.

In witness thereof the parties have duly executed this Agreement this _____ day of _____, 1972.

Florham Falls University

By_____
Dean of Students

_____
Campus Provost

_____
Vice President for Financial Affairs

Automatic Foods, Inc.

By_____

AGREEMENT

AGREEMENT: made and entered into as of the first day of July, 1973, by and between the Florham Falls University, an educational institution organized under the laws of the state of New Jersey, hereinafter referred to as the University, and Black & Nugent Bookstores, Inc., a corporation duly organized and existing under the laws of New York State with its office and principal place of business at 107A Fifth Avenue, New York, hereinafter referred to as the College Store.

WITNESSETH: That the parties hereto do mutually convenant and agree as follows:

(1) The University shall make available to the College Store at the Florham Falls campus a space approximately forty-three feet by fifty-two feet in the existing student center lounge. The University shall provide retaining walls on both sides of this space. This space shall be designated as College Store space, and the College Store shall use the same to stock, display, and sell books, and other items usually sold by college stores. The University shall provide, at its sole expense, with respect to such space, electricity, heat, air conditioning, and rubbish removal from a designated area. The University shall reserve the right of approval for all items offered for sale in the College Store.

(2) The College Store agrees to provide at its sole expense the following:

(a) all fixtures and equipment necessary to operate a functional and attractive bookstore, and further agrees to sustain all costs for modifications necessary for the installation of said equipment;

(b) the redesign and conversion of existing lighting fixtures to fixtures suitable for bookstore operations;

(c) qualified bookstore personnel to operate the College Store at all times;

(d) the collection of proceeds of sales and banking thereof;

(e) the accounting, tax reporting, and supervision of such operations;

(f) all other operations and procedures necessary to provide bookstore service to the faculty, staff, and students at Florham Falls University;

(g) cleaning and maintenance of the College Store.

All changes and modifications to the existing physical facilities, at any time, must have the prior written approval of the director of physical facilities and campus services. All costs of renovations and alterations must be backed by paid receipts, copies of which must be forwarded to the director of physical facilities and campus services upon payment of said receipts.

(3) The College Store shall pay to the University the following percentages of all net sales made during each fiscal year (July 1 to June 30):

(a) 3% of all sales up to $400,000,

(b) 4% of all sales between $401,000 and $800,000,

(c) 5% of all sales over $800,000.

Net sales are defined as gross sales less refunds and voids.

(4) Sales shall be made by the College Store on the following basis:

(a) new textbooks at current publisher's list price;

(b) used texts books at 75% of current publisher's list price;

(c) all other merchandise at competitive prices, subject to review of campus business manager;

(d) faculty and full-time staff shall receive an additional 10% discount on all merchandise.

(5) The College Store shall purchase books from the faculty, staff, and students at the following prices:

(a) at 50% of the publisher's list price, provided the book is a good used copy and is on the University book list for the current semester;

(b) in the absence of such notification, or if the book will not be used the following year, or is to be replaced shortly by a revised edition according to announcement of the publisher, at the price listed in the current Black & Nugent buying guide.

(6) The College Store shall make payments to the University on the following dates:

(a) November 15 for all sales recorded in July, August, September, and October;

(b) March 15 for all sales recorded in November, December, January, and February;

    (c) July 15 for all sales recorded in March, April, May, and June.

    (d) The College Store guarantees the University a minimum payment of $10,000 for the first year of the contract. The subsequent $10,000 minimum yearly payments for the running length of the contract shall be increased at an annual rate of 5% per year or as mutually negotiated. Payments to the University will be in equal amounts on November 15, March 15, and July 15 of each year. The final payment on July 15 shall reflect the "plus" differential, if any, as per schedule under item (3) of this contract.

       The College Store shall make available all register tapes, daily reports, bank depository receipts, and sales journals to show how commissions have been arrived at.

  (7) This agreement, which is executed by the parties hereto, shall become effective as of July 1, 1973 and shall continue in effect until June 30, 1978.

  (8) The University may cancel this agreement by written notice to the College Store within ninety (90) days of the date of such cancellation. The University agrees to reimburse the College Store the unamortized value of all fixtures, equipment, and leasehold improvements made by the College Store in the event of such cancellation. The College Store agrees to depreciate all such improvements one-fifth per year over the course of this contract.

  (9) In the event of cancellation of this agreement by the University, the University agrees to repurchase College Store inventories at full invoice cost value paid by the College Store. Payments will be made over a graduated period of three years as stated under item (11).

  (10) The College store shall pay the University for all bookstore inventory presently on hand at the following values:

    (a) full invoice cost value for all salable inventory of school supplies and miscellaneous merchandise.

    (b) full invoice cost value for all textbooks and paperbacks required for the summer and fall semesters of 1973.

The cost to relocate any and all University inventory purchased by Black & Nugent and any other items from the current bookstore location will be at the expense of Black & Nugent.

(11) The College Store will reimburse the University for above inventory in six equal payments, commencing November 15 and each succeeding November 15 and March 15 for the next three years or upon termination of contract.

(12) The College Store shall be open for business at such times as may be required to satisfy the needs of the University, its students, faculty, and staff, as determined by the University. Store hours will be extended during each registration period and the first two weeks of classes to accommodate the students.

(13) The College Store agrees to provide a check-cashing service for students and faculty at a charge of ten cents for checks up to twenty-five dollars.

(14) It is agreed that the College Store shall be responsible for the salary of any and all of its employees, charges, or any other liabilities or obligations incurred by said College Store, and for the cost of any merchandise which the College Store may purchase. The College Store agrees to hold the University harmless from liabilities and to indemnify them any such claims. The College Store further agrees that it shall obtain all appropriate policies of insurance including workmen's compensation, fire, premises and tort liability insurance in adequate amounts to cover any and all claims which might result from the operation of the bookstore. The College Store further agrees to hold the University harmless for any and all claims asserted against the University arising in and out of the operation of said bookstore. A copy of the certificate of insurance shall be on file with the campus business manager. The University is not responsible for loss or damage of College Store property or any interruption of service by fire or any other cause, including the interruption of the furnishing of such utilities as heat, air conditioning, and electricity.

The minimum limits of insurance coverage will be $300,000/$500,000 Public Liability and $50,000 Property Damage.

(15) The College Store further covenants and agrees that it will not in any manner use the credit or name of the Florham Falls University in connection with its said business or affairs, except as may be from time to time specifically authorized by the campus

business manager in writing. The College Store further covenants that it will purchase merchandise and sign contracts only in its own name and at its own cost and expense and on its own sole credit, and that it will promptly make full payment thereof in accordance with the terms of the purchase.

(16) The College Store further agrees to observe and obey, and to compel its employees to observe and obey, and at all times to be subject to and conform with all rules and regulations promulgated by the president and/or campus business manager of the Florham Falls University for the government and control of all employees engaged by the University or others in the said premises — it being understood and agreed, however, that the president or campus business manager of the Florham Falls University shall have no personal control, direction, or supervision, except as herein specifically provided for, over the business of the College Store. The College Store agrees to conform to all fire and public safety laws, regulations, and ordinances of the borough of Florham Falls and the state of New Jersey.

(17) The College Store pledges its cooperation with any faculty or faculty-student committee created by Florham Falls University.

(18) The College Store agrees to permit an auditor appointed by the University to examine the financial statements of the College Store, its records, and its operations at any given and reasonable time.

(19) The College Store agrees to refund or exchange without penalty any textbook within ten days of date classes begin provided said book is still in same condition as when purchased and is accompanied by the sales receipt.

(20) The College Store agrees to post conspicuously and without equivocation, store policies concerning discounts, refunds, and exchanges, and buy-backs.

(21) The College Store agrees to place special personal orders for books requested by faculty, students, and staff. Appropriate deposit requirements as a protection to the store are authorized.

(22) The College Store agrees to maintain proper standards of courtesy, services, and professional standards in all of its dealings with members of the total University community.

(23) The parties do further agree that this agreement cannot be

changed, modified, or discharged, unless such agreement of change, modification, or discharge is reduced to writing and signed by the party against whom such change, modification, or discharge is sought.

(24) The College Store agrees and warrants that in the performance of this contract they will not discriminate or permit discrimination against any person or group of persons on the grounds of race, color, religion, national origin, or sex in any manner prohibited by the laws of the United States or the state of New Jersey, and furthermore agrees to provide the Commission on Human Rights and Opportunities or any other governmental agency having jurisdiction with such information requested by the commission concerning the employment practices and procedures of the College Store as related to the provisions of this section.

(25) In the event of the breach of this contract or any tortious claims arising in and out of the college bookstore, the law of the state of New Jersey shall be controlling.

(26) Black & Nugent assumes full responsibility for any and all losses due to theft. The University will not provide security for the College Store other than the normal routine currently followed. In witness whereof the parties hereto have caused this agreement to be executed as of the day and year first above mentioned.

Florham Falls University

By_____
Dean of Students

By_____
Provost

By_____
Vice President for Financial Affairs

Black & Nugent Bookstores, Inc.

By_____
President

CHAPTER SIX

STUDENTS IN THE CLASSROOM

CONFRONTATIONS between students and administrators were not infrequent during the 1960's. Indeed, the sixties represent a time frame in which the constitutional requirements of free speech and due process served to dilute administrative discretion, and generally realigned students and administrators as equal persons before the law.

Historically, the courts have avoided controversies between students, teachers, and advisors. Public interest in civil liberties in the recent past precipitated judicial examination particularly of student relationships and activities outside the classroom. Given legal adulthood for almost all college students, and judicial *desiderata* of the 1960's and early 1970's, faculty and advisor prerogatives with regard to students and their academic status may now face new limitations.

College regulations involving grades, course credit, and graduation obviously must be applied consistently and responsibly. Faculty and staff advisors themselves must assume the shortcomings and inadequacy of their advice to and direction of students as well as their interpretation of academic and administrative regulations.

While due process including notice and hearing is not yet required for students expelled for scholastic reasons, the courts have not excluded themselves from examining scholastic dismissals. Indeed, if a student were expelled for reasons which involve criteria other than oral and written work produced in a class, or if a student's grade was in some way affected by a professor's bad faith, passion, or prejudice, the courts will in all likelihood order a fair and impartial hearing. It is well to understand, however, that claims of bad faith and prejudice are extremely difficult to maintain in a legal proceeding because of the intangibility of such practices. Issues which are more palpable and amenable to a due process proceeding, such as a student's failure to attend class regularly or to submit additional test scores after admission to the institution has been effected are matters of fact and will in most instances require a fair hearing.

Academic advice and guidance when articulated by a faculty or staff member and relied upon by an advisee is said then to have binding effect upon the institution. *Blank v. Board of Education of the city of New York,* 51 Misc. 2d 724 (1966). An implied contract between student and institution is said to *exist* where a faculty advisor, for example, directs a student to take certain courses within a major for degree satisfaction, and upon such instruction the student completes certain prescribed academic work. The advisor cannot at a later point without a contractual breach hold up graduation by claiming student failure to complete departmental requirements. University officials, then, are generally precluded from changing degree requirements once they have been articulated to students.*

Courts will reluctantly hear cases involving grades and institutional requirements, and will do so only when such controversies are based upon the arbitrary and capricious acts of university officials. College administrators are urged, therefore, to carefully note institutional standards and requirements in appropriate bulletins and handbooks. Procedures for academic review should be made available to students. Good faith on the part of college officials also would require that students who are dissatisfied with decisions about their academic status should be permitted to discuss their claim before an appropriate faculty-administrative committee.

MEMORANDA ON THE LEGAL IMPLICATIONS OF GRADING AND ADVISING

The courts of most judicial systems have customarily restricted their jurisdiction in matters of scholastic affairs where circum-

---

*In *Mahavongsana v. Hall,* 401 F. Supp. 381, U. S. District Court, N. D. of Georgia, Atlanta Division, (1975), the court found that Georgia State University Officials violated the due process right of a student when they required for graduation successful performance on a comprehensive examination not specifically noted in the university catalog.

stances have clearly indicated that a college or university has abused its prerogatives of discretion. Among the infractions for which courts will seize jurisdiction are cases of discriminatory grading practices or arbitrary and capricious evaluation of a student's performance.

In all of these situations, judges are notoriously hesitant and will not enter a controversy unless a clear and substantial abuse of administrative discretion is alleged and visible. Thus, it is easy to conclude that even given today's judicial interest in students' civil liberties, courts will rarely intervene in conflicts involving scholastic affairs.

A series of recent cases now will be analyzed to better demonstrate these parameters of judicial nonintervention set by the various federal and state courts. In *Connelly v. University of Vermont*. 244 F. Supp. 156 (1965), a third-year medical student was refused his request to repeat his previous year's work even though the poor quality of his work could have been ascribed to an illness. The court refused the student's petition and ruled that college officers have absolute discretion in determining the qualifications of a student. The court reasoned that school authorities are especially qualified by training and experience to make such judgments. Only when a college or university clearly abuses this discretion will courts interfere.

A student's delinquency in his studies has been the subject of important litigation in recent years. An increasing number of students who were dismissed from college for low grades have brought legal actions in support of their request of reentry on denial of due process and the inequity of professors' grading systems. Both in *Mustell v. Rose,* 211 So. 2d 498 (1968), and in *Militana v. University of Miami*, 236 So. 2d 162 (1970), such requests by medical students were categorically refused. To the student allegation in *Mustell* that due process had been violated since the decision to dismiss was made in his absence and he had been refused attendance at the hearing, the Supreme Court of Alabama reaffirmed that due process is not required in scholastic dismissal cases as opposed to those dismissals based on misconduct. The court went on to say that such a failure to attain a standard of excellence in academic studies is a very different matter than misconduct. There was, however, an implication that the right of due process could become a future reality in such cases of academic dismissal. In both *Mustell* and *Militana*, the courts supported the dismissals for failure to meet academic standards since no finding of capricious, prejudicial, or arbitrary conduct was found in the actions of institutional officers.

In the companion case to *Militana*, the district Court of Appeals of Florida unequivocally supported the right of private institutions to establish the criteria under which its students should graduate. The court went on to say that the terms and conditions for graduation are offered by the publications of the college at the time of enrollment with many of the characteristics of a legally binding contract. See *University of Miami v. Militana*, 184 So. 2d 701 (1966).

Public institutions have been brought under the contract theory as well as private institutions. In addition to the concept of express contract the Supreme Court of New York in *Healy v. Larsson*, 323 N. Y. S. 2d 625, held that there can be an implied contract between a student and a college predicated upon the consultations and advisement of administrators. In *Healy*, a student prior to enrollment consulted with the dean, director of admissions, and other college officers. With their guidance, he chose courses required for graduation. When he was later denied his degree for failure to take the proper credits, he brought suit against the college. The court, in an interesting and important case, ruled that an implied-in-fact contract was created by the consultations and that no additional requirements could be imposed upon the student for his degree. The key factor here was that the student followed requirements outlined by *proper* officials in prior consultations.

In addition to the performance of a student in a formal classroom setting, the courts have extended the prerogatives of appropriate professorial evaluation to the performance of a student in field work as well. In *Bower v. O'Reilly*, 318 N. Y. S. 2d 242 (1971), the court sustained the dismissal of a student from further studies because of his unsatisfactory field work. Affidavits were submitted by professors attesting to the fact of the student's unsatisfactory performance. The student claimed his dismissal was arbitrary and in violation of his contractual rights since his academic grades were generally *B*'s and that he was in good academic standing at the time. This argument was refuted by the court in its finding that since no arbitrary action was involved, it was the right of the faculty to review the total record and potential of a student and make its decision of dismissal accordingly.

It has been quite clearly established that so long as the same procedures of grading are applied equally to all members of a class, the judgments of professors and officials in academic matters would be supported unless there can be proved arbitrary, capricious, or prejudicial behavior by the student who has the burden of proof in such cases. See *Balogun v. Cornell,* 333 N. Y. S. 2d 878 (1971).

CASE: GRADING

Balogun v. Cornell University, 333 N. Y. S. 2d 838, Supreme Court, Special Term, Madison County, 1971.

Justice, Howard A. Zeller, presiding.

This action has been brought to compel the defendants to issue plaintiff a Doctor of Veterinary Medicine degree and to recover $95,000.00 in damages for alleged reduced earnings. Defendant Poppensiek is dean of the defendant State Veterinary College, which is a college in the defendant Cornell University.

The defendants moved to dismiss the complaint upon the grounds the action may not be maintained because of the statute of limitations and because of failure to state a cause of action.

There is no dispute over the factual events. Plaintiff Peter G. Balogun, a native of Nigeria, registered as a special student at the university from September 1960 through June 1961 taking primarily academic studies to meet entrance requirements of the New York State Veterinary College of the university. From September 1961 through June 1966, he pursued a regular course of study at the Veterinary College, including repeating his third year of veterinary studies because of initial failing grades in those courses. Plaintiff did complete the veterinary curriculum with "passing" grades in the required courses in the month of June 1966.

By a 39 to 1 vote on June 9, 1966 of the Veterinary College faculty, based upon a prior unanimous recommendation of the faculty class committee for the class of 1966, it was decided that the plaintiff should not be graduated from the Veterinary College due to unsatisfactory academic performance, particularly in the two semesters of his senior year. The plaintiff then ranked fifty-fourth in a class of fifty-four with a first senior semester academic point average of 1.681 and a last semester point average of 1.352. The lowest final semester point average of graduates of the class of 1966 was 1.895. The faculty committee also found Mr. Balogun should not be permitted to reregister.

The lowest final semester average of students permitted to graduate from 1960 through 1969 are:

1960	1.650
1961	1.979
1962	1.931
1963	1.764
1964	2.183
1965	1.812
1966	1.895
1967	1.635
1968	1.733
1969	1.857

Thus, during this ten-year period no student graduated whose final semester average was less than 1.635.

(1) The thrust of the plaintiff's complaint and of his affidavit in opposition to its dismissal is sound in contract (law) and thus is timely brought. The plaintiff contends that he duly completed the requisite number of courses with passing grades, spent more than the requisite number of years in residency at the college, and otherwise met the "Requirements for Graduation (D.V.M.)" as outlined in a New York State University College bulletin in effect at all times here pertinent.

On February 10, 1966 Dr. A. G. Danks, then chairman of the committee on deficient students of the veterinary college (among other offices), replied to an inquiry from the Nigerian Consulate concerning Peter Balogun as follows in part:

> —Mr. Peter Balogun has completed the fall term of the 1965-66 academic year in a satisfactory manner. It would be nice if he had higher averages—. At the end of his third year in the professional school, Mr. Balogun was ranked forty-second in a class of fifty-four. For the seventh term, just completed, he ranked fifty-fourth in a class of fifty-four. He must continue to do at least as well as he is presently doing in order to graduate—.

Such performance did not occur. From a fall senior semester point average of 1.681 Mr. Balogun dropped to a spring senior semester point average of 1.352.

(2) The plaintiff now contends that the point standards applied to him added an additional requirement for graduation to those set out in the noted college bulletin, and that its application

was "malicious, arbitrary, and capricious."

This argument ignores the standards of "Scholastic Requirements" set out in the Student Information Booklet issued to each student at registration each term. Paragraph 4 of the "Scholastic Requirements" standards states:

> Although a weighted average of 70 percent is passing, the determination of whether or not a student has done satisfactory or unsatisfactory work is not based on any set percentile grade but rather upon the appraisal of the student's record and potential. *The New York State Veterinary College has a responsibility to maintain a standard of excellence determined by the faculty."* (Emphasis supplied.) This is a clear reservation of a right of review.

The affidavit of Dean Poppensiek points out that a quality point value of 1.7 is the equivalent of 70 percent. Mr. Balogun's senior year quality point arithmetic average was 1.516.

As also noted in the affidavit of Dr. Danks, the junior and senior years' curricula deal with acquiring the type of knowledge, information, and skills (the clinical ones) required of practicing veterinarians in their daily rounds. And it was in these areas that student Balogun was most deficient; the records show that in the academic and basic fields, as opposed to the clinical areas, he could be classed as a good student. But this serves only to illustrate the necessity for the veterinary college faculty to review student performance and potential in order to maintain a minimum standard of excellence for its graduates.

Regular student review procedures existed and exist to this end and, without refutation, Dr. Danks' affidavit states "this normal procedure for academic rating of students was employed with respect to plaintiff and all other students in his class." These review procedures involve a regular faculty class committee which functions in an advisory and recommendatory capacity to a committee of the body of the college faculty, in which final determination lies. These procedures and committee actions were fully applied to Mr. Balogun's case.

Beyond the mere allegation, there is no showing that denial of plaintiff's degree was arbitrary, malicious, capricious, or in any way discriminatory. The unrefuted evidence is that standard procedures of review of academic achievement and professional potential were equally applied to all members of Mr. Balogun's class and that the decision to withhold a degree from him resulted from the rightful exercise of honest discretion based upon justifying facts. Abuse of discretion or gross error has not been shown.

(3) In a statement (labeled an affidavit) signed by Mr. Balogun and witnessed on July 15, 1971, he states "my character was assassinated by Dr. A. G. Danks" . . . in that he falsely "called me a Communist," and further that Dean Poppensiek had been told that Mr. Balogun had engaged in interracial dating. Mr. Balogun also contends that the action in denying him a degree was vindictive and would not have occurred if he were not black and that it was the result of a conspiracy between Dr. Danks and Dean Poppensiek. These are conclusionary allegations. "Suspicion, surmise, and accusation are not enough" to defeat a motion for summary judgment.

This is not a case where the court may further review the discretionary acts of the college's academic committee or substitute its judgment for theirs.

CASE: ADVISING

Healy v. Larsson, 323 N. Y. S. 2d 625, Supreme Court, Special Term, Schenectady County, 1971.

John J. O'Brien, Justice.

The petitioner in this proceeding seeks an order directing the respondents to grant the petitioner a degree of Associate of Arts.

The petitioner enrolled in Schenectady County Community College in September, 1969 as a full-time student for the purpose of securing an Associate of Arts degree in liberal arts. Prior to his enrollment at the respondent college, the petitioner had attended two other colleges and was given certain transfer credits for this prior work. The petitioner claims that he consulted with the dean, director of admissions, acting president, guidance counselor and chairman of the mathematics department of the respondent college in an effort to establish a course of study which would enable him to meet the degree requirements of Schenectady Community College. Copies of statements from these officials submitted with the motion papers tend to support the petitioner's contention as to prior consultation concerning his proposed course of study.

The moving papers recite that the respondent college was in its first year of operation, and as a result of this, the petitioner was limited as to subjects or courses available to him. The petitioner claims that he took and successfully completed all of the subjects he was directed to take and was then denied his degree. The respondents' position essentially is that the petitioner failed to take proper credits within the area of concentration leading to an Associate of Arts degree.

(1, 2) *It has been held that when a student is duly admitted by a private university, there is an implied contract between the student and the university that if he complies with the terms prescribed by the university, he will obtain the degree which is sought.* There is no reason why this principle should not apply to a public university or community college. The factual situation in the instant case is similar to that presented in the case of *Matter of Blank v. Bd. of Higher Education of City of New York*, 51 Misc. 2d 724, 273, N. Y. S. 2d 796. *In the* Blank *case, the court found that the petitioner was entitled to his degree after taking certain courses in a manner prescribed by university officials.* The officials were considered by the court to be agents of the respondent board of education and the respondent was estopped from denying the acts of the agents. The rationale of the *Blank* decision is grounded in the familiar principle of law that the authority of an agent is not only that conferred upon him by his principal, but also as to third persons, that authority which he is held out as possessing.

(3) *Upon the evidence presented on the motion and on the rationale of the* Blank *decision (supra), I find that the petitioner has satisfactorily completed a course of study at the respondent community college as prescribed to him by authorized representatives of the college, and I find that the petitioner is entitled to receive his Associate of Arts degree.*

Motion is granted without costs.

JOSEPH BEVILACQUA

STUDENTS, PROFESSORS, AND
THE CURRICULA

The following note on students and the classroom was prepared by Joseph Bevilacqua, Assistant Vice President for Student Affairs, Villanova University.

Courts, traditionally, have been reluctant to interfere with controversies involving the quality of a student's academic work. The courts have held that individual faculty should make judgments within their academic expertise free from judicial interference.

Nevertheless, as in controversies involving social behavior, the judiciary has indicated that even the discretion accorded faculty members is subject to review when arbitrarily exercised. In the case of *Connelly v. the University of Vermont,* 244 F. Supp. 156 (1965), the U. S. District court ruled that college authorities have "absolute authority in determining if a student has been delinquent in his studies, and the burden of proof is on the student to show arbitrariness, capriciousness, and bad faith. Only when the college abuses this discretion will the courts interfere." *Connelly* has been reaffirmed in other reviews of scholastic affairs. In *Mustell v. Rose,* 211 So. 2d 498 (1968), the Supreme Court of Alabama supported the doctrine of judicial nonintervention in academic affairs, and perceived no need for due process systems within academic concerns. In *Healy v. Larsson,* 323 N. Y. S. 2d 625 (1971), however, the New York Supreme Court was not reluctant to rule in favor of a student who claimed he had been misadvised by college officials. *Healy* points out the existence of an implied contractual relationship between a college and student, when college advisors and deans instruct students concerning degree requirements. This case has implications for all academic areas, and reinforces the concept of a college's obligation to act in accordance with academic requirements and regulations stated in its bulletins. Furthermore, it implicitly adds credence to the growing concern for clear specifications of academic standards within the classroom.

Limits to the academic authority of a university also were illustrated in a New York State case, *Blank v. Board of Education,* 273 N. Y. S. 2d 796 (1966), which ruled that the academic authority of an institution and its officials is not absolute. Although courts are currently reluctant to interfere in academic processes of the classroom, they have shown some interest in judging the propriety of decision making in areas of academic administration. In several recent cases involving grading practices and academic dishonesty, however, the courts have upheld the precedent that academic judgments in grading are a matter of discretion, provided the grading standards are not vague or overly broad, and that institutional resolution of classroom cheating is justified, provided there is adherence to procedural due process.

The American Association of University Professors has encouraged faculty to react positively toward changing student expectations. The AAUP Committee on College and University Teaching, Research, and Publication approved a "Statement on Teaching Evaluation" in April, 1974 which mentions the need to include in the evaluation process "first-hand data from various sources including students."[1] The statement further describes perceptions as a prime source of information in teacher evaluation. This statement considers as important the teacher's ability to contribute to the student's learning outside the classroom. It would appear that the profession is already asking itself serious questions about the value of good teaching, and is aware of impending change within the classroom. The AAUP also has emphasized that students are entitled to "even-handed treatment in all aspects of the teacher-students relationship."[2]

It appears that judicial and legislative involvement in academic matters, and the concern of the profession itself, may be more indicative of changes in American society and the advent of the student as consumer/citizen. With the great majority of students over eighteen years of age and often actively recruited by educa-

---

[1]AAUP Committee on College and University Teaching, Research, and Publication, "Statement on Teaching Evaluation," *AAUP Bulletin,* June, 1974, pp. 186-170.

[2]AAUP A Statement of the Association's Council, "Freedom and Responsibility," *Policy Documents and Reports,* (Washington, D. C., 1973) p. 61.

tional institutions, the idea of the student as a contractor of educational services carries significant meaning.

The 1960's substantially modified relationships between universities and their students. Students now may more readily look to the courts for redress of their consumer interests, especially if the universities do not move to provide clear information regarding academic requirements and standards. As a consumer of educational services the student is entitled to a fair return for his money and efforts through truthful advertising, equity in admission standards, student aid and loans, open methods of evaluation, meaningful advising, specific regulations on dishonesty, and a clear delineation of all academic rules and expectations.

The courts already have heard several cases in this area of honesty in educational advertising. Colleges and universities have been patently misleading with regard to prospective candidates. Pamphlets, brochures, and booklets used to interest students in particular college programs often contain information which can be generously described as romanticized. Catalogues, handbooks, and bulletins often contain vague, generalized information. The promises of unlimited career opportunities that obstensibly accompany the award of a degree are often more of a potentiality than a reality. Students who have withdrawn or transferred have frequently indicated that one of the precipitating reasons for their departure was the fact of unrealized academic career objectives. Chickering and Hannah, in studying thirteen liberal arts colleges, found that students who had withdrawn gave as their reason for leaving their disenchantment with the disparity between their college's description of itself and reality.[3]

The area of faculty advising presents another potential example of misleading advertising. Academic advising traditionally considered an important area of student-faculty relationships has been criticized as generally ineffective. In addition, faculty members have not been perceived as influential in the student's personal growth outside the classroom.

The 1973 Student Task Force at Stanford studied the question of student-faculty relationships. Their findings indicated that

---

[3]A. W. Chickering, and W. Hannah, "The Process of Withdrawal," *Liberal Education*, 55:552, 1969.

only 30 percent of the undergraduates were satisfied with student-faculty relationships and the academic advising system. Fewer than 25 percent thought the faculty tried to know undergraduates as people or that advisers gave them better advice than did their peers.[4] Even with this decline in faculty-student contract, college catalogues continue to portray academic advising and other student-faculty relationships as an integral part of the learning process. The lack of appropriate faculty advising will be an increasing source of irritation to students unless more realistic catalogue statements are developed.

The increased incidence of academic dishonesty within the classroom environment has been generated by a variety of causes, including a depressed economy and restricted professional and employment opportunities. The courts have recently reviewed cases questioning the appropriateness of due process procedures when applied to controversies involving student dishonesty.[*] Although the courts have upheld the primacy of institutions to make judgments in each case, they also have noted whether due process has been satisfied or should in fact be applied. Incidentally, the courts have preserved for themselves the ultimate review where a student claims that his constitutional guarantees have been violated.

University grading systems, obviously of important concern to students, now have become a probable area of judicial review. Previously the methodology of grading was the exclusive prerogative of an instructor. Only recently have the courts considered this a new justiciable issue. In general the courts have remained reluctant to intervene unless professors were found to have acted arbitrarily or capriciously. Students as sophisticated consumers are liable to continue to challenge procedures for academic evaluation. The AAUP itself has repeatedly spoken against prejudiced or capricious academic evaluation.

The student as consumer of educational services is entitled to be aware of the standards and expectations of the professor. Students

---

[4]"The Student Task Force on Education at Stanford — The Other Stanford," *Stanford Workshop on Political and Social Issues* (SWOPSI), 1973, p. 56.

[*]*McDonald v. Board of Trustees of University of Illinois*, 375 F. Supp. 95 United States District Court, N. D. Illinois, E. D. 1974.

will become more effective in securing explicit and clear statements of academic requirements as they participate more in course and teacher evaluations. The AAUP indeed has recognized that student course evaluations are valid and should be used as a factor in evaluating teachers' performance. Colleges which fail to appropriately utilize student course evaluations will be more liable to student dissent over dissatisfaction in their curriculum expectations. Colleges which fail to specify academic requirements for successful progression in the various disciplines will find themselves more open to complaint and judicial interference.

As faculties wrest control of curricula from administrations and limit the exercise of this control to themselves, they may inadvertently become more liable to student groups who wish more opportunities to participate in curriculum design. The Carnegie Commission, in fact, has stated that relevance is achieved when courses and programs relate directly to individual student interests and current societal needs.[5] Because of this, faculties may eventually allow more constructive student involvement in curriculum development areas, similar to that which occurred in the student service area in the 1960's.

---

[5]L. B. Mayhew, *The Carnegie Commission on Higher Education*, (San Francisco, Jossey-Bass, 1973) p. 61.

CHAPTER SEVEN

STUDENT ORGANIZATIONS

STUDENTS are generally free to organize and to associate with each other.* University regulations, in fact, may not arbitrarily deny recognition to clubs or associations. Regulations which proscribe a particular group of students from organizing on campus must be based not on predetermined conclusions as to a group's willingness to respect institutional regulations, but upon clear and convincing evidence that the organization in question has refused to abide by the rules of the institution. Decisions by college administrators which deny recognition, funding, and/or facility usage to student organizations without proper notice and impartial hearing will not be supported in the judicial arena. Unless student organizations are likely to substantially interfere with the normal functioning of the college or university, the courts most likely will not respect arbitrary or unilateral administrative action which restricts or precludes selected students from organizing themselves and seeking the use of student fee monies.

Student organizations obviously may not use university monies or facilities to support partisan political activities. All facilities and services used by student groups in support of a political group or candidate should be paid for according to appropriate campus rates. Prolonged use of facilities particularly by non-members of the university community also should be avoided, even though payment for such use is made.

Student organizations when using university monies or campus facilities may not, of course, discriminate on the basis of race, sex, or creed. Organizations whose membership is restricted to students of a particular race or sex are vulnerable to judicial review under Title VI of The Civil Rights Act of 1964 and Title IX of the Education Amendments Act of 1972. A March 1969 memorandum from the Office for Civil Rights of the Department of Health, Education, and Welfare emphasizes that institutions of

---

*See *Healy v. James*, 408 U.S. 169 (1972).

higher education must make available to all students "every service and benefit offered...without regard to race, color, or national origin." Federal regulations under Title IX expressly prohibit support or assistance to "organizations, agencies, or persons which discriminate on the basis of sex," except for social fraternities and sororities.*

College and university counsel have traditionally maintained that student activity fees charged and collected by the university are the property of that university. Institutional responsibility for fee-funded campus organizations and their activities remains intact in most jurisdictions, not withstanding the substantial discretion given student governing bodies in terms of the expenditure of student activities' monies.

The question of mandatory student activity fees for all undergraduates has been vigorously tested in a number of recent cases. Students have challenged the constitutionality of mandatory fees on the grounds that such fees have been used to pay speakers who advocate philosophies repugnant to certain individuals. The courts have ruled that so long as the university does not assume an advocacy role for a particular philosophy, and where no association by the university with a particular philosophy can be shown, no violation of First Amendment rights can be said to exist. The courts, moreover, have maintained that universities represent a free marketplace of ideas where controversial and disagreeable issues may be discussed and debated, and, even paid for with student fee funds. Such discussion and debate is said to be validly related to a university's educational program.

Certain categories of students, particularly those who live off campus, have complained that mandatory student activity fees are incidental to the educational process, costly, and unnecessary. Although most college administrators maintain that extracurricular activities are highly beneficial to student life in general and to a student's personal growth in particular, voluntary student activity fees may well be more appropriate for the new student clientele now attending colleges and universities, i.e. adult women, midcareer executives, and senior citizens. It is well to note

---

*See the material from the *HEW Fact Sheet* in this chapter for a discussion of Title IX regulations and selected excerpts.

that without mandatory activity fee charges, the financial base for most student life programming would be seriously eroded.

The advent of collective bargaining on many college campuses, interestingly enough, is likely to have some impact upon mandatory fee policies and the ways in which student fee monies are collected and disbursed. Crystallization of issues and of campus constituencies is a probable consequence of faculty and/or staff unionization. Once faculty have unionized, professional staff generally will seek some form of collectivity. Students also will recognize sooner or later the potential strength of group alignment. Such alignment may take the form of student unions or student collective bargaining committees supported, perhaps, by a voluntary fee structure.

Student requests to be seated at faculty-administrative bargaining tables have been initiated at a number of institutions. Although students share many of the same interests which faculty and administrators may discuss, observer and/or participant status for students generally will be resisted by faculty as well as administrative negotiators. Student participation in faculty status committees, budget committees, campus councils, and university senates, therefore, will provide the only formal, albeit diluted, forum for student, faculty, and administrative issue resolution.

Athletics

Title IX of the Education Amendments Act of 1972 provides that with certain limited exceptions

> No person in the United States, shall, on the basis of sex, be excluded from participation in, be denied the benefits of, or be subjected to discrimination under any education program or activity receiving Federal financial assistance...

The Department of Health, Education, and Welfare in 1975 promulgated regulations specifying sex nondiscrimination standards for education programs and activities receiving federal financial assistance. Title IX regulations expressly prohibit support of extracurricular activities which discriminate on the basis of sex. In general, colleges and universities may not use sexual criteria in granting access to or providing for participation in social organizations, athletic activities and class work. The objective of HEW regulations reviewed at the end of this chapter is to secure equal opportunity for males and females who seek support and training in all student activities, intramural athletics, and competitive athletics.

College administrators, in light of recent legislation and judicial policy, can no longer arbitrarily allocate and distribute educational resources when such would serve to deny equal opportunity to all those excluded on the basis of sex or race. University officials therefore, must go beyond mere historical precedent and *due process* in developing educational programs and activities. Educators must now make affirmative attempts to integrate institutional objectives with current legal guidelines and regulations.

Title IX of the Educational Amendments Act of 1972: Toward the Elimination of Sex Bias in Education

In 1972 President Richard Nixon signed into law Title IX of the Educational Amendments Act of 1972. Title IX specified sex non-discrimination standards for educational programs and activities receiving, directly or indirectly, federal financial assistance. Initial proposals published by the Department of Health, Education, and Welfare on June 18, 1974 aroused some 10,000 responses from interested citizens, educational institutions, and professional organizations strongly urging modifications of proposed legislation. Legislation ultimately signed by President Gerald Ford in the summer of 1975 was in fact modified substantially. Modifications included congressional amendment removing social fraternities and sororities from Title IX jurisdiction. Additional changes by the Department of Health, Education, and Welfare as a response to areas most commented upon by affected publics related specifically to physical education classes, sex education, scholarship and financial assistance, athletics, and pension benefits. Contact sports, although not the most important educational subject under Title IX, raised the most public controversy and involved some of the most difficult and obstruse legal points.

The sponsors of Title IX perceived their legislative effort as a means to close a statutory loophole of Title VI of the Civil Rights Act of 1964. Interestingly enough, a male-dominated Congress, in passing the controversial Civil Rights Act, failed to include regulations prohibiting discrimination on the basis of sex. In preparing the final rules for presidential approval, HEW Secretary Caspar Weinberger noted specifically the failure of Congress to discuss in detail the difficult problems of administrative control and implementation of sex discrimination legislation. Congressional sponsors were eager, nevertheless, to enact antisex legislation. It was assumed that previous failures of voluntary control required a strong and immediate legislative remedy. Indeed, no matter what voluntary controls might exist, sex discrimination even in educational institutions, it was believed, would not abate in the foreseeable future. It is important to note that final enforcement procedures under Title IX still require substantial voluntary compliance by affected institutions. Indeed, certain requirements of Title IX are unenforceable for transitional periods up to three years.

Title IX regulations although initially written to totally prevent discrimination on the basis of sex, after substantial public and even congressional disapproval, were rewritten to accommodate anticipated difficulties of implementation, subtlely compromising the seemingly original goals of congressional sponsors. Major regulations under Title IX and supplemental materials, including a history of this important legislation, are abstracted and outlined below.*

TITLE IX: SEX DISCRIMINATION

In June 1972, the Congress passed Title IX of the Education Amendments, a law which affects virtually every educational institution in the country. The law prohibits discrimination by sex in educational programs that receive federal money.

The spirit of the law is reflected in this opening statement:

---

*U. S. Department of Health, Education, and Welfare, *HEW Fact Sheet*, June, 1975.

Under Title IX, "No person in the United States shall on the basis of sex be excluded from participation in, be denied the benefits of, or be subjected to discrimination under any education program or activity receiving federal financial assistance..."

The law was originally introduced in 1971 as an amendment to the Civil Rights Act of 1964. Following Congressional debate and changes, the law, signed on June 23, 1972, emerged as Title IX of the Education Amendments of 1972, a broad-scale bill covering a range of federal assistance programs.

During the deliberations on the new law, individuals and organizations testified to existing conditions which they believed made the passage of such a law essential.

Examples

Testimony indicated that girls were frequently denied the opportunity to enroll in traditionally male courses such as industrial arts, and boys the opportunity to enroll in courses such as home economics because of overtly discriminatory secondary school policies. Even if such course enrollment restrictions were not present and a student interest existed, boys and girls would be counseled to enroll in traditionally male and female career development courses.

Evidence concerning physical education activities indicated that women and girls were shortchanged. A school in a Midwestern district, for example, operated a program for girls that was substantially inferior to that operated for boys. In another case, rules in one state forced a high school to deny its best tennis player both coaching and a chance to compete on the school's tennis team because that athlete was female.

A national survey conducted in 1970-71 by the National Education Association showed that, while women constituted 67 percent of all public school teachers, they accounted for only 15 percent of the principals and 0.6 percent of the superintendents. Most of the women holding administrative positions were confined to the elementary school level. Specifically, women represented 19 percent of the nation's elementary school principals; but only 3.5 percent of the junior high principals and 3 percent at the senior high level.

A study by the National Center for Educational Statistics revealed that, as of 1973, women college faculty members received average salaries almost $2,500 less than those of their male counterparts. The study also showed that 9.7 percent of female faculty members had achieved the rank of professor, contrasted with 25.5 percent of males.

Development of Regulations

This was the setting under which HEW's Office for Civil Rights drew up the proposed regulation to carry out the nondiscrimination principles of Title IX. It applied, with a few specific exceptions, to all aspects of education programs or activities carried on by federally assisted school districts, institutions of higher learning, or others receiving federal financial aid. Generally, it covered admissions, treatment of students, and employment.

On June 20, 1974, a proposed regulation was published in the *Federal Register* and public comment was invited. To assist the public in understanding the proposed regulations, representatives from the Office for Civil Rights conducted extensive briefings in twelve major cities throughout the country.

From the publication of the proposed regulations in June to the close of the comment period in October, HEW received nearly 10,000 public comments. The heaviest volume of comment came in six areas on the following issues:

(a) sex discrimination in sports and athletic programs,
(b) coeducational physical education classes,
(c) sex stereotyping in textbooks,
(d) the possible impact of the law on fraternities and sororities,
(e) scholarships, and
(f) employment issues.

Drafted on the basis of the proposed regulation issued in June of 1974 and reflecting a number of changes suggested by concerned citizens, organizations, and institutions, the final regulation has been signed by the President as required by the statute. *Effective July 21, 1975,* the final regulation prohibits, with certain exceptions, sex discrimination in education programs or activities which receive federal financial assistance. The regulation will be administered by the Office for Civil Rights of the U. S. Department of Health, Education, and Welfare.

Substantive Provisions

The final regulation covers the following areas with respect to recipients of federal financial assistance for educational programs or activities:
  (a) coverage,
  (b) admission of students,
  (c) treatment of students,
  (d) employment, and
  (e) procedures.

Coverage

Except for the specific limited exemptions set forth below, the final regulation applies to all aspects of all education programs or activities of a school district, institution of higher education, or other entity which received federal funds for any of those programs.

With respect to *admissions to educational institutions,* the final regulation applies *only* to: vocational, professional, and graduate schools and to institutions of public undergraduate education (except those few public undergraduate schools which have been traditionally and continually single sex).

The final regulation *does not cover admission to:* recipient preschools, elementary and secondary schools (except to vocational schools), private undergraduate institutions and, as noted above, those few public undergraduate educational institutions that have been traditionally and continually single sex.

Even institutions whose admissions are exempt from coverage must treat all students nondiscriminatorily once they have admitted members of both sexes.

Military institutions at both the secondary and higher education level are *entirely exempt* from coverage under Title IX. *Practices in schools run by religious organizations* also are *exempt to the extent compliance would be inconsistent* with religious tenets. Thus, for example, if a religious tenet relates only to employment, the institution would still be prohibited from discrimination against students.

Admissions

The final regulation covers *recruitment as well as all admissions policies and practices* of those recipients *not exempt as to admissions.* It includes specific prohibitions of sex discrimination through separate ranking of applicants, application of sex-based quotas, administration of sex-biased tests or selection criteria, and granting of preference to applicants based on their attendance at particular institutions if the preference results in sex discrimination. The final regulation also forbids application in a discriminatory manner of rules concerning marital or parental status, and prohibits discrimination on the basis of pregnancy and related conditions, providing that recipients shall treat pregnancy and disabilities related to pregnancy in the same way as any other temporary disability or physical condition.

Generally, *comparable efforts* must be made by recipients *to recruit* members of each sex. Where discrimination previously existed, *additional recruitment efforts* directed primarily toward members of one sex *must be undertaken to remedy the effects of the past discrimination.*

Examples

An institution whose admissions are covered by the regulation *may not set quotas* on the number of men or women who will be admitted. Thus, a medical school may not set such quotas, although a private undergraduate school may do so.

An institution whose admissions are covered *may not set different standards* of admission for one sex than for the other. Thus, a graduate school may not require a lower grade point average for men than for women, although a private undergraduate school may do so.

An institution of graduate, professional, or vocational education which prior to enactment of Title IX had limited its admissions primarily to members of one sex *must* undertake special efforts to notify and recruit members of the sex previously barred or restricted in order to overcome the effects of past discrimination. Thus, a professional school which previously purposely limited the proportion of females in each entering class to approximately 15 percent would be required to initiate special recruitment efforts to attract qualified female students. A similar institution whose admissions had not been subject to such a quota arrangement, but had admitted students without discrimination on the basis of sex, would be required only to make comparable efforts to attract members of each sex.

Treatment

As stated before, although some schools are exempt from Title IX with regard to admissions, *all* schools must *treat* their admitted students *without discrimination* on the basis of sex. With regard to treatment of students, therefore, the final regulation applies to recipient preschools, elementary and secondary schools, vocational schools, colleges, and universities at the undergraduate, graduate, and professional levels, as well as to other agencies, organizations, and persons which receive federal funds for educational programs and activities.

Specifically, the treatment sections of the regulation cover the following areas:

(1) access to and participation in course offerings and extracurricular activities, including campus organizations and competitive athletics;

(2) eligibility for and receipt or enjoyment of benefits, services, and financial aid; and

(3) use of facilities, and comparability of, availability of, and rules concerning housing (except that single-sex housing is permissible).

The final regulation incorporates a Congressional *exemption* enacted into law in 1974 for the *membership practices of social fraternities and sororities at the postsecondary level, the Boy Scouts, Girl Scouts, Campfire Girls, Young Women's Christians*

Association (Y.W.C.A.), Young Men's Christian Association (Y.M.C.A.), and certain voluntary youth services organizations. Thus, a recipient educational institution may provide assistance to such specifically exempted single-sex organizations without violating the nondiscrimination requirements of the statute.

Classes in health education, if offered, may not be conducted separately on the basis of sex, but the final regulation allows separate sessions for boys and girls at the elementary and secondary school level during times when the materials and discussion deal exclusively with human sexuality. There is, of course, nothing in the law or the final regulation requiring schools to conduct sex education classes. This is a matter for local determination.

Physical Education

While generally prohibiting sex-segregated physical education classes, the final regulations *do* allow separation by sex in physical education classes during competition in wrestling, boxing, basketball, football, and other sports involving bodily contact. Schools must comply fully with the regulation with the respect to physical education as soon as possible. In the case of physical education classes, elementary schools must be in full compliance no later than one year from the effective date of the regulation. In the case of physical education classes at the secondary and postsecondary level, schools must be in compliance no later than three years from the effective date of the regulation. During these periods, while making necessary adjustments, any physical education classes or activities which are separate must be comparable for each sex.

Athletics

Where selection is based on *competitive skill* or the activity involved is a *contact* sport, athletics *may* be provided through *separate* teams for males and females or through a single team open to both sexes. If separate teams are offered, a recipient institution may not discriminate on the basis of sex in provision of necessary equipment or supplies, or in any other way, *but equal aggregate expenditures are not required.* The goal of the final regulation in the area of athletics is to secure equal opportunity for males and females while allowing schools and colleges flexibility in determining how best to provide such opportunity.

In determining whether equal opportunities are available, such factors as these will be considered:

(a) whether the sports selected reflect the interests and abilities of both sexes,

(b) provision of supplies and equipment,

(c) game and practice schedules,

(d) travel and per diem allowances,

(e) coaching and academic tutoring opportunities and the assignment and pay of the coaches and tutors,

(f) locker rooms, practice and competitive facilities,

(g) medical and training services,

(h) housing and dining facilities and services, and

(i) publicity.

Where a team in a noncontact sport, the membership of which is based on skill, is offered for members of one sex and not for members of the other sex, and athletic opportunities for the sex for whom no team is available have previously been limited, individuals of that sex must be allowed to compete for the team offered. For example, if tennis is offered for men and not for women and a woman wishes to play on the tennis team, if women's sports have previously been limited at the institution in question, that woman may compete for a place on the men's team. However, this provision does not alter the responsibility which a recipient has with regard to the provision of equal opportunity. Recipients are requested to "select sports and levels of competition which effectively accommodate the interests and abilities of members of both sexes." Thus, an institution would be required to provide separate teams for men and women in situations where the provision of only one team would not "accommodate the interests and abilities of members of both sexes." This provision applies whether sports are contact or noncontact.

In the case of athletics, like physical education, elementary schools will have up to a year from the effective date of the regulations to comply; and secondary and postsecondary schools will have up to three years.

Organizations

Generally, a recipient may not, in connection with its education program or activity, provide significant assistance to any organization, agency, or person which discriminates on the basis of sex. Such forms of assistance to discriminatory groups as faculty sponsors, facilities, administrative staff, etc., may, on a case-by-case basis, be determined to be significant enough to render the organization subject to the nondiscrimination requirements of the regulation. As noted previously, the final regulation incorporates an exemption for the membership practices of social fraternities and sororities at the postsecondary level, the Boy Scouts, Girl Scouts, Campfire Girls, Y.W.C.A., Y.M.C.A., and certain voluntary youth service organizations. However, recipients continue to be prohibited from providing significant assistance to professional or honorary fraternal organizations.

Benefits, Services, and Financial Aid

Generally, a recipient subject to the regulation is prohibited from discriminating in making available, in connection with its educational program or activity, any benefits, services, or financial aid, although "pooling" of certain sex-restrictive scholarships is permitted. Benefits and services include medical and insurance policies and services for students, counseling, and assistance in obtaining employment. Financial aid includes scholarships, loans, grants-in-aid, and work-study programs.

Facilities

Generally, all facilities must be available without discrimination on the basis of sex. As provided in the statute, however, *the regulation permits separate housing based on sex as well as separate locker rooms, toilets, and showers.* A recipient may not make available to members of one sex locker rooms, toilets, and showers which are not comparable to those provided to members of the other sex. With respect to housing, the regulation requires comparability as to the facilities themselves and nondiscrimination as to their availability and as to the rules under which they are operated, including fees, hours, and requirements for off-campus housing.

Curricular Materials

The final regulation includes a provision which states that "nothing in this regulation shall be interpreted as requiring or prohibiting or abridging in any way the use of particulr textbooks or curricular materials." As noted in the preamble to the final regulation, the Department (HEW) recognizes that sex stereotyping in curricula is a serious matter, but notes that the imposition of restrictions in this area would inevitably limit communication and would thrust the Department into the role of federal censor. The Department assumes that recipients will deal with this problem in the exercise of their general authority and control over curricula and course content. For its part, the Department will increase its efforts, through the Office of Education, to provide research, assistance, and guidance to local educational agencies in eliminating sex bias from curricula and educational material.

Examples

A recipient school district may not require boys to take shop and girls to take home economics, exclude girls from shop and boys from home economics, or operate separate home economics or shop classes for boys and girls.

A recipient vocational or other educational institution may not state in its catalog or elsewhere that a course is solely or primarily for persons of one sex.

Male and female students shall not be discriminated against on the basis of sex in counseling. Generally, a counselor may not use different materials in testing or guidance based on the student's sex unless this is essential in eliminating bias and then, provided the materials cover the same occupations and interest areas. Also, if a school finds that a class contains a disproportionate number of students of one sex, it must be sure that this disproportion is not the result of sex-biased counseling or materials.

A recipient school district may not require segregation of boys into one health, physical education, or other class, and segregation of girls into another such class.

Where men are afforded opportunities for athletic scholarships, the final regulation requires that women also be afforded these opportunities. Specifically, the regulation provides, "To the extent that a recipient awards athletic scholarships or grants-in-aid, it must provide reasonable opportunities for such awards for members of each sex in proportion to the number of students of each sex participating in interscholastic or intercollegiate athletics."

Locker rooms, showers, and other facilities provided for women must be comparable to those provided for men.

A recipient educational institution would be *prohibited from providing financial support* for an all-female hiking club, an all-male language club, or a single-sex honorary society. *However, a nonexempt organization whose membership was restricted* to members of one sex *could adhere to its restrictive policies,* and operate on the campus of a recipient university, *if it received* no *assistance from the university.*

Male and female students must be eligible for benefits, services, and financial aid without discrimination on the basis of sex. Where colleges administer scholarships designated exclusively for one sex or the other, the scholarship recipients should initially be chosen without regard to sex. Then when the time comes to award the money, sex may be taken into consideration in matching available monies to the students chosen. No person may be denied financial aid merely because no aid for his or her sex is available. Prizes, awards, and scholarships not established under a will or trust must be administered without regard to sex.

An institution which has one swimming pool *must* provide for use by members of both sexes on a nondiscriminatory basis.

An institution which lists off-campus housing for its students *must ensure* that, *in the aggregate, comparable off-campus housing is available in equal proportion to those members of each sex expressing an interest in it.*

Administration by a recipient institution of different rules based on sex regarding eligibility for living off campus, curfews, availability of cleaning and janitorial assistance, etc., would violate the regulation.

Employment

All employees in *all* institutions are covered, both full and part-time, except those in military schools, and in religious schools, to the extent compliance would be inconsistent with the controlling religious tenets. Employment coverage under the proposed regulation generally follows the policies of the Equal Employment Opportunity Commission and the Department of Labor's Office of Federal Contract Compliance. Specifically, the proposal covers

(a) employment criteria,
(b) recruitment,
(c) compensation,
(d) job classification and structure,
(e) fringe benefits,
(f) marital or parental status,
(g) effect of state or local law or other requirements,
(h) advertising,
(i) preemployment inquiries,
(j) sex as a bona fide occupational qualification.

As to fringe benefits, employers must provide either equal contributions to or equal benefits under pension plans for male and female employees; as to pregnancy, leave, and fringe benefits to pregnant employees must be offered in the same manner as are leave and benefits to temporarily disabled employees.

Examples

A recipient employer may not recruit and hire employees solely from discriminatory sources in connection with its educational program or activity.

A recipient employer must provide *equal* pay to male and female employees performing the *same work* in connection with its educational program or activity.

A recipient employer may not discriminate against or exclude from employment any employee or applicant for employment on the basis of pregnancy or related conditions.

Enforcement Procedures

The final regulation incorporates by reference a procedural section which includes among other things, compliance reviews, access to information, administrative termination procedures (hearings), decisions, administrative and judicial reviews, and posttermination proceedings.

Should a violation of the statute occur, the Department is obligated to seek voluntary compliance. If attempts to secure voluntary compliance fail, enforcement action may be taken:

(1) by administrative proceedings to terminate federal financial assistance until the institution ceases its discriminatory conduct, or

(2) by other means authorized by law, including referral of the matter to the Department of Justice with a recommendation for initiation of court proceedings. Under the latter mode of enforcement, the recipient's federal funds are not jeopardized.

Questions and Answers

Question:

What is Title IX?

Answer:

Title IX is that portion of the Education Amendments of 1972 which forbids discrimination on the basis of sex in educational programs or activities which receive federal funds.

Question:

Who is covered by Title IX?

Answer:

Virtually every college, university, elementary and secondary school, and preschool is covered by some portion of the law. Many clubs and other organizations receive federal funds for educational programs and activities and likewise are covered by Title IX in some manner.

Question:

Who is exempt from Title IX's provisions?

Answer:

Congress has specifically exempted all military schools and has exempted religious schools to the extent that the provisions of Title IX would be inconsistent with the basic religious tenets of the school.

Not included with regard to admission requirements *only* are private undergraduate colleges, nonvocational elementary and secondary schools, and those public undergraduate schools which have been traditionally and continuously single sex since their establishment.

However, even institutions whose admissions are exempt from coverage must treat all students without discrimination once they have admitted members of both sexes.

Question:

Does the law cover social sororities and fraternities?

Answer:

Congress has exempted the membership practices of social fraternities and sororities at the postsecondary level, the Boy Scouts, Girl Scouts, Camp Fire Girls, Y.W.C.A., Y.M.C.A., and certain voluntary youth services organizations. However, if any of these organizations conduct educational programs which receive federal funds open to nonmembers, those programs must be operated in a nondiscriminatory manner.

Question:

May a vocational school limit enrollment of members of one sex because of limited availability of job opportunities for members of that sex?

Answer:

No. Further, a school may not assist a discriminatory employer by referral of students or any other manner.

Question:

In athletics, what is equal opportunity?

Answer:

In determining whether equal opportunities are available, such factors as these will be considered:

(a) whether the sports selected reflect the interests and abilities of both sexes,
(b) provision of supplies and equipment,
(c) game and practice schedules,
(d) travel and per diem allowances,
(e) coaching and academic tutoring opportunities and the assignment and pay of the coaches and tutors,
(f) locker rooms, practice and competitive facilities,
(g) medical and training services,
(h) housing and dining facilities and services, and
(i) publicity.

Question:

Must an institution provide equal opportunities in each of these categories?

Answer:

Yes. However, equal expenditures in each category are not required.

Question:

What sports does the term "athletics" encompass?

Answer:

The term "athletics" encompasses sports which are a part of interscholastic, intercollegiate, club, or intramural programs.

Question:

When are separate teams for men and women allowed?

Answer:

When selection is based on competitive skill or the activity involved is a contact sport, separate teams may be provided for males and females, or a single team may be provided which is open to both sexes. If separate teams are offered, a recipient institution may not discriminate on the basis of sex in providing equipment or supplies or in any other manner.

Moreover, the institution must assure that the sports offered effectively accommodate the interest and abilities of members of both sexes.

Question:

If there are sufficient numbers of women interested in basketball to form a viable women's basketball team, is an institution which fields a men's basketball team required to provide such a team for women?

Answer:

One of the factors to be considered by the director of HEW in determining whether equal opportunities are provided is whether the selection of sports and levels of competition effectively accommodate the interests and abilities of members of both sexes. Therefore, if a school offers basketball for men and the only way in which the institution can accommodate the interests and abilities of women is by offering a separate basketball team for women, such a team must be provided.

Question:

If there are insufficient women interested in participating on a women's track team, must the institution allow an interested woman to compete for a slot on the men's track team?

Answer:

If athletic opportunities have previously been limited for women at that school, it must allow women to compete for the men's team if the sport is a noncontact sport such as track. The school may preclude women from participating on a men's team in a contact sport. A school may preclude men or women from participating on teams for the other sex if athletic opportunities have not been limited in the past for them, regardless of whether the sport is contact or noncontact.

Question:

Can a school be exempt from Title IX if its athletic conference forbids men and women on the same noncontact team?

Answer:

No. Title IX preempts all state or local laws or other requirements which conflict with Title IX.

Question:

How can a school athletics department be covered by Title IX if the department itself receives no direct federal aid?

Answer:

Section 844 of the Education Amendments of 1974 specifically states, "The Secretary shall prepare and publish . . . proposed regulations implementing the provisions of Title IX of the Education Amendments of 1972 relating to the prohibition of sex discrimination in federally assisted education programs which shall include with respect to intercollegiate athletic activities reasonable provisions considering the nature of particular sports."

In addition, athletics constitutes an integral part of the educational processes of schools and colleges and, thus, are fully subject to the requirements of Title IX, even in absence of federal funds going directly to the athletic programs.

The courts have consistently considered athletics sponsored by an educational institution to be an integral part of the institution's education program and, therefore, have required institutions to provide equal opportunity.

Question:

Does a school have to provide athletic scholarships for women?

Answer:

Specifically, the regulation provides, "To the extent that a recipient awards athletic scholarships or grants-in-aid, it must provide reasonable opportunities for such awards for members of each sex in proportion to the number of students of each sex participating in interscholastic or intercollegiate athletics."

Question:

How can schools and colleges interested in a positive approach to Title IX deal with its provisions?

Answer:

To encourage each school and college to look at its policies in light of the law, the final regulation now includes a self-evaluation provision. This requires that during the next year the educational institution look at its policies and modify them to comply with the law as expressed by the regulation. This includes remedying the effects of any past discrimination.

Question:

Does Title IX cover textbooks?

Answer:

No. While the Department recognizes that sex stereotyping in curricula and educational material is a serious matter, it is of the view that any specific regulatory requirement in this area raises constitutional questions under the First Amendment. The Department believes that local education agencies must deal with this problem in the exercise of their traditional authority and control over curriculum and course content.

Question:

Many universities administer substantial sums of scholarship money created by wills and trusts which are restricted to one sex. If the will or trust cannot be changed to remove the restriction, must the universities cease administration of the scholarship?

Answer:

Where colleges administer domestic or foreign scholarships designated by a will, trust, or similar legal instrument exclusively for one sex or the other, the scholarship recipients should initially be chosen without regard to sex. Then, when the time comes to award the money, sex may be taken into consideration in matching available money with students to be awarded the money. Scholarships, awards, or prizes which are not created by a will, trust, or similar legal instrument, may not be sex restricted.

Question:

What are the Title IX requirements for counseling in schools and colleges?

Answer:

An institution using testing or other materials for counseling may not use different materials for males and females, nor may it use materials which lead to different treatment of students on the basis of sex.

If there is a class or course of study which has a disproportionate number of members of one sex, the school is required to assure that the disproportion does not stem from discrimination by counselors or materials.

Question:

May a college administer or assist in the administration of sex-restrictive scholarships, such as the Rhodes, which provide opportunities for students to study abroad?

Answer:

Yes, if (1) the scholarship was created by a will, trust, or similar legal instrument, or by an act of foreign government, and (2) the institution otherwise makes available reasonable opportunities for similar studies abroad by members of the other sex. Such opportunities may be derived from either domestic or foreign sources.

CASE: STUDENT FEES — USES AND ABUSES

Lace V. University of Vermont, 303 A. 2d 475, Supreme Court of Vermont, 1973.

Smith, Justice.

This is an appeal by the defendant, University of Vermont and State Agricultural College, from a judgment of the Franklin County Court of Chancery declaring that the mandatory assessment of the student activities fee (also known as the student association fee) by the defendant university against the plaintiffs to be unconstitutional.

The plaintiffs, at the time this action was commenced, were students at the defendant university. As a requirement of enrollment, the plaintiffs were obliged to pay a student activities fee in the amount of $21.50 per student. This fee was collected by the defendant university along with the tuition fee and all other enrollment fees and deposited into and with its other accounts. The defendant university then transferred from its deposits to accounts designated for student association use amounts equal to the sums collected by it as student activities fees. In the academic year preceding this action, the total amount collected as student activities fees amounted to $112,000.00. The student activities fee was found by the county court to be "assessed and allocated by the student association toward the support of student organizations and student activities."

There were at the time this action was commenced approximately one hundred and five student organizations on the campus of the defendant university. The only organizations which received financial aid from the student association were those which submitted requests and obtained approval from both the student senate and the budget or finance committee of the student association. However, before any funds could be expended by a student organization, such expenditure required the signature of the faculty, administrative, or student advisor of that organization. The board of trustees of the defendant university also maintained a continuing student activities committee, whose members were all trustees of the defendant university.

The mandatory student activities fee was voted on by the student senate, which is the legislative body of the student association. When this action was commenced, the student senators were elected by the students of the defendant university in proportion to the occupancy of dormitories and housing units, both on and off campus. In order to speak before the student senate, one had to be a student senator, an advisor, an officer, or one petitioning the student senate. All others wishing to speak before the student senate were required to request and receive a two-thirds majority approval from the senate itself.

Disbursement of the student association funds, after having been segregated and designated as such, was the responsibility of the bursar's office of the defendant university at the commencement of this action. Its interest in such disbursement was confined to bookkeeping procedures; examining vouchers and requests for funds, and issuing checks for the disbursement of these funds. It did not inquire into the purpose and nature of the expenditures.

On February 26, 1971, the plaintiffs instituted this action by bringing a petition for declaratory judgment praying that the chancellor of the Franklin County Court in Chancery declare that the student activities fee was not a lawful mandatory fee or, in the alternative, that the trustees of the defendant university

> ... be charged with the responsibility of supervising the expenditure of said fees and that the said funds not be disbursed without the Trustees first making a determination that the purpose for which the funds are to be expended are educational, cultural, recreational, or social in nature.

The heart of the plaintiffs' objection to the assessment of the mandatory student activities fee was found in paragraph eight of their petition:

> These named Plaintiffs and all other students similarly situated have been forced to finance, through the assessment of the mandatory activities fee, actions and activities which they wholly and totally disapprove; have been compelled to give financial support to persons advocating positions and views with which they wholly disagree; and have, by reason of said unauthorized and improper expenditure of funds, been cast in a public image of nonpatriotism, lack of respect for duly constituted authority, and utter disregard for the rights and responsi-

bilities of others — an image which these Plaintiffs abhor and reject.

The principal objections of the plaintiffs were to the expenditure of funds by the student association through the speakers bureau, for the campus newspaper entitled the *Cynic,* for defraying the expenses of the president of the student association for attending a national student conference at the University of Michigan, and the purchase of certain films.

The speakers bureau was established for the purpose of coordinating requests for speakers by the various organizations on campus. The trustees of the defendant university promulgated a speaker's policy in 1965. It provided, among other things, that (1) the opportunity be offered to balance a speaker with one of differing opinions, (2) the meeting be chaired by a tenured faculty member, and (3) the speaker be subject to interrogation by the audience. During the time preceding the institution of this action, the county court found that speakers were presented on the defendant university's campus and reimbursed out of student association funds "who by their conduct, views, and political philosophy have become and are highly controversial individuals."

The *Cynic,* the campus newspaper, to which $21,000.00 of the student association funds were appropriated during the academic year immediately preceding this action, was found by the county court to have

> ... consistently published editorials of a radical persuasion; espoused the causes of radical student unions; used its editorial pages to advocate political activism; published articles that have resulted in embarrassment to the plaintiffs; accepted advertisements for contraceptives; ridiculed and accused the President of the county of political guttersnipery and attacked him for 'politicking' ...

The court went on to find that the *Cynic*

> ... has pursued a course of blatant abuse of its rights as a free press and has evidenced a narrow-minded, dogmatic disgust with anything and anyone disagreeing with its policy, its beliefs and opinion, all contra to the pronounced policy of a free and independent campus publication.

The national student conference, attended by the president of the student association, was found by the county court to be where demonstrations were planned to be held in Washington, D. C. The county court also found that the expenditure of student association funds for the purpose of defraying the expenses of the attendance of the president of the student association to attend this conference was approved by an individual who held both the posts of student advisor and director of student acitvities.

The films to which the plaintiffs objected to the purchase of with student association funds were found by the county court to be "revolutionary."

The county court found that not only were such functionalisms and behaviors repugnant to the plaintiffs "as loyal and patriotic citizens," but also because they were compelled to contribute their money to the defendant university in support of them by payment of the student activities fee required by the defendant university.

The county court, in its judgment order, found that the mandatory assessment of the student activities fee by the defendant university "to be in violation of the due process clause of the Constitution of Vermont and the Constitution of the United States" as long as the present method of supervision, control, and responsibility for the expenditure and disbursement of the funds derived from the student activities fee should continue. The court also ordered the trustees of the defendant university to assume the responsibility, control, and supervision of the expenditure and disbursement of the funds for uses and purposes "as in their sound practical judgment will contribute in the greatest degree to the educational, cultural, social, and recreational activities and functions of the Defendant University campus community."

The plaintiffs herein maintain that they were being forced to support financially causes or philosophies with which they disagree as the claim adequate for judicial determination. The legal right claimed violated is freedom of association guaranteed in Article 20 of the Declaration of Rights of the Vermont Constitution and the First Amendment of the United States Constitution.

However, we cannot find from the record that the plaintiffs either pled or proved that they were required through the assessment of the mandatory student activities fee to finance the promo-

tion of religious, political, or philosophical causes. The plaintiffs have shown that the funds derived from the mandatory student activities fee were utilized for the introduction of certain positions and views with which they disagreed into the campus community of the defendant university by student organizations through speech, press, films, and associations with students of other educational institutions. As the "speakers corner" of Hyde Park in London provides a platform for the espousing of social, religious, and political ideas by various and divergent individuals, so the student association funds provide the monetary platform for various and divergent student organizations to inject a spectrum of ideas into the campus community. In noting this function of the disbursement of the student association funds, the dissenting opinion of Mr. Justice Holmes in *Abrams v. United States,* 250 U. S. 616, 630, 40 S. Ct. 17, 22, 63 L. Ed. 1173 (1919), comes to mind:

> ...But when men have realized that time has upset many fighting faiths, they may come to believe even more than they believe the very foundations of their own conduct that the ultimate good desired is better reached by free trade in ideas — that the best test of truth is the power of the thought to get itself accepted in the competition of the market, and that truth is the only ground upon which their wishes safely can be carried out.

The plaintiffs do not show that they were denied equal and proportional access to the same student association funds utilized by student organizations to advocate "positions and views with which they wholly disagree" in order to advocate positions and views with which they wholly agree. Nor do they show that the defendant university had taken any action to forbid the making of their views known to others in the campus community through the use of speech, press, films, and association. See *Tinker v. Des Moines Community School.* Minus the allegation and proof of these conditions, the plaintiffs did not present the county court with a justiciable controversy and the county court, and therefore, did not have the jurisdiction to entertain the plaintiffs' petition for declaratory judgment.

The plaintiffs also imply that the expenditures of student association funds in the above manners with which they disagree was lacking in educational, cultural, and recreational value. The county court, in discussing some of the functions for which these funds were expended, found, "Few would seriously contend that (anything was contributed) to the University Campus that could be termed 'cultural, educational, or recreational.' " The county court also ordered the trustees of the defendant university to intervene in the expenditures of those funds to determine in their judgment what "will contribute in the greatest degree to the educational, cultural, social, and recreational activities and functions of the Defendant University campus community."

However, the fact that certain ideas are controversial and wholly disagreed with does not automatically make them noneducational. Mr. Justice Brennan, writing for the court in Keyishian v. Board of Regents of New York, *385 U. S. 589, regarded the introduction of controversial ideas into the eductional process in this light:*

> ... The classroom is peculiarly the "marketplace of ideas." The Nation's future depends upon leaders trained through wide exposure to that robust exchange of ideas which discovers truth "out of a multitude of tongues, (rather) than through any kind of authoritative selection."

We here hold that the Franklin County Court was without jurisdiction to entertain this petition for declaratory judgment *sans* a justiciable controversy on the authority of *French v. French*, 128 Vt. 138, 139, 259 A. 2d 778 (1969). As such, the judgment order of the Franklin County Court is invalid and held for naught.

NEIL S. BUCKLEW

UNIONIZED STUDENTS ON CAMPUS

Doctor Bucklew's article "Unionized Students on Campus" appeared in the Fall 1973 issue of the Educational Record. *Permission to reprint has been granted by the American Council on Education, Washington, D. C. Doctor Bucklew's article discusses the implications of collective bargaining with regard to faculty-student relationships. The author particularly notes the potential use of a union model for students in their various campus roles. When this article was prepared, Doctor Bucklew was visiting professor at the Center for the Study of Higher Education, Pennsylvania State University.*

ALAN SHARK, a student leader at the City University of New York, recently predicted that:

> The day may very well be approaching when students will be manning picket lines of their own. The signs they carry will read "On Strike," "Unfair Learning Conditions," "Support Your Local Student Association." The issues and demands will be made by responsible students who have been awakened to the fact that collective bargaining offers the possibility of making colleges and universities recognize and honor student prerogatives.[1]

The potential impact of this prediction is the motivation for this article.

Mr. Shark may be right. The chronology of student activism over the last half-century indicates a trend to increased willingness on the part of students to adopt an independent, adversarial posture toward the university, and the labor relations model is a pattern for student activism receiving quite visible discussion at this time.

Use of the union model in student-university relations has until now been for the most part only a matter of theoretical

---

[1]"The Student's Right to Collective Bargaining," *Change*, April 1973, p. 9.

discussion. Various labor relations techniques have been adopted on an *ad hoc* basis, but in no instance has a comprehensive labor-management relationship been implemented. However, the national student government movement has considered establishing such a relationship a top priority issue, and there is a call for official recognition by the university community of a union of students as the exclusive bargaining agent for the student body. The intent is that a bargaining relationship will ensue and that a written collective bargaining agreement will be drawn. The rhetoric of this movement is that of the traditional labor-mangement relations system. W. Max Wise refers to the opinion of an individual close to the student movement when he notes:

> One experienced observer of student efforts at collective action, who is also attorney to several student governments, has recently said, "I suspect that what is going to occur, and what is in fact already occurring, is that students will engage in collective activity analogous to that of labor unions.... In my opinion, collective activity and negotiations by student 'unions' constitute the wave of the future."[2]

The evolution of such a movement and the acceptance of the labor relations model would involve the adoption of established principles. The traditional labor relations model has the concept of collective bargaining as its keystone. Collective bargaining is viewed as a system of bipartite decision making evoked within a sanctioned infrastructure for the purpose of mutual determination of wages, fringe benefits, and related conditions of employment. Traditional labor-management relationships involve the following principles:

1. *The determination of an appropriate bargaining unit.* This unit comprises the individuals to be covered by the resulting labor-management relationship. A unit may be agreed upon by the two parties involved in the labor-management relationship or may require establishment by a third-party mechanism (employment relations board).
2. *Free election/decertification.* The individuals in an appropriate unit determine through a secret ballot election whether

---

[2]"The Student Corporation: A New Prospect for American Colleges and Universities," *Journal of Higher Education,* January 1973, p. 33.

they wish to be represented exclusively by a particular bargaining agent. This same system provides a structure for decertification of an exclusive bargaining agent.

3. *Recognition of an exclusive bargaining agent.* The labor-management model stipulates that the individuals in an appropriate bargaining unit are represented exclusively, for the purposes of determination of specific matters, by their elected agent. Individual members of the unit no longer can reach individual determinations of bargained conditions but must grant such determination rights to the selected representative.

4. *Bipartite negotiations.* The two parties (employer-union) are required to negotiate in good faith in an attempt to reach agreement over the appropriate subject of bargaining. There is no requirement to reach agreement, only a requirement to negotiate in good faith.

5. *Mediation/ fact finding /compulsory arbitration.* Traditional systems of dispute settlement are used to encourage agreement between the parties. These systems use third-party involvement as the key to bringing the two affected parties into agreement. The techniques range from "gentle assistance" to granting the third party the right to make substantive decisions binding the two parties.

6. *Written binding contract.* Labor-management relations are based on the principle that the agreement between the parties must be reduced to a written, legally binding contract.

7. *Grievance/grievance arbitration.* Neither party is ultimately free to independently interpret the binding contract. A system of "contractual jurisprudence" is used for the determination of contract interpretation questions.

The labor relations model can be applied to the student in three contexts: as university employee, as affected third party, and as student. The following discussion will indicate the scope of current and possible future activities in each of these areas, and the advantages and disadvantages of the labor relations model in these contexts.

Students as Employees

The use of student employees is a widespread practice within universities. In some situations students are used as temporary relief or "fill-in" employees in an area regularly staffed by non-student employees. Student employees in this type of work arena have often found themselves in conflict with the goals and needs of regular staff employees, particularly over the issue of "job jurisdiction." When the traditional labor relations model is in use by the staff employees, this student-staff conflict is often manifested in a collective bargaining agreement that imposes quota systems and other protective devices. In some of these situations, the bargaining unit definition includes part-time employees so that student relief employees actually become members of the bargaining unit itself although they have only a minor impact on the political operation of the union.

Positions as student assistants or aides within academic units are a second form of student employment. The work is normally associated with a particular faculty member or academic department and consists of such duties as grading exams, typing, conducting library research, and preparing laboratories for student use. The employment relationship is basically a one-to-one situation; appointments are often influenced by the academic promise of the student. Significant pressure exists for including such appointments in the general financial-aid package of the university.

Employment Prerequisite

A third basic form of student employment is the routine employment of students in areas such as food service operations. Usually student status is a prerequisite for obtaining such employment and, in many of these arrangements, students represent the basic working force with staff employees a distinct minority. The staff employees perform specialized tasks or have supervisory-management responsibilities. Wages, fringe benefits, and other conditions of employment in such situations have traditionally been determined by the university as employer. The last two decades have witnessed increased student worker involvement in these matters, reflecting the implementation of contemporary management principles of "employee motivation." This involvement has brought the expectation and even the demand that students be involved in the determination of employment policies and practices directly affecting them in their role as employees. The forms of involvement requested have included (1) an improved dialogue between individual student employee and the immediate supervisor, (2) the increased use of student "lead workers" or supervisors, and (3) the establishment of advisory councils or committees of student employees to assure that management is aware of student worker interests.

Between the university and such student-based work forces, a new type of relationship has started to evolve. Student employees have joined together to deal with the university as an employer in the determination of conditions of employment. In some instances, student employees have grouped together to resolve particular working issues; in other cases, the new association assumes an ongoing concern with the total scope of student employee issues. These latter groups have sometimes called themselves unions. In spite of the occasional use of the union designation, the university as an employer has seldom granted such groups any form of recognition. Under pressure, the employer has met with these groups but has normally insisted that it met with them only as groups of "interested student employees" and not as labor organizations. Despite the absence of recognition, these groups have regularly submitted "demands," which the university calls "recommendations." These matters are discussed by the two parties, and there is evidence of their capacity to reach agreement. However, the employer's decision to implement any of these agreements is actually unilateral. If these agreements are placed in written form, they are normally considered a management policy rather than a bilateral binding agreement.

University as Employer

Even though these groups or "unions" of student employees are growing and becoming more common, their relationship with the university as an employer is not characterized by many of the principles of the traditional labor relations model. They seldom have any form of recognition — and definitely do not have exclusive bargaining recognition. Rarely is there any third-party determination of an appropriate bargaining unit, nor is there any form of election or certification. Although a form of negotiations occurs, there is no legal requirement to negotiate in good faith, nor is any agreement statutorily required to be reduced to a written binding contract. Grievance procedures are not an uncommon outcome of this relationship, but the use of an outside binding arbitrator is quite uncommon.

Student employees have adopted the full form of the labor relations model in a few situations. The University of Wisconsin represents the most comprehensive implementation of this relationship to date. In 1969 the university granted recognition to the Teaching Assistant Association as the exclusive bargaining agent for teaching assistants on the Madison campus. This recognition did not take place under state law but under a special structure negotiated by the parties for this purpose. The certification election was held by the state employment relations commission as a service to the parties. Negotiations took place and a written binding agreement was developed (after a traditional labor relations strike). The parties have renegotiated twice since the conclusion of the first agreement.

Exclusive Bargaining Rights

In 1970 student employees in the residence halls system and the student union system of the Madison campus of the University of Wisconsin sought exclusive bargaining agent rights under the state labor law. Two bargaining units were sought: The Residence Halls Student Labor Organization (RHSLO) petitioned to represent student employees in the residence halls system of the university; the Memorial Union Labor Organization (MULO) petitioned to represent both student employees and "limited-term" staff employees. (The majority of the members of the MULO were students.) The State Employment Relations Commission found that student employees were covered under the existing public employee labor law, and certification elections were held. The employees selected the exclusive bargaining agent in each case, and the university entered into a legally defined bargaining relationship with student employees.

Negotiations with RHSLO resulted in an agreement, but only after a rather bitter strike. The MULO settled without use of a strike. The contracts represented the first instance of collective negotiations under the sanction of a labor law between a university and units of student employees.

In July 1972, Wisconsin adopted a new public employee labor law (Wisconsin Statutes 111.80, amended), which excluded students from coverage. Existing contracts under the previous statute were permitted to be in effect until July 1973. The original contract for 1971-72 with the Residence Halls Student Labor Organization had expired and had not been renewed. Although RHSLO has maintained a skeleton organization, presently it is not sanctioned under law as a legal bargaining unit, nor does it appear that the university will enter into any form of voluntary recognition.

The Memorial Union Labor Organization and the university did have a contract at the time the revised labor law came into effect. That contract has a reopener clause, and the union will probably request continued negotiations. It is possible that the university will extend voluntary recognition similar to that existing with the Teaching Assistant Association.[3]

There are instances of collective bargaining with student employee groups at other institutions. The University of California, Berkeley has had semiofficial relations with student employee groups calling themselves unions. These relations have resulted in new policy statements by the university but not in collectively bargained contracts.

In July 1971 the University of Oregon entered into a collective bargaining relationship with a union consisting of student food service workers. The union, Local 1893 of the American Federation of State, County, and Municipal Employees, AFL-CIO, represented student employees in both the dormitory and student union food service systems of the university. The agreement reached, as reported by Richard C. Reynolds, director of the Erle

---

[3]Interview with Edward Corcoran, personnel administrator, personnel office of the University of Wisconsin — Madison, 13 March 1973.

Memorial Union at the University of Oregon, dealt with the issues of recognition, check-off, work rules, uniforms, seniority, discipline, grievance procedure, sick leave, leaves of absence, and wages.[4]

The Oregon and Wisconsin cases represent the situation where a labor-management relationship involving student employees developed under law. The revised labor law in Wisconsin now excludes students. There is little evidence to indicate that student employees will be interpreted as covered by most state labor relations acts. It is also fairly clear that voluntary recognition of student labor groups by universities as employers will not be widespread. Although there has been increased involvement of student employees in the decision-making processes affecting their conditions of employment, there is no indication at this time that the student employee union pattern is spreading. It is important to note, however, that previous experiences in the general society (private sector, 1930s; public sector, 1960s) indicate that where there is an interest, the labor relations model will eventually be adopted. As the existence of a labor relations statute increases union organization, so the desire for unionization eventually leads to the passage of enabling legislation.

Staff Employee Sector

The adoption of the labor relations model within the general university community has basically been a phenomenon of the 1960s and has been largely limited to the staff employee sector. The parties to this relationship, the university and staff employee unions, have acknowledged no role for students. It has not been unheard of, however, for either party to use "student interest" as an argument in support of a particular bargaining position. Student involvement in these negotiations, which affect them, has been nonexistent. Limited student services and higher tuition rates are partly explained by the cost associated with the collective bargaining agreements. Universities faced with fixed income

---

[4]"Labor Relations, Labor Unions, and Student Labor Unions," speech delivered at the annual meeting of the Association of College Unions International, St. Louis, Mo., March 1972.

have either had to reduce services or increase fees or tuition to meet the increased personnel cost of contracts. In some cases, as noted before, staff employee unions have negotiated settlements that affect the employment possibilities of students.

In at least one other way the labor relations model has involved or "used" students. This involvement has taken place normally when the parties to the labor-management relationship have become involved in a conflict. In cases where this conflict has taken the form of a work stoppage, it has not been uncommon for student involvement to become an issue. Unions at times have either urged or accepted student support of a strike. The university has not been above the use of student labor to replace the striking staff employees. There have also been grievance cases where student support was evident.

Third-party Observers

With the advent of faculty unionism in four-year institutions of higher education, the possibility of using students as third-party observers has become a question of renewed interest. Use of the labor relations model by faculty has a much higher level of interest, if not impact, for students than use of the model by staff employees. Students have traditionally expressed an interest in various faculty employee policies and practices. Most campuses could describe a case, if not several, where student expression of discontent with the continuation or discontinuation of a faculty member has occurred. Various faculty employment conditions (e.g. office hours, counseling responsibility) have been the subject of student newspaper editorials and general student complaints for some time. Many students would indicate not only an interest but also a sense of deserved involvement in such matters for negotiation as faculty workload and class size. Because of the significant impact of bargaining on the academic personnel budget, students can also view their tuition costs as being directly affected by collective bargaining negotiations with faculty.

The rights and structure of student participation in faculty-university collective bargaining have yet to take any general form. Of the four-year institutions with faculty bargaining agreements, only a handful have experienced situations where students had any direct role in the negotiation or ratification of the contract. Students, along with alumni, were observer/commentators of the faculty collective bargaining process at the Brooklyn Center of Long Island University. At two of the Massachusetts state college campuses (Boston State and Worcester State), students have had the responsibility for ratifying those portions of the collective bargaining contract that describe their role in institutional governance. More recently, students there were included in the actual negotiations and were permitted to participate in all discussions. At Central Michigan University, students hold membership on specified contractual committees. The student appointees are named by the student government association. Students also hold membership in the academic senate.

Bipartite Bargaining

Some observers of the faculty bargaining activity point out that the labor relations model is essentially a bipartite system and that multiparty negotiations have traditionally been unsuccessful. Although faculty bargaining is still a limited phenomenon, it is growing. Experiences with student involvement have been even more limited, but models depicting how such involvement might occur can be drawn. Three such models are:

1. *Indirect representation.* This model is based on the assumption that the two parties directly involved in the negotiations (faculty union and university administration) will be able to represent adequately student concerns without involving students in the actual negotiations. This representation could be accomplished in several ways. The bargaining teams could develop mechanisms to assure student inputs into the respective bargaining positions; such involvement could take place away from the bargaining table and be part of the preparation process. The consultation with students would be limited to those subjects directly affecting students. Another option is to assign a bargaining agent, such as a student affairs officer, the specific task of

evaluating bargaining issues in regard to their effect on students and student life.

2. *Observer/participant.* Through some mechanism, this model would involve students in the actual negotiation of the collective bargaining agreement. Students could be included as third-party silent observers of the actual negotiations to assure that students' interests are considered and protected. An optional form of this approach would allow the student observers to discuss only those subjects directly affecting students. Another option would grant students the opportunity to participate fully in discussions.

An alternate to having students as third-party observers would be to include student membership on either or both bargaining teams. This option would be permissible under law, but would raise the issue of whether the student members were advocates of the students or of one of the parties to negotiation.

3. *Full participation.* The full involvement of a third bargaining team in negotiations is another possible model. The new bargaining team would consist of students or student representatives. The actual collective bargaining would be tripartite bargaining, or some modification of such a system. The student team could have the power to present counterproposals but not to initiate original demands, or it could be granted approval/veto power over any bargaining agreement directly affecting students. As another option, the team could be granted full bargaining team rights including the power to present, demand, and ratify any final contract agreement.

The legal status of tripartite negotiations is unclear. Labor relations statutes are written to describe a bipartite decision-making system. A third party would have no legal status under law. The parties could agree to a third-party involvement, but whether such a party could be involved to an extent that would limit the power of the original two parties to reach agreement becomes an unanswered legal question.

Students as Students

The implementation of student involvement in the labor relations system, using the models described above or alternatives to those models, lies basically in the future. As noted, there has been limited student involvement in both the actual bargaining process (Boston State College, Worcester State College, and Long Island University) and in the formulation of the contract itself (Central Michigan University, Boston State, and Worcester State). It is possible that the future thrust for student involvement may be through separate bipartite negotiations with the university administration.

Students in their role as members of the university community are beginning to express distinct interest in, and even commitment to, the adoption of the labor relations model. Even though it is not clear to what extent the traditional union model is being sought, it is clear that traditional labor movement terminology and rhetoric are being used to herald a new type of student movement. Alan Shark, while chairman of the City University of New York Student Senate, described this desire:

> The formal recognition and relationship of students would best be served through a collective bargaining unit of students. The terms and conditions of the contract would be collectively bargained for by a tripartite body of students, faculty, and administrators subject to the Board of Higher Education and the State Legislature.[5]

The adoption of the labor relations model is not a totally new development. Students, as a special interest group within a diverse community, have previously adopted various aspects of the model. The concepts of "demands" and "negotiations" over those demands have appeared before. The concepts of "mediating" differences and "grieving" an issue of concern have been part of previous student-university relationships. They provide a base of experience that allows for the ultimate call for "unionism" as an exclusive bargaining process.

The call for a "contract" is not a totally new concept either. The concept of a contract as a binding, if not always written, agreement is finding increased application in nonlabor relations situations. In many ways, students have been affected by the increasingly contractual nature of life in our society.

---

[5]"A Student's Collective Thought on Bargaining," *Journal of Higher Education,* October 1972, p. 557.

Implied "Contracts"

The catalog or bulletin of the contemporary university represents a "curriculum contract." This agreement is not the same as a written contract, which is part of labor relations, but it is a guarantee of most university policies, and it represents a contractual obligation on the part of the university. Another form of contractual relationship has developed in the form of a "living contract." Students, who by choice or requirement live in university dorms and use university food facilities, enter into a "contract" covering the rules and obligations of dormitory life. In residence councils and other systems, students have an increasing role in the description of this contract. The tenant union movement represents another form of student influence on "living contracts." To a large extent, the efforts of such consumer groups have been directed toward external landlords, but the university as a landlord has not escaped the attention of such combines. Student codes of conduct in many ways represent a "behavioral contract." The events of the past decade have placed these codes within the general principles and jurisdiction of due process rights of the broader society. Nevertheless, they continue, and student involvement in the description of these codes has increased. Grievance and appeal systems for the interpretation and application of these various forms of contractual relationships have grown within universities.

Another form of contractual relationship that is on the rise is the concept of "educational contract" between individual students and faculty members. This concept is expanded in various universities to include a "negotiated set of degree requirements."

Suitability of the Model

It is often pointed out that the student-university relationship is not well described by the use of the employer-employee system. Some suggest that a more appropriate model is the consumer-vendor relationship. Clearly, the relationship between students and university is not within the traditional view or practice of labor-management relationships in the United States, but it should be noted that many argued that the traditional private-sector labor-management relationship model was inappropriate for the public sector. That position has become an historical phenomenon in the face of public-sector unionism. The argument that the labor relations model is not acceptable for application to the faculty-university relationship also has been widespread, but the evidence of the last few years does not support any such conclusion.

Various pieces and parts of the traditional labor relations model do exist in the relationship of "students as students" to the university. There is no experience to date where the labor relations model in its entirety has been applied to this relationship. Nevertheless, it is possible, using the principles of the labor relations framework, to acknowledge some of the theoretical advantages and disadvantages of such an application. However, it should be remembered that what is categorized as an advantage or disadvantage obviously differs according to the perspective of the individual reader.

Advantages

1. The union model holds the promise of more clout for students as they attempt to obtain special interest desires. Some sense that a union model will better permit students to "get it together" and to pursue their own particular interests in the complex give and take of the university. Currently, significant student input is normally limited to crisis situations. Bargaining would provide an ongoing process of involvement.

2. The union model is consistent with the general philosophy, held by many students, that students should have an equal voice in decision making.

3. The union model could be structured to preserve small-group and special-group interests.

4. The union model would give students a concerted-action power base in order to assist them in gaining consideration of their demands. For instance, the withholding of tuition payments or room payments by a significant number of students could

conceivably provide students with adequate leverage to achieve desired ends.

5. Various characteristics or principles of traditional labor-management relationships would, at least on the surface, appear to be applicable to the student-university setting. Conceivably, such principles as collective bargaining negotiations, collectively bargained agreements, mediation, fact finding, grievance systems, etc., could function adequately in the arena of student-university relations.

6. The use of the union model by "students as students" is consistent in some ways with its expanded uses by other groups within the university (e.g. faculty, staff personnel).

7. There is educational value in the negotiating experience that would be functional for students as they enter into an increasingly adversarial society.

Disadvantages

1. The use of the union model might be detrimental to traditional relationships within the university. Some of the roles and relationships that might be adversely affected by the presence of an exclusive bargaining agent for students would be the relationship of students to faculty members, the role of student government, and the role of students in university governance mechanisms such as the academic senate.

2. The labor relations model involves granting exclusive bargaining power to a particular organization. This action implies, perhaps fallaciously, that such an organization will be able to represent the diverse interests and needs of the students.

3. The union model implies a moderate degree of stability on the part of the bargaining unit membership. It is assumed that the bargaining agent has the capacity to make and keep agreements. The short-term status of students as students is contrary to most of these assumptions.

4. Many issues of interest to students do not by their nature lend themselves to being resolved in the bipartite arena of collective bargaining negotiations. Instead they require the deliberative involvement of various groups.

5. Collective bargaining negotiations imply a two-way contract. There is an assumption that each party is able to provide a service or a good that is necessary to the other party's welfare. In exchange, the parties attempt to determine a mutually satisfactory relationship. If the parties do not have a roughly equal "exchange currency," negotiations are unbalanced and traditionally unsuccessful.

6. No legal structure exists for controlling and monitoring a labor union relationship with students as students. There is evidence that the absence of a monitoring unit (employment relations commission) creates difficulties for the accomplishment of an effective labor-management relationship.

7. Involvement in the collective bargaining process represents a diversion of interest and energy from the student's primary role as student.

The categorization of these pros and cons of applying the labor relations model to students in their role as students is not intended to provide a firm set of conclusions. Application of the model has not been subjected to the test of experience. Selected aspects of the model have been used and found satifying, if not promising. The rhetoric in support of the adoption of the union structure continues. If tradition can provide insight into the future, it would appear to indicate that where the labor relations model has been sought by a constituency, it has eventually been applied — first informally and then by law.

ALAN C. COE

THE IMPACT OF COLLECTIVE BARGAINING ON STUDENTS

In the following article, "The Impact of Collective Bartaining on Students," Professor Alan C. Coe of Kent State University reviews the development of collective bargaining in higher education and focuses on its impact upon students and the negotiations process.

Since 1965 faculty unions and the accompanying process of collective bargaining have emerged as significant forces in higher education. Instructors in community colleges were the first group to turn to unions for representation in negotiations with governing boards followed by faculty in four-year universities. In private schools, trustees are legally required to engage in good faith negotiations with unions under the National Labor Relations Act (NLRA). Enabling legislation in more than twenty states provides faculty members in public universities with the opportunity to unionize. The major faculty organizations have endorsed collective bargaining and have committed additional resources to organizing the professoriate.

Collective bargaining has an impact on all members of the university community. The role of trustees and administrators is altered because they must adhere to a legally binding contract. The relationship of the faculty to the university is no longer defined by tradition but by the terms of the agreement. Student personnel administrators are affected while they articulate, advocate, and mediate relationships between students, faculty, and administrators. And students are becoming increasingly concerned about the impact of collective bargaining on their lives on a unionized campus. The purpose of this article is to review the development of collective bargaining in higher education and to focus on its impact on students and in turn their effect on the negotiations process.

An Era of Bargaining

The causes of faculty unionization have been researched by the scholars, reviewed by the literature, and reacted to by administrators. The extreme view of some trustees is characterized by, "They want more money for less work and instant job security." The union leader may respond with the statement, "We want to assist the administration in a team effort to manage the university and to secure more money for all of us from the state legislature." However, the causes of bargaining are complex and encompass more than salaries, governance, and job security. The extension of the NLRA to faculties in private institutions, the enabling legislation for public employees, the environment of higher education, the problems of individual institutions, the attitudes of faculty members, and the activities of faculty organizations are some of the contributing influences which have resulted in the unionization of the professoriate.

Labor unions have existed in various forms and have had varying degrees of success since the 1800's. It was not until 1935 when the National Labor Relations Act was passed that employers in the private sector were required to recognize and bargain with employee groups. In private universities, coverage under the NLRA was generally denied faculty members until 1970, when the National Labor Relations Board extended its jurisdiction to include institutions with a gross annual revenue of at least one million dollars for operating expenses. This standard covers approximately 80 percent of the private schools in the United States.

Collective action in the form of lobbying has had a long history with employee groups in the federal service and to a lesser extent in other areas of public employment. Public employee groups have recently achieved legal standing as states have passed enabling legislation requiring employers to negotiate a contract with a recognized union. Currently, twenty-three states have laws which permit bargaining by faculty members in public universities. Most of these laws have been passed in the last decade.

The current environment of higher education has been an important determinant in the development of bargaining. Inflationary pressures, lobbying efforts by groups representing new social priorities, and reduced federal and foundation support have contributed to the financial problems of many universities. State legislatures and coordinating agencies are seen as becoming involved in the traditional decision-making prerogatives of the faculty. At the same time, public attitudes concerning the value of a college degree have become increasingly negative, and the public seems to be losing its confidence in higher education.

Many universities are beset with difficult problems. Declining enrollments, inflation, and reductions in funding have resulted in retrenchment, small salary increases, and a variety of related problems that surface in institutions confronted with financial pressures. Insensitive governing boards, unpopular presidents, and ineffective administrators have been contributing causes in several universities. On some campuses, faculty governing bodies have not been able to survive credibility crises with their constituents and have lost their power to union leaders. Former state teachers' colleges are now universities with aspirations to become more like the great educational institutions of the country. Many of these schools are apt to remain modest in size and prestige. Adjusting to this new role will be difficult for many institutions.

The apprehensions of individual faculty members have also contributed to the emergence of bargaining. Young faculty members may see their careers being determined by senior professors. Older faculty members who once held the leadership positions on the campus may have lost their influence to ambitious and aggressive junior colleagues. Both groups may view bargaining as a way of protecting their careers and leadership roles. Finally, many faculty members have feelings of anxiety, frustration, and fear for the higher education enterprise itself and their role in it in the future.

The efforts of the American Association of University Professors (AAUP), the American Federation of Teachers (AFT) and the National Education Association (NEA) have contributed to the growth of faculty unions. These groups are giving the organizing of the professoriate a high priority. The NEA (1857) historically viewed itself as a professional organization focusing its efforts on the problems of elementary and secondary school teachers. In the early 1960's, the AFT was successful in organizing these teachers, and the NEA responded by seeking to represent faculty first in elementary and secondary schools, then in community colleges in the mid-1960's, and finally in four-year institutions. The AFT was established in 1916 and was the first group to become actively involved in organizing the education profession. The AAUP (1915) has been concerned with governance and the prerogatives of faculty members in four-year institutions. Bargaining was viewed by the AAUP as incompatible with academe until 1969, when it took the position that negotiations might have a significant role, and in 1972 it resolved to pursue bargaining as a major way of achieving its goals. While these organizations have established positions on various issues, they are not reliable predictors of contract provisions negotiated by their local chapters.[1]

The NEA has been the most successful of the three organizations in unionizing community colleges. These colleges are the most heavily organized sector of higher education, where bargaining first emerged in the mid-1960's. Bargaining in two-year schools has centered in Illinois, Kansas, Michigan, New Jersey, New York, Pennsylvania, Washington, and Wisconsin. According to the National Center for the Study of Collective Bargaining, agents had been named in 180 two-year institutions and contracts covering 227 campuses had been negotiated in 145 of these schools as of September 1975.

In the late 1960's bargaining expanded to four-year institutions. The most heavily organized states are Massachusetts, Michigan, New Jersey, New York, and Pennsylvania. Agents have been named in 97 four-year universities and contracts covering 140 campuses have been negotiated in 66 of these institutions. The AAUP and NEA have been more successful than the AFT in organizing four-year schools.

Bargaining in private schools has grown, but at a modest rate despite the expanded jurisdictional standard of the (National Labor Relations Bureau) NLRB. Of the 97 four-year universities with agents, 46 are private colleges; and of the 66 institutions that have negotiated contracts, only 28 are private. "No-agent"

---

[1]Virginia Lee Lussier, "Faculty Bargaining Associations," *The Journal of Higher Education*, 46:507-518, Sept./Oct., 1975.

votes have also occurred with a greater frequency in private schools than in public institutions.

Although academic unionism exists primarily in community colleges, four-year universities, and primarily in states having enabling legislation, the potential for the organization of the professoriate remains great. In a 1975 survey of 4,000 professors in all types of institutions by Everett C. Ladd, Jr., and Seymour M. Lipset, 72 percent stated that they would vote for a union if an election were held on their campus.[2] The effect of recently passed legislation is starting to have an impact on many campuses, and public employee bargaining laws are being contemplated in several states. The national faculty organizations are also committing additional resources to organizing faculty members. The unionization of the nation's colleges and universities can be expected to continue as new states pass public employee bargaining legislation and as the causes for unionization continue to exist. The rate of growth from year to year may be slow, but it will persist.

Impact on Students

Students will be affected by collective bargaining. The phrase "wages, hours, terms, and conditions of employment" is often used to define the scope of negotiations. This phrase is difficult to define with precision and unions have interpreted it to mean that anything from class size to office hours can be introduced in negotiations. Issues which directly or indirectly affect the interests, rights, and welfare of students will be subjects for bargaining.

A major concern of students regarding the impact of bargaining has been that it will increase their share of the cost of higher education. Collective bargaining costs money. Direct costs include increases in salaries and fringe benefits. When a reduced student-faculty ratio is negotiated into the contract, the university incurs the cost of hiring additional faculty. The expense of bargaining and administering a contract can also be significant. The time required of administrators, the new staff needed to bargain

---

[2]Everett Carll Ladd, Jr., and Seymour Martin Lipset, "The Growth of Faculty Unions," *The Chronicle of Higher Education* (January 26, 1976), p. 11.

and administer an agreement, and legal fees can easily exceed $100,000 per year for an institution of modest size.

There is little evidence that state legislatures have increased subsidy levels for universities involved in faculty bargaining, even in states where bargaining has occurred on a system-wide basis. Institutions confronted with financial problems may find that the only alternative to meeting the cost of bargaining will be to pass it on to the already hard-pressed student consumer. This cause and-effect relationship is not easy to determine in a period when the cost of higher education has been rising along with inflation. Nonetheless, student consumers are aware of the practice of many industries where the cost of a labor agreement is ultimately reflected in the price of the product.

Another major impact of bargaining on students focuses on the issue of governance. In the past ten to fifteen years, the role of the student underwent a careful and often emotional examination. The result was that students are now involved in many areas of institutional decision making which were previously the exclusive prerogatives of the faculty or administration. On many campuses, traditional forms of student government have been supplemented with participation in institutional governance. The symbolic student on the governing board is only an example of a wider range of student involvement in the decision-making processes of the institution. For example, students have become involved in influencing course requirements, evaluating faculty members, and selecting administrators. Many administrators and faculty leaders have publicly supported student representation in a variety of other areas. Wary administrators are well aware of the reactions of students to policies that have been developed in the absence of student input.

Because collective bargaining is a decision-making process in which the exclusive agent of the employees and representatives of management reach agreements that are incorporated into a legally binding contract, they are not required to consider the concerns of any other group in their agreement. The continued and meaningful existence of traditional forms of governance may well be determined by the scope of the union's demands at the bargaining table. Senates, committees, and other decision-making groups will no longer be viable when their previous prerogatives become the subjects for bargaining and when agreements regarding these subjects are included in the contract. Student participation in governance will decrease when the issues that were decided by groups on which they were represented are replaced by the bargaining process. Finally, if a cause of unionization is a faculty concern over the new role of the student in the institution, then there is little likelihood that the union will support student representation on committees that are often established through negotiations.

Recent research reported by Shark reveals that the parties to the negotiations process have given little consideration to student rights in the contract. An analysis of 145 contracts revealed that only 40 contracts referred to student rights. The areas referred to pertained to student evaluation of faculty and student governance. Student input in admissions, academic standards, educational research, and/or the institutional calendar was mentioned in 15 agreements. Students were given voting rights on committees in 6 four-year and 2 two-year college contracts. No student representative was present during the negotiation of these 145 contracts.[3]

Students may also be the victims when student life programs are curtailed to meet the costs of bargaining. In the past, programs designed to enchance student services, student affairs, and student development were often the first to be cut when universities have had severe financial pressures. The same may be true under collective bargaining as adjustments are made in the budget to accommodate the costs of negotiating.

The direct impact of bargaining on instructional quality is difficult to determine, and any conclusions at this time are premature. The following "if's" do suggest themselves as examples of the possible consequences bargaining may have upon quality:

(1) If the contract contains a generous sick-leave policy, then educational quality is diminished by the overuse of substitute teachers.

---

[3]Alan Shark, *Current Status of College Students in Academic Collective Bargaining*, special report no. 2 (Washington, D. C., Academic Collective Bargaining Information Service, July, 1976), p. 2.

(2) If faculty members are promoted only on the basis of due process without regard to performance, then the ineffective faculty member is promoted along with the effective teacher.

(3) If unions must protect all members equally, then the mediocre are retained along with the faculty member exemplifying excellence.

Students may find the campaign rhetoric of the union and the charges and counter-charges of the parties amusing. This will change when impasse leads to strike. Despite the illegality of strikes by public employees in most states, this has not prevented them from occurring. The turmoil of a strike will affect campus morale and possibly the sense of commitment and community feeling for the university among administrators, faculty, and students. The students' education will be interrupted and an extended calendar will interfere with obtaining their summer employment. Alternative living arrangements will be required when residence halls are closed. The lingering effect of a strike will be one of disillusionment for all segments of the university community.

Student Impact on Bargaining

Students have become increasingly aware of the impact of bargaining on them, in contrast to the early days of union activity when students were not acutely aware of what bargaining meant for them and their institutions. Now, conferences are being devoted to the subject. The Fund for the Improvement of Secondary Education is sponsoring a study entitled, "A Research Project on Students and Collective Bargaining," and articles on the topic are appearing with increasing frequency.

As the level of student awareness has increased, so have their attempts to influence the bargaining process. These attempts have taken a variety of forms:

(1) lobbying to affect state legislation,
(2) seeking injunctive relief from the courts,
(3) participating as a third party in bargaining,
(4) serving as consultants to the bargaining process,

(5) observing negotiations,

(6) serving on the management or union bargaining team,

(7) forming student government unions,

(8) establishing student employee unions, and

(9) using third-party pressure tactics.

In several states, students have attempted to influence the bargaining by lobbying to shape the nature of the governing state legislation. Student lobbying has been reported in California, Maine, Michigan, New York, Texas, Washington, and Wisconsin.[4,5] While the number of successes have been few, where they have occurred the results have been dramatic.

The 1975 public employee bargaining statute in Montana gave student governments the right to meet with the board of regents and the union prior to negotiations, to observe bargaining sessions, and to participate in employer caucuses. They are also guaranteed the right to meet with the regents prior to the ratification of the contract. The law requires the students to maintain confidentiality.

The statute passed in Oregon in 1975 also guarantees student representation in negotiations. The student government of each institution is entitled to name three representatives to meet and confer with the employer and agent prior to bargaining. They can attend all bargaining sessions, have access to all written documents exchanged between the employer and agent pertaining to negotiations, comment during bargaining sessions, and caucus with either party prior to the execution of a contract. The student representatives must maintain confidentiality. While the statutes in Montana and Oregon represent new guarantees for student rights, most state legislation does not protect them at the bargaining table.

Another form of participation has been through the courts when students have sought legal relief from the results of collective bargaining. In 1972, students from the Chicago City Colleges obtained an injunction after a four-week strike by the faculty. Open negotiations were held under the auspices of the Cook

---

[4]Joseph W. Garabino and Bill Aussieker, *Faculty Bargaining* (New York, McGraw, 1975), p. 121.

[5]Shark, *Current Status of College Students in Academic Collective Bargaining*, p. 4.

County Circuit Judge, and an agreement was reached shortly thereafter. Suits were also brought by students to prevent faculty strikes from closing the Pennsylvania community colleges of Allegheny County and Philadelphia in 1972. At Allegheny, students charged that the strike was illegal and that closing the college was a threat to their welfare, since it would deny them an education. In Philadelphia, the students argued that the trustees could not legally close the college, and if they did, they were in effect expelling students without due process. Agreements were reached at both colleges before the courts ruled on the suits.

Students were also active in bringing about a settlement in the 1974 strike at the eight New Jersey state colleges. According to Begin, Settle, and Alexander in *Academics on Strike,* the student government association from Kean College filed a suit seeking an injunction to order the faculty back to work. Student governments at other colleges hired attorneys, contemplated court action, and were considering demonstrations to force an end to the strike. Begin, Settle, and Alexander concluded, "By the end of the strike it appeared as if the student leadership on many campuses was an independent force for settlement derived out of a concern for losing a semester's work."[6]

A third method for student participation in bargaining has occurred when students have sought to function at the table as independent third parties. Where this has occurred, it has been with the consent of the principal parties to the negotiations process. In tripartite bargaining, the parties negotiate simultaneously with each having veto power. There is no evidence that pure tripartite bargaining has taken place. Students have been involved in negotiations and have voted to ratify some contract provisions in the Massachusetts State Colleges of Boston, Worcester, and Fitchburg. But Aussieker reports that students at these colleges have not negotiated directly with the administration or faculty.[7]

In bargaining, two parties often encounter difficulties in

[6]James P. Begin, Theodore Settle, and Paula Alexander, *Academics on Strike,* (New Brunswick, Institute of Management and Labor Relations, 1975), p. 113.
[7]Bill Aussieker, "Student Involvement with Collective Bargaining," *The Journal of Higher Education,* 46:533-547, Sept./Oct., 1975.

reaching a settlement. Pure tripartite bargaining could be chaotic and increase the problems in reaching a settlement. Effective negotiations also require considerable staff work and other resources. Students have other priorities and may find it difficult to effectively prepare for bargaining.

The consultant approach to participation in bargaining was used at Youngstown State University in 1975. Student leaders did not attend bargaining sessions, but met with the chief spokesmen from both parties for briefings on the progress of negotiations. The student leaders were able to comment on the positions of the parties and suggest their own proposals. Kemer and Baldridge report that in the New Jersey state colleges and at Southeastern Massachusetts University, students have an agreement with the AFT to consult on union goals and activities.[8] At Kent State University, the union has consulted with student leaders about their goals.

Perhaps the most frequent form of student participation has been that of an observer. For example, students have served as observers at the Chicago City Colleges, the University of Bridgeport, Kent State University, the University of Cincinnati, and Long Island University. The role of these observers has covered a continuum ranging from silence to the introduction of proposals. This role may be the most acceptable to the parties, but students may reject it, particularly if they must remain silent during negotiations.

In at least one institution, students served as members of the negotiating team. At Ferris State University, the president of the student government was a member of the management team. He participated as a full member of the team, engaged in negotiations and attended caucuses. A modification of this form of participation has been categorized as coalition bargaining. According to Garbarino and Aussieker, this form of bargaining occurs when students support one or the other of the parties. They argue that student-faculty or student-administration coalitions will depend on the issues. Students may support the administra-

---

[8]Frank R. Kemerer, and Victor J. Baldridge, *Unions on Campus,* (San Francisco, Jossey-Bass, 1975), pp. 204, 205.

tion when the issue is student participation in evaluation of teaching, and the faculty when the dispute focuses on tuition.[9]

Student unions may emerge as a new alternative for protecting student interests and rights. Student governments may seek to negotiate a contract with the administration and faculty to guarantee certain services. Student governments will encounter numerous obstacles to this approach. These groups tend to have diverse interests and a relatively high turnover in membership. State labor laws exclude students from coverage since they are not employees of the institution. Administrators and faculty union leaders may be reluctant to enter into a contract with a student government on a voluntary basis.

Students who are also employees of the university may seek to bargain an agreement with the institution. Teaching assistants have engaged in bargaining at the University of California at Berkeley, University of Indiana, Stanford, University of Colorado, University of Washington, University of Wisconsin, and Harvard.[10] The Graduate Employees Organization at the University of Michigan won recognition rights and struck to support their demands. A significant element in the future success of student employee unions will be the decision of state labor boards to either grant or withhold recognition rights for these groups. However, it is conceivable that university administrators will voluntarily recognize and engage in bargaining with a student employee union which is threatening to strike, when its members account for 50 percent of the food service staff or teach 75 percent of the freshman English courses.

The bargaining process may also be influenced by pressures brought to bear on the parties by students. These pressures may influence the course of negotiations to ensure that the students' concerns, interests, and welfare are considered at the bargaining table. Administrators and faculty are aware of the power students can command using a variety of pressure tactics. For example, during a lengthy strike at Lake Michigan Community College, students lobbied with legislators and congressmen and circulated

---

[9]Garbarino and Aussieker, *Faculty Bargaining*, pp. 122-123.
[10]Garbarino and Aussieker, *Faculty Bargaining*, p. 119.

petitions to recall the board of trustees. Students have picketed to influence negotiations at the City University of New York. The range of alternatives in the form of pressure tactics are many and varied, as evidenced by the student disruptions of the 1960's. In a more rational era, perhaps enlightened administrators and faculty leaders will fulfill their public commitment to student participation in governance by responding to their concerns in the bargaining process.

Summary

The prospects for the continued growth of faculty unions remains good, because the causes of collective bargaining are likely to continue. The most significant impact of bargaining on students will probably be their disenfranchisement in many areas of governance. The financial consequences are more difficult to determine, but bargaining costs money. Strikes will be detrimental to the morale of the campus community. Unions are apt to claim that the negative impact of bargaining is the result of poor management and unresponsive legislatures. Administrators may focus the blame on the exhorbitant demands of the union.

The role of students in bargaining has taken several forms with the most frequent one being that of an observer. On most campuses, the nature of student participation has been determined by the parties. Students, faculty, and administrators will continue to experiment with alternative forms of student representation in negotiations. Experimentation will occur within the framework of laws, such as those in Oregon and Montana, in response to the good faith attitudes of administrators and union leaders, and in reaction to effective pressures brought to bear on the parties by students. Whatever role students have in the process, they must be wary of attempts by the parties to manipulate them.

While only a few contracts have been negotiated that specifically provide rights for students, bargaining has the potential of protecting their interests and providing beneficial outcomes for them. Bargaining is primarily a two-party process involving the employer and employee, but administrators and union leaders must concern themselves with its impact on all members of the university community. The statesmenship of the parties will be tested if students are to become more than the neglected consumers of higher education.

CHAPTER EIGHT

TOWARD CONTRACTUAL COMMITMENT

ENVIRONMENT may be defined as the aggregate of surrounding conditions and influences. One of the most significant influences for the educational administrator is, of course, the law. The law defines, directs, and regulates administrative modes, shaping values and standards. It effectively provides a framework for legitimate and authoritative courses of action and provides the means to achieve personal and institutional goals.

The citizens of a campus community, faculty, students, and administrators have special legal obligations with each other. Such obligations are a result of judicial interpretation derived from the Federal Constitution, statutory law, the policies of state higher educational authorities, and college and university documents.

Within the last two decades, the Federal Constitution has been the most significant source for the rearticulation of legal obligations between students, their teachers, and the institution they may attend. The Bill of Rights and the equal protection and due process clauses of the Fourteenth Amendment have become the fundamental means in shaping such legal obligations, as has the Twenty-Sixth Amendment to the Federal Constitution which gave eighteen-year-olds the right to vote in both state and federal elections and which encouraged an increasing number of states to confer legal adult status upon eighteen-year-olds. Therefore traditional roles and relationships must be reexamined in the light of both legislative and judicial *desiderata*. Certain conventional administrative practices, such as the sending of bills, records, and reports to parents, the supervision of certain student activities, and the manner in which medical and residence services may be delivered, now require review and appropriate modification.

Laws and policies will increasingly have an important impact upon college and university policy formulation, especially with regard to the financing of higher education. Higher educational authorities generally have the power to approve of academic programming at public institutions and certain private institutions whose charter requires state review and approval. With the advent of collective bargaining and faculty unionization, it is expected that state legislatures will become even more involved than they already may be in the educational process. State legislatures may now attempt to define and direct the bargaining process, particularly with regard to the question of tenure, and the allocation of legal prerogatives. Since state funding is obviously critical to the maintenance of public institutions and generally important to private institutions, particularly with regard to financial aid for students, legislative intervention in the educational process cannot easily be avoided.

Institutional documents, most notably the college or university catalog, traditionally little more than educational directories, now should be construed as tripartite contractual agreements — agreements which establish the legal obligations of campus citizens, students, faculty, and administration.

Each campus citizen because of his recently altered legal posture stands precariously in balance with his colleagues, each positioned within a matrix of needs and expectations, each attempting to create institutional policies which will serve his own interests. The administrative chief executive, therefore, has the responsibility of fusing the self-interest of students, faculty, and other administrators with institutional objective. Given an environment where diverse interests struggle to acheive goals often antithetical to the goals of others, what legal and administrative means are likely to favorably identify self-interest with institutional objectives?

Judicial *desiderata* of the last twelve to fourteen years, particularly with regard to First Amendment freedoms and the equal protection and due process clauses of the Fourteenth Amendment, has thoroughly shaken the aura of faculty expertise, especially in areas outside the classroom. Administrative authority stands on shifting judicial and legislative sands. Supreme Court policy making of the 1960's generally heightened an awareness of the individual's worth and place, and such an awareness has been notably evident on college and university campuses. Together with student disruptions in the middle and late 1960's, judicial decisions, and particularly those of the Supreme Court, helped determine a new legal footing for both students and administrators. With students as well as administrators now legitimately and closely tied to legal processes, a new administrative mode in educational institutions can be said to exist — it is parallel and horizontal, not vertical and hierarchical. Student lifestyles, academic programming, and administrative policy formulation now seem to run on much more of a horizontal plane, i.e. students, faculty, and administrators are more likely to sit together, work together, and decide together — on judicial tribunals, on admission committees, on academic programming committees, and even on faculty status committees.

Two judicial decisions, *Tinker v. Independent School District of Des Moines, Iowa,* 393 U. S. 503, 1969, and *Dixon v. Alabama,* 294 F. 2d 150, 1961, have effectively eliminated the privileged status of educators with regard to student clientele. With *Dixon,* due process of law for the first time in the history of American public education became applicable to students. With *Tinker,* personal intercommunication among students became immunized from official sanctions. The Supreme Court noted that personal intercommunication was as much a part of the educational process as formal classroom teaching. Prohibition of a particular expression of opinion would be justifiable only in those instances where material and substantial interference with a school's operation could be shown.

Universities, then, no longer enjoy a special relationship to the state or with the courts. Vast amounts of power over the lives of students previously vested in college administrators has been stripped away. Students are persons, administrators are persons, faculty are persons — and all live within the same legal environment.

The courts have said, for all practical purposes, that campus citizens are on common ground, i.e. each has equal legal footing. Not all campus citizens can be colleagues, but all can become contractually committed to each other. Contractors, of course, will play different roles, but in concert will prepare, offer, and accept learning and living contracts encompassing all institutional instruction and residence modes. Some contractors may recruit and advise consumers who seek particular sets of skills and expertise. Others will provide whatever services, materials, and learning experiences are required to meet contractual commitments between students and institution. The relationship between student and institution, then, will be characterized by contractual commitment and a sense of mutual and reciprocal interest.

It is really possible to create such a contractual relationship among campus citizens? Is it likely that such a relationship will help identify self-interest with institutional objective? Contracts for room and board are, of course, common on many college campuses. Contracts to finish academic obligations essentially exist already, but are not articulated as such and therefore promote little, if any, sense of contractual commitment. Student, faculty, and administrative committees generally range from admissions to graduation in variety but often seem to lack a spirit of mutual interest and advantage.

A number of institutions have initiated the use of learning contracts in which students and professors jointly agree to achieve a particular academic goal. Some, like Empire State and Edison College, use the learning contract idea as an essential means to achieve institutional objective, i.e. all admitted students meet with college counselors and thereby develop a program or contract which will lead to a particular degree.

The process of communitization, meaning a process of defining and meeting the mutual needs of student and institution through a reciprocal exchange of goods and services, has been discussed widely by college administrators, but rarely, if ever, finds spokesmen who actually articulate the *means* by which such communitization can take place. Communitization by contractual commitment, especially in light of recent judicial policy making, has, at the very least, promising potential. Amendments to the Higher Education Act of 1972, especially as they relate to sex discrimination, make it clear that equal opportunity, equal access, equal use, and equal rewards for all students will tend to limit faculty and administrative discretion vis-à-vis students, and tend to promote more horizontal relationships among all campus

citizens. Statutory law, indeed, will be a new legislative touchstone in equalizing the options and power of those who wish to
offer and accept educational services.

Legislation in some forty-four states establishes the age of majority as eighteen. The extension of voting rights at age eighteen
by constitutional amendment, moreover, encourages acceptance
of college age youth as more independent of their families. The
trend toward independence of students in college as established in
majority age legislation also finds support in student assistance
programs. Requirements for full-time study have been dropped
for those students receiving Educational Opportunity Grants,
work-study funds, and Guaranteed Student Loan program
monies. Veterans, in addition, must by law be considered independent of their parents. The need qualification for National
Defense Student Loan monies also is described in existing law in
terms of an individual's need rather than in terms of parental
income. Emphasis on individual need rather than family income
is specifically noted in the Guaranteed Student Loan program.
Individual determination of need opens, rather than denies, access to specific members of social groups and relieves the uncer-
tainties of distributing financial aid among students classified by
family income. Deficiencies in resources to meet college costs, in
fact, may be greater among students in the $3,000 to $12,000
family income bracket than among students with family incomes
of less than $3,000.

Emphasis on the individual and independence from parents
percolates through the legislative history of the Education
Amendments Act of 1972. Student assistance from federal sources
now comes to the student in primarily voucher terms and on the
basis of individual qualification. Aid to the individual then
rather than the institution now seems to be a fixed national objective. Such an objective supports, moreover, the idea of the student
as consumer-contractor who comes to an educational institution
with a specific means of exchange.

The new forms of contractual association emerging on the
college campus vastly complicate traditional and conventional
forms of association between and among administrators, faculty,
students, and parents. Once faculty and administrators stood primarily as surrogate agents for parents, both defining and pre-

senting the values, goals, and proper procedures underlying the achievement of a college degree. Now the student himself arrives on the campus with specific rights of his own — rights supported by judicial and legislative directives, and rights which make the student an equal bargaining agent in the determination not only of living arrangements and extracurricula opportunities, but of the essential goals and priorities of the educational process itself. Herein lies the fundamental dilemma confronting the university today. Many have traditionally believed that the educational process assumes by its very nature a hierarchical arrangement, incompatible with democratic decision making. The professor, by virtue of extended training and expertise, knows more than the student. The student comes to the university with the intention of absorbing that knowledge, on whatever basis the professor chooses to provide it, the benefits of the latter's superior knowledge. Now with the student assuming the status of equal partner, all of these assumptions are open to question.

The disorders of the 1960's clearly indicated, moreover, that the educational priorities frequently presented by faculty were incompatible with the student's own expectations, purposes, and objectives in coming to college. Nevertheless, is the student alone to become sole arbiter of his own educational input? The economic exigencies which seem to have created a buyer's market for students certainly has and will continue to temper the once autocratic control of faculty and administration over the educational offerings and direction of the university. Replacing faculty and administrative autocracy with a new form of student control where universities exist only to provide students with whatever they happen to want at any given time seems inappropriate and counterproductive. Given the new legal footing of campus citizens, and especially the array of rights now specifically guaranteed to students, the framework of contractual commitment where campus citizens sit together and decide together is particularly appropriate at this time. Relationships characterized by contractual commitment and reciprocity are the best means to ensure the fullest accommodation of the real and legitimate needs of students with the continuing institutional objectives of the university.

IRVING BUCHEN

THE SWINGING MONK, OR
THE DEAN OF THE FUTURE

In "The Swinging Monk, or the Dean of the Future," Dr. Irving Buchen, of Fairleigh Dickinson University, describes the future dean as an academic broker between disciplines and colleges who assumes change as the only constant. Decision making becomes a horizontal rather than vertical process. Authority to make unilateral decisions no longer exists, and academic as well as student personnel deans should recognize the erosion of previously held authority, and seek thereby new and legitimate sources for their future role in the campus and civic community. Permission to reprint Dr. Buchen's article, which appeared in the May 1974 issue of Intellect, has been secured from Intellect: The Magazine of Educational and Social Affairs.

To assess what is going on in higher education, we should examine what has been happening to college deans in longitudinal portraiture. The anchor image is the Dean of the Past (circa 1950); the transitional, the Dean of the Present (1974); and the projected, the Dean of the Future (1980-85). I will postpone the last portrait somewhat to suggest the extent to which education and society will be increasingly aligned in the future, with the former already providing the embryonic shape of the latter, as well as the profile of the Dean of the Future.

The Dean of the Past was seldom, if ever, a member of a minority group, nearly always used a middle initial, and often taught at least one course or still engaged in limited research. Dean Chester B. Ivy, as I shall call him, was often an elegant speaker, never gave orders, seldom looked rumpled or hurried, held his own nicely at faculty lunch tables, and would often surprisingly show up at poetry readings where only nine students were intensely enjoying their isolation from the Philistine world. I had such a dean as an undergraduate — in fact, it was he who explained to me that etymologically the word "dean" came from the Latin *decem,* to signify a person in charge of ten monks or soldiers, and then quipped, "sort of an academic Salvation Army." It was one of those small, elegant jokes that seemed appropriate to the stability and sophistication of a university, a little bit of derision born of comfort and security. Such deans are gone. In fact, even more striking, so is increasingly this type of school. What his passing from the scene underscores for a portrait of the Dean of the Present is the extent to which being a dean with academic credentials may have made sense then, but one questions whether such credentials are indispensable in making decisions on sewerage systems, parking lots, and three-year budgets.

To help shape my portrait of the Dean of the Present, I sent a letter to certain deans I know. One immediately phoned me to tell me that he was too busy to respond, and, in rather pungent language, wished me and my curiosity ill. Another scribbled his answer on the bottom and back of my letter, itemizing an unbelievable list of meetings and concluded that he was dashing off to yet another blasted meeting.

The third dean has three secretaries, and asked his third secretary to type up a typical weekly schedule (so much for order of priorities). The schedule was horrendous. According to it, the dean is really a monk in at least two respects. He is constantly fasting and, although he may be married and have children, for all practical purposes he is celibate. The writing and routing of paper work takes some twenty to thirty hours a week. His days are jammed with meetings on and off campus. At least three evenings a week are taken up with community-related matters affecting the university. Not unusually, he has at least one social obligation for the university on the weekends, and sometimes two or three. In short, the Dean of the Present is not so much incomplete as incapacitated.

The Dean of the Present, whom I shall call Dean Mike Bunker, has been trained to be anything but a dean. He no longer teaches, and, if he was engaged in research, it terminated the moment he took office. He is one of the few people around who has a real overview of the entire situation, but that is constantly subjected to fragmentation by the diverse constituencies of students, faculty, staff, and administrators he has to serve. He appears to work a minimum of one hundred hours a week, and his vacations are always in jeopardy. I would call this a Pathmark schedule, after the pattern recently established by Pathmark supermarkets of remaining open seven days a week, twenty-four hours a day, nearly three hundred and sixty-five days a year. In fact, the Pathmark dean probably can only shop at Pathmark during its zanier hours.

The standard solution to this overwhelming problem has taken the form of a fusion of the overkill and Peter principles; when one dean cannot handle it all, multiply the number of deans, who then will be overwhelmed collectively. Thus, we now have an intense proliferation of deans — of men, of women, of students, of student services, etc. Added to this is a vast number of semiadministrators — coordinators of volunteer programs, counseling services, development offices, alumni groups, parents' committees, etc. Whatever gains have accrued by this creation of corps of paraprofessionals unique in higher education, the particular price the Dean of the Present has paid for this parcelling out of services is that he is further and further removed from the unique overview which is his sole responsibility to communicate and to administer. Such fragmentation also extends to his role as an academic leader. If he is not a swinger, the students will not listen to him; if he is, the faculty will not. If he asserts academic leadership on behalf of students, the faculty will accuse him of poaching on their preserve. If he asserts academic leadership on behalf of the faculty, the students harden and want to do away with all required courses and tenure. His dealings with other administrators on his own level are strictly a political log-rolling game. On top of this, the staff regularly complains, often rightly, that they have no representative and direct their complaints to the dean. Any student rebel who wishes to take over the university by targeting on the dean is totally naive, for he probably does not possess power even as a source of consolation — nor does the faculty. The only ones with real power are the students, and they either do not know it or do not know what to do with it.

Perhaps there are some practical suggestions that could be made to alleviate the plight of the dean, but to deal with the present without looking ahead to the future may be comparable to devising a tax shelter for someone who may become unemployed. In other words, the worst mistake is to create permanent solutions to temporary problems. When a problem is solved or goes away by itself, one is left with a permanent solution which can really be a problem. Moreover, I am not just talking about the future of education, but of education for the future, for education already is an early warning institution and is operating along futuristic lines which will increasingly surface in society.

I will limit myself to two trends, tightly packed with supporting subtrends, both of which converge to accent the increasing interaction between society and education in the future. The first could be called the disconnect pattern, which subsumes under it a number of disconnects. The principle behind this trend is simply that, if enough people are broken off in the same time frame or in the same place, they collectively constitute a disconnect culture. A fundamental ingredient is the familiar agent of mobility, now gone international, except that it finally has characterized higher education as well. Increasingly, the college student does not graduate from the one in which he was initially enrolled — many have attended as many as four or five colleges before they finally graduate or drop out. That trend has been enormously intensified by the increase in two-year colleges that have fed into the academic mainstream the new norm of the 1970's — the transfer student. In short, the disconnect inherent in mobility or transience is no longer determined solely by money or the lack of it. The out-of-towner and the local student are alike in that their education is increasingly becoming not a terminal, but a transitional arrangement; not a single whole, but a continuum of parts.

The national disconnect appears in the many and various subgroups which have separated themselves from the mainstream of the melting pot, including various minority groups, Gay Liberation, rebel priests, Women's Lib, and bachelor parents. Such separations already have been sanctioned by the Federal government's proportionate hiring programs and reinforced by the studying of these movements in college curricula. One disconnect pattern that is seldom noted or, when it is, not factored into planning or curricula development is the substantial increase in the number of divorcees. That many then remarry does not alter the disconnect pattern, but merely puts it within the more complex and meaningful framework of serial monogamy. What is regularly overlooked is the extent to which a correlation seems to be developing between changing partners and changing careers, especially for women. In short, what is steadily emerging is an apparently new educational rhythm which alternates between continuity and discontinuity, with the transfer student serving as the trafficking mediator between the two. Significantly, enrollment figures support the interpretation. According to the Census Bureau's most recent report,* from 1966 to 1971, four-year college enrollment rose from 3,300,000 to 4,100,000. In the same period, two-year college enrollment rose from 1,000,000 to 1,700,000. Equally as important, two-year college students accounted for 31 percent of the total number of freshmen and sophomores in 1966, but jumped to 42 percent in 1971. Moreover, comparable students in two-year colleges tend to be older than their counterparts in four-year colleges, and two-year colleges educate nearly twice the number of men and three times the number of women who fall into the twenty-two to thirty-four-year-old bracket. Finally, 34 percent of all two-year college freshmen and sophomores attended classes part-time in 1971, as compared to 21 percent in four-year colleges.

This signifies that two-year colleges are rarely operating along the futuristic model of educating part-timers, including both younger and older students. In addition, they are futuristic in their flexible capacity to design, implement, and specialize in transitional programs. Indeed, if it chooses, a two-year college can be enormously experimental without risk. They are set up on a plug-in, plug-out basis — they control the disconnects. However, they have two serious problems — lacking depth, they tend to impart to programs a premature intellectual or employment constriction, and, having to satisfy admission requirements for their transfer students, the integrity of their programs is not totally self-determined. In my judgment, the mistake was in creating two-year colleges as entities separate from colleges and

---

*Undergraduate Enrollment in Two-Year and Four-Year Colleges, No. 26 (October, 1971). p. 21.

universities in the first place. What I would propose is that every college and university restructure itself to create a two-year college as part of the four-year and graduate program of the university.

The full design would resemble that of three concentric rings orbiting around, and drawing upon the resources of, the individual colleges. The outermost ring would be, in effect, a two-year college, but recast to become essentially a part-time college operating along the Pathmark model of twenty-four hours a day, seven days a week, nearly three hundred and sixty-five days of the year. As such, it would absorb so-called evening programs, early-admission or early-bird programs, adult education extension programs, open admissions, weekend colleges, etc., under one overall structure which would operate as a maximum disconnect-and-connect college. It would be a way station for road scholars and, because its periphery would be enormous and varied, it would be the principal cutting edge into the community, especially if its periphery were dotted with structural sensors like cooperative education programs, community services, and the like.

The middle ring would be that of half-time students, designed especially to accommodate women, senior citizens, and individuals involved in career conversions or paraprofessional programs. Finally, the innermost ring would be for full-time students, especially those committed to careers. Students here would be given the full options of honors work, accelerated programs through self-pacing, research-oriented projects, and the prospect of merging undergraduate and graduate work in the senior year. The three styles of education — part-time, half-time, and full-time — would not be mutually exclusive. Bridges between all three rings would be permanently available so that a part-time student could move into, or have access to, the full-time program. Thus, if full-time students became disenchanted or wanted a less rigid arrangement, instead of dropping out completely, they could nicely be caught and sustained in the outer part-time net. Such an arrangement does not cut off part-time programs and students from access to depth anymore than it cuts off full-time students from involvement in current issues in the community. Indeed, it is quite conceivable that a student could essentially be operating along all three lines simultaneously, and thus embody in his educational life exactly the kind of diversity or apportionment of time, energy, and interests that occur in his private life. Above all, such a multiple structure could multiply the sources of students along a total chronological line and eliminate the present artificial restriction of limiting enrollment to young adults.

The second trend is, strictly speaking, not so much a trend as a tracer — a conceptual time frame within which major shifts can be comprehended. Historically, Western civilization has been oriented along a vertical time-line. Its source is in the evolutionary distinction of humankind standing erect, and appears structurally in the creation of pyramids, Towers of Babel, contemporary skyscrapers, and organizational charts. Verticality compels hierarchies — once man stood erect, he put a top over a bottom, spirit over matter, man over woman, and he had no peace until he created postmortal equivalents in the hierarchy of heaven over hell. Verticality is also tied to singularity — to monotheism — and to intense stress on individuality. Modern society basically has been set up along the goals of the vertical or singular model: One God, One Love, One Career, One College, One Country, One Planet. Individual colleges are really vertical monoliths within which are nested double hierarchies — those of departmental units and of academic ranks. What I have been trying to suggest is that the vertical line is being leveled to the horizontal — we now have an intersect of horizontal (multiple) and vertical (singular) lines. Specifically, the catechism for the future is Many Gods, Many Loves, Many Colleges, Many Careers, Many Countries, Many Planets.

What this pattern portends for higher education is the new structural concept of an intercollege college. This goes way beyond the fashionable stress on interdisciplinary programs, which operate within safe parameters, to interdepartmental programs, which cut across college lines. What is the point, for example, of developing the group transactional process if one of the aims is to bring about a new negotiated relationship between environmentalists and business managers, and then to contain the entire process within the College of Liberal Arts? The intercollege concept would not destroy the integrity of separate disciplines or colleges anymore than communal imperatives would compromise the separateness of each person. What would be created is an intersect of the vertical and the horizontal. Such education would be entangling and permanently open-ended. It is relatively easy to disconnect from a vertical monolith or to be absorbed into an anarchistic blur, but one that involves the individual and the communal, the specific and the general, has holding power. To be sure, such a dovetailing presupposes the existence of an intersecting or integrating discipline that can create and sustain bridges within and between colleges. Naturally, I am partisan, but I would suggest that the academic discipline to accomplish these aims is futurism. Moreover, as long as my bias is so transparent, let me return to the protrait of the Dean of the Future and state that such a dean will be a futurist. Chances also are good that he will be a she, because women seem more interested in futurism, more flexible in handling change, and closer, because of Women's Liberation, to questioning basic or hidden assumptions. One of his/her first official acts will be to push for a degree-granting program in futurism, especially a doctoral program which is designed exclusively for working professionals and which admits students from all colleges and areas of interest.

If the Dean of the Past was basically independent and the Dean of the Present has become increasingly dependent, the Dean of the Future should pledge allegiance in 1976 to a New Declaration of Interdependence. Specifically, the Dean of the Future should have as his academic discipline that of futurism, which is predicated on a wholistic view. His administrative training should consist of designing interdependent structures and relationships that facilitate and manage change and innovation. Moreover, both dimensions should reinforce each other. For example, the emphasis on acquiring basic managerial skills such as accounting, statistics, computer scheduling, and systems theory would be related to the academic emphasis on the futuristic techniques of short and long-range planning of how to get from here to there. The skill of shaping a budget would be tied to the futuristic view of budgets as really means for ordering academic priorities and for accommo-

dating the consensus process by faculty and students of determining educational goals.

Reinforced alliances of this sort could be multiplied, but they
would only further detail what is perhaps already apparent —
that, with such training, the aim of the Dean of the Future will be
to press for the study of the future as a legitimate and rigorous
concern of every academic discipline, including that of history.
His principal academic function will be to serve as broker or
synthesizer between faculty, departments, colleges, and between
the academic and the actual communities. Specifically, he will
arrange partnerships between the college and the community, but
only if they are academically charged with the commitment to
solving, rather than perpetuating, problems, to study followed by
implementation, rather than to study followed by further study.
Above all, he will have to wade in and help to bridge disciplines
that should have been joined a long time ago. The so-called conflict between the two cultures is a neat example of what not to do.
Scientists in the future can no more skirt the moral implications
of their work than humanists can irresponsibly bewail the threats
of technological dehumanization while they use concordances
produced by computers. What was, and remains, stupid about the
conflict between the two cultures is that it was seen as a conflict
between right and wrong, whereas it really is a conflict between
rights. Moreover, the differences took place in a vertical structure
that was so inherently polarizing that neither side could recognize
the legitimate integrity of the other, and what could have taken
the form of a common cause emerged as an unbridgeable gulf.

Most important of all, the Dean of the Future should see, and be
able to project, a vision of higher education which, far from being
dreadful, is really splendid, precisely because the future of higher
education, more than ever before, has the promise of becoming
aligned with the future of society. What we do not need now is a
wringing of hands and a wishing for the good old days when our
lives were as neat as our students' appearances. What we certainly
do not need are those who are engaged in a desperate search for
miracle workers, or Jesus Christ Superstars who magically will
cure all future ills. Those who traffic in the past should not be

deans, but morticians. Those who always need messiahs are inevitably set up to be taken in by Big Brothers waiting to make an offer they cannot refuse.

Swinging monks, in contrast, are professional straddlers — synthesizers of the best of the old and the new. They are temporary transitional types who will no longer be singular wholes, but a continuum of parts — a constellation of multiple selves. Such Deans of the Future, for all their adventuresome swingingness, will be consciously and intentionally invisible. They will become not indispensable, but dispensable models. Such withdrawal will enable them to accomplish their principal academic and administrative function — to provide students with the full state to create the future they will have to live.

I conclude by updating an old Talmudic tale. It was announced from Heaven that, within a few days, the entire earth would be inundated under 20,000 fathoms of water. Those committed to the old ways went off to pray. Those committed to the new ways became hedonists. The futurists met, wrinkled their brows, talked it over, and finally issued a counterproclamation: "It will be difficult to live under 20,000 fathoms of water."

ROBERT AND ELEANOR LAUDICINA

THE DECLINE OF UNIVERSITY AUTHORITY: SOME IMPLICATIONS OF ACADEMIC EGALITARIANISM

The following article, "The Decline of University Authority: Some Implications of Academic Egalitarianism," by Robert and Eleanor Laudicina of Fairleigh Dickinson University and Kean College, respectively, examines the implications of changing academic demands on students and the difficulties engendered by the demise of traditional curricula, course requirements, and grading systems. The decline of university authority in academic areas parallels the similar decline, discussed elsewhere in this volume, of its authoritative role in relation to student lifestyles. In both areas, the deterioration of traditional patterns has left a serious void. The authors examine the importance of developing new patterns of interaction and, new contractual relationships between student and institution in the academic as well as other arenas. The article originally appeared in the March 1973 issue of the Rutgers University Magazine.

The concept of individual responsibility is deeply imbedded in American culture. In the belief system of a rapidly developing nation, the idea that a man, through his own will, fortitude, and natural capacities, could become whatever he wished to be was greatly valued. Some, today, still maintain the belief that success or failure in life is directly dependent upon the way in which the individual freely chooses to manipulate the personal and environmental resources at his disposal. Events occurring during the past half-century, however, have sharply undermined this belief in total individual responsibility. The Depression years, in particular, indicated to many the importance of vast, impersonal social and economic forces as they mold and shape individual destinies. No matter how strong the desire to work and to succeed, the absence of jobs could thwart any individual will. World War II and the complex problems of the postwar era increased awareness of the vast network of national and international forces capable of influencing and determining the course of many lives. The social upheavals of the 1960's underscored the extent to which racial and ethnic minorities had endured the impact of cultural and historical forces not amenable to individual control. All of these experiences helped to shift the earlier emphasis on individual responsibility toward a growing awareness of social accountability. A "sociological perspective" emerged, i.e. an understanding of the individual, his motivations, capabilities, interests, and opportunities — as a product of the complex web of social relationships in which he is enmeshed.

The new perspective on social responsibility and accountability had many positive effects: more enlightened governmental action to reverse the discriminatory effects of history and tradition; a growing cohesion and sense of identity among many previously fragmented groups, who as individuals, began to perceive themselves not as discrete outcasts but as members of a group sharing common problems; and a growing sophistication among many people concerning the environmental influences helping to shape the course of their own lives. Nevertheless, some thoughtful observers of contemporary American life have concluded that the pendulum has swung too far toward social accountability, with devastating effects on the standards for judging individual success and excellence. Daniel Bell, a prominent sociologist, argues that emphasis on equality of opportunity for groups previously excluded from full participation, has been replaced by a growing emphasis on providing "equality of result" — that is, the notion that every person, because of his membership in a group formerly subject to discrimination, is entitled to some of life's rewards, i.e. good jobs, high status positions, and access to the academic degrees which make these possible. Rewards are compelled, not by the individual's own personal achievements and capabilities, but by social, economic, and personal needs. In higher education particularly, the subtle effects of perhaps inadvertent absorption of the doctrine of equality of result or need are becoming apparent.

In the postwar world, massive changes overtook educational institutions, altering their character and operation irrevocably. A complex, technological age demanded skilled personnel to man its bureaucratic and managerial apparatus. Colleges and universities accepted students in ever increasing numbers in order to provide the skills and techniques required by the world beyond their boundaries. Growing emphasis on equality of opportunity firmly established the idea that a college education was not the prerogative of an elite few, but an intrinsic right of all who desired it. The result was a rapid democratization of higher education as county colleges, state colleges, public and private universities grew in size and scope to accommodate students at whatever level their financial and academic capacities made possible. The rapid influx of new student constituencies drastically altered the character of higher education. Vocationally oriented students, seeking a means of upward economic and social mobility, questioned the validity and usefulness of traditional liberal arts curricula. The demands of specialized business and professional areas, combined with a steadily diminishing need for unskilled workers, made college a necessity for many, not the luxury of a relative few.

As the element of necessity in higher education became increasingly apparent, the relationship between the student and the university changed considerably, initiating the transformation from equality of opportunity to equality of need. Students, traditionally have been a relatively passive element in the university community, staying for four years, then moving on without insignificantly altering ongoing intellectual and professional pursuits. The new student constituency of the 1960's were not only more obvious in their large numbers, but more vocal and tenacious in their questioning of the value of the curricula to which they were exposed. As a result, the powers within the university not only became aware of students as a competing constituent force, but also as a necessary economic and social condition for institutional survival.

Students rapidly became a significant force within the university and its resources increasingly were channeled to service their needs. The office of the Dean of Students, formerly a purely ceremonial or disciplinary function, was expanded to include many student services, counseling facilities, recreational opportunities, and financial and career guidance — all intended to help the student adjust to the rigors of student life and to succeed. Faculty, particularly younger faculty, became more responsive to student needs, developing a personal relationship, a willingness to hear students' problems, and to accommodate course requirements to individual circumstances.

The emphasis upon maximizing the opportunity for all students to succeed provided innumerable benefits for many students, greatly increasing the scope and value of the educational experience. But just as equality of opportunity has begun to give way to equality of need in a broad social context, similar changes are occurring within the university. In a knowledge-based society, in which the need for academic credentials alone frequently compels attendance at college, it is perhaps inevitable that need, not achievement, should become the ultimate criterion of success, i.e. graduation. Many of the academic innovations introduced recently, i.e. the pass-fail system of grading, elimination of required liberal arts courses and core curricula, lightened course loads, "second chance" colleges and special programs, have operated in fact, if not in intent, to make it easier for the student to succeed and virtually impossible for him to fail. Average grades at most institutions have risen from "*C*" to "*B*." The reason lies less in a higher level of competence among today's students than in an increasing responsiveness of faculty members to their students' need for academic success as a basic requirement for entry into adult life.

Is an emphasis on need rather than achievement necessarily an undesirable trend? Despite the mystique of individual responsibility we recognize that ascriptive criteria, i.e. accidents of birth, family, and status have provided rewards at least as frequently as hard work and individual achievement. Moreover, the courses previously dictated by required curricula clearly are unnecessary, irrelevant, and insignificant as preparation for later economic or even social roles. Who remembers anything specific from that Western Civilization course, or can speak two words of the language so arduously pursued for two years? Proponents of academic innovation, in addition, argue that loosening academic restrictions allows the student freedom to pursue his own intellectual inclinations, to study in some depth the subjects which interest him, and to explore new areas of learning without fearing the consequences of a bad grade.

All of the arguments supporting basic changes in traditional procedures are justified, and support abandonment of academic forms more encrusted with tradition than imbued with any purpose. Nevertheless, serious problems remain, problems related especially to the university's role in making of its students responsible, mature adults, and related as well to the responsibility of the university itself to establish objective criteria by which the world beyond its walls can judge the competence of its graduates. Many of the hopes of academic innovators that a more flexible, less demanding course load would encourage students to work harder in their areas of interest and to explore new fields have yet to be realized. On few campuses is there any indication of a heightened intellectual atmosphere or greater seriousness of purpose among the student body. To the contrary, most instructors probably would agree that the quality of work received, even in specialized courses, has declined and that students seem determined to evade even the minimal responsibilities currently demanded of them. Elimination of required skills courses, such as English Composition, leaves little to help the student organize and express his ideas on paper, transferring the burden for that instructor on to instructors who should spend their time teaching the substantive matter which is their primary area of competence. The small percentage of students who have taken advantage of liberalized requirements to expand their intellectual horizons probably would have done so whatever academic demands were imposed upon them. Meanwhile, the growth and success of organizations providing ready-made term papers testifies to the unwillingness of many students to probe deeply even the subject matter of courses they themselves have chosen.

The dissatisfactions of faculty with the quality of work received find few avenues of expression. Changing role relationships within the classroom — from authoritarian to a basic egalitarianism limits the willingness and capacity of the instructor to impose rigorous demands in the face of student opposition.

Course evaluations published by students exert a subtle pressure to remain popular and to make the course requirements palatable to students, in the interests of keeping the chairs filled and one's job intact. Self-doubts among faculty members themselves, encouraged by current challenges to the very cognitive foundations of existing knowledge, further inhibit imposition of rigorous demands. Faculty, unwilling and unable to hold students responsible for their own inner turmoil or for the turmoil facing contemporary education, and recognizing the economic and social needs which compel the student's presence in his class, liberalize their grading and help everyone get through.

The crucial and necessary factor which many academic innovations unfortunately have removed from academic demands is the element of discipline — not the discipline of corporal punishment or expulsion from school, but discipline in the academic or artistic sense, i.e. creative work within a structured framework of previously acquired knowledge. Current innovations, in attempting to promote creativity, have abandoned structure, with the result that neither remains. Obviously the older structure of traditional liberal arts requirements is obsolete and irrelevant. But in eliminating the old structure, we have neglected to establish another.

The basic problem may be that we have attempted to graft earlier concepts of education and learning onto a student body for whom they are largely meaningless. If even the few remaining academic demands are evaded and circumscribed by students, perhaps the answer is not to eliminate even these requirements, but to question whether the kinds of academic discipline required by the university in the form of courses and requirements actually supports the kinds of learning for which students wish to be made responsible. If equality of need means that all students feel entitled to a college education because of their importance in the outside world, and if students seem unwilling to be evaluated for their success or failure in fulfilling existing academic demands, can it be that the kinds of demands and the kinds of achievements being evaluated in the academic context have little relationship to the kinds of standards being applied outside the university? Is the diploma issued by the university, rather than the learning transmitted within it, the one thing students find valuable in their educational experience?

The solution to the problem of student responsibility does not lie in attempting to make it even easier for them to swallow the course work and to meet the kinds of academic demands deeply established within the university. To this point, academic innovation has been accomplished without seriously challenging the interests or concerns of faculty. If required courses have been abolished, the impetus for abolition came as much from faculty who were bored with them as from students who were harrassed by them. Not having to teach low-level requirements leaves more time for specialized courses. But how many faculty have been forced to consider the importance — or lack of importance — of their own concerns to the needs of students about to enter the adult world? The solution must be found in new structures of learning, embodying new forms of discipline, and a more realistic synthesis between what the university offers and what the student needs to succeed in the world beyond its boundaries. Students are unwilling to accept any longer the disciplines and forms of evaluation traditionally used in the university because they recognize how unimportant particular grades are for success in later life. They recognize that the important output of their college years is not their grade average, but their diploma. Of all the studies undertaken, none indicates any correlation between high grades in college and achievement — at least achievement measurable in dollars and cents — in later life.

Despite students' awareness of the unimportance of academic grades for later success, the movement to eliminate traditional standards has begun to create substantial unforeseen problems as students enter the job market. Emphasis on equality of need, meaning that virtually everyone who enters college, graduates, and the elimination of traditional grade requirements and standardized courses, leaves prospective employers and professional schools with few criteria upon which to base their judgment of an individual's potential. With the tightening of both job opportunities and openings in postgraduate education, there are many more applicants than places to be filled. As a result, criteria even more arbitrary and less concerned with individual qualities than grades, come into play, i.e. the reputation of the school from which the individual graduated, the recommendation of one or two instructors, preferably those widely known or known to the person seeking to fill a position, become decisive. In a very paradoxical way, the effort to democratize education, by allowing every one the fruits of a college degree, is creating a highly inegalitarian situation, as persons from prestige schools, with contacts among well-known faculty have a substantial edge over those who may have worked hard at a smaller school, but have fewer contacts and little to distinguish them from other students.

If a college education is to remain a significant and meaningful individual experience, if the college years are to be something more than a device to keep young people out of the job market for four years, and if universities are to retain their traditional role in encouraging and rewarding excellence, then new structures of learning, embodying new standards of discipline and achievement, meaningful to both students and faculty, must be developed. Obviously there is a need for a new way to delineate academic success compatible to some degree with the demands of learning and the acquisition of knowledge, but also compatible with the students' need to find in college the bridge for their entry into adult life. Very little thought or experimentation has been directed to forms of academic innovation conforming to these criteria, but several promising developments have begun. The movement toward cooperative education is one of these. The student actively works in the area of his career interests at the same time as he is taking course work, or during alternate academic terms. Although these experiments have provided important individual benefits, few criteria have yet been developed to provide objective assessment of the student's degree of success, apart from the simple fact of his participation.

Universities, student groups, and alumni should begin to work together to construct viable options to existing educational forms, options which can help to bridge the gap between the demands of academic and of nonacademic life, and which can develop in students the desire to achieve within the discipline of new structures, and to have their achievements realistically and objectively assessed. Failure can be recognized as a possibility, but only if the tangible results of academic success are sufficiently important to encourage students to assume responsibility for individual achievement.

INDEX

297

Date Due

JAN 3 0 1979			
DEC 21 1979			
DEC 4 1979			

ORANGE MEMORIAL LIBRARY
WITHDRAWN
THE COLLEGE AT BROCKPORT

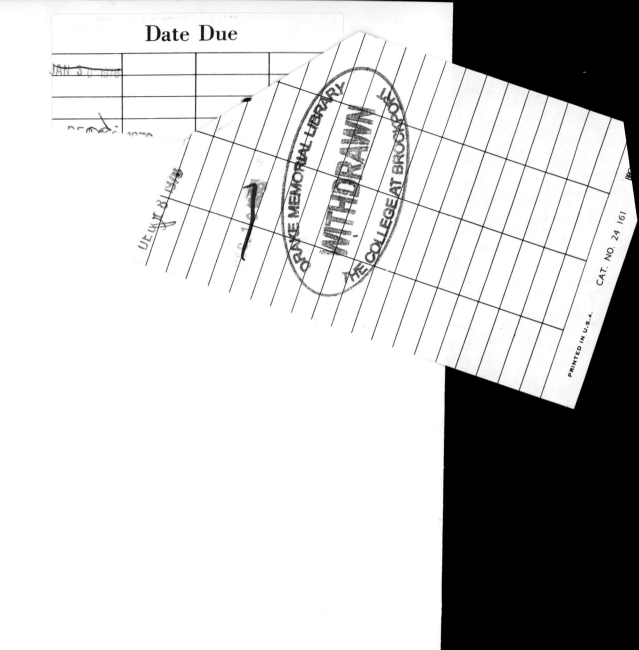

PRINTED IN U.S.A.   CAT. NO. 24 161